EVIDENCE-BASED PARENTING

FROM TODDLER TO PRE-TEEN

MATILDA GOSLING

Swift

SWIFT PRESS

First published in Great Britain by Swift Press 2024

1 3 5 7 9 8 6 4 2

Typeset by Tetragon, London
Printed and bound in Great Britain by CPI Group (UK) Ltd, Croydon, CR0 4YY

A CIP catalogue record for this book is available from the British Library

ISBN: 9781800752368
eISBN: 9781800752375

For Pete, Lola and Ivy

CONTENTS

INTRODUCTION

The concept

This book aims to answer one question: what actually works when it comes to parenting? It draws on thousands of pieces of research on subjects such as child development, family systems, relationships, mental health and genetics. The evidence has been distilled into simple, practical suggestions to support children's relationships, physical health, learning and play, behaviour, and happiness and well-being. All families are different – what works for one may be ineffectual or impractical to another – and this book recognises this by offering a variety of evidence-based alternatives. Parents can select ideas using their expert knowledge of what's most likely to work for their own children.

The need for an evidence base

Given the fundamental importance of parenting to almost every human on this planet – if not as a parent, then as a child of one – an overview of the parenting evidence base is remarkably absent.

As a parent and professional social researcher, I spent years trying to find something that condensed high-quality research and evidence on how to bring up a child to be a happy, healthy adult in a way that preserves parents' sanity. I found lots of books that took a particular philosophy and used it as a cornerstone for recommendations. I read in-depth descriptions of the different stages of a child's development and how these relate to parenting. I found excellent work using the principles of economics to create decision-making frameworks for families. I discovered a huge range of writing by psychologists and parenting experts who used lessons from their own practice to construct advice for parents.

What I couldn't find was a concrete summary of what works according to the vast academic and expert evidence base, much less a version of this distilled into a selection of ideas from which parents can choose according to their knowledge of what's likely to work best. Parents are, after all, authorities on their own children. I also couldn't find anything that attempted to paint the whole picture, drawing not only on parenting research but also on the full range of social sciences research, and even on other academic disciplines such as biology and history. If I'm writing about how to reduce arguments within a family, I need to understand the research on conflict. An overview of genetics research helps me to fathom out where a child's environment can make a positive difference to their health. Knowing how to support children's behaviour means I need an understanding of research on psychology and child development.

This book emerged from these gaps. The variety of research findings also informs the idea that what works for one child or family may be completely inappropriate for another. Parents need a range of evidence-based options. The most successful approach might work for sixty out of a hundred children, but what about the other forty?

The various ideas offered in this book help answer this question. What works in parenting can cut across different philosophies and concepts. Taking high-quality research as a starting point equips parents with the knowledge of what's likely to work for them and their children, according to their particular circumstances. And my children have benefited from this approach, even if they roll their eyes every time I try something new on the back of the latest research paper.

What this book covers and what it leaves out

This book draws directly on well over a thousand studies and indirectly on thousands more to create an evidence-based reference manual for busy parents. It focuses on children between the ages of two and ten. There's already a vast literature on babies, including reasonable evidence summaries, and teenagers are sufficiently different from younger children to deserve their own dedicated follow-up. I occasionally draw from research on teenagers and adults when I look at long-term outcomes of individual parenting decisions.

The geographic focus of the research reviewed for this book is mainly Anglophone countries – the UK, Ireland, the United States, Canada, Australia and New Zealand – because culture has a strong bearing on which parenting practices work best.

I talk about *parents* and *parenting* in the interests of simplicity of language, but of course the ideas in here apply just as much to other caregivers. If you're a step-parent or other guardian, please know that I include you when I talk about parents.

Finally, and importantly, this book focuses on positive strategies and things that can be changed. Those that can't, such as how much money a family has or where they live, are irrelevant to what parents can do to make life at home easier or to support their children better.

How to use this book

Practical suggestions drawn from evidence are presented according to three levels of research quality:

- ▶ **High-quality research evidence**: meta-analyses, systematic reviews, randomised controlled trials or longitudinal studies of more than 1,000 people.
- ▶ **Moderate-quality research evidence**: studies showing links but not causality.
- ▶ **Anecdotal research or expert advice**: suggestions based on clinical practice or similar.

Presenting the research in this way enables parents to make up their own minds about how to interpret the information. Most study findings apply to children in general, but no child is an average. In each section of the book, a number of approaches are covered. If one suggestion doesn't work for you and your family, you can experiment with other ideas.

This book illustrates the evidence in a particular way, although there are many ways it could have been presented. Under any way of structuring the evidence, though, there's inevitable overlap. There's also debate within the research about precisely what it is that makes a positive difference to child outcomes. In some cases, particularly for lower-quality evidence, links between parenting decisions and outcomes for children may be due to some other, underlying factor. A link between children playing in nature and having higher levels of resilience might be explained by adventurousness. It's not absurd to suggest that when parents model adventurousness, their children are more likely to be resilient, and adventurous parents are more likely to encourage their children to play in nature.

Nothing has been suggested in this book that's likely to harm your child. While you may want to prioritise suggestions based on the highest-quality evidence, it's still worth looking at the other options in here. Sometimes the most interesting ideas come from lower-quality studies. These may contain evidence of things too specific to be tested in a big research trial, or perhaps it wouldn't be ethical to test the findings in this way.

The book is organised into two main parts. The first covers universal approaches: these can be helpful for many children across multiple aspects of their lives. Avoiding harsh discipline, for example, is linked to better outcomes for children across a range of areas, including physical health, mental well-being and behaviour. When using this section of the book, it's important to think about whether and how any recommendations apply to your own situation. Even some of these more universal approaches may not work for every family and every child. For instance, some children find making decisions difficult and stressful. Giving these children autonomy and room to make choices, unless done carefully and gradually, may not be helpful for them. That said, the diversity of ideas should mean you find plenty you can use. This part of the book is arranged into things you can do as an individual, within the structure of your home and family, and as a parent. There are concrete suggestions for each area, and thoughts on how you can put these into practice, such as looking at how you can dial down tempers when family members keep arguing. I'd have had no idea where to start with calming family conflict without having pored over the research. I've also seen how sorely clarity is needed in the research literature about what the findings mean, practically, for individual families. When the research says that household chaos is bad for children, what does that mean in terms of the day-to-day changes parents can make to make things a little less chaotic? In every case, the book draws out practical implications and examples. Theory is as good as useless if it's not clear how to apply it.

The second part contains focused approaches for supporting your child with specific outcomes, namely:

▶ **Relationships:** how to build your relationship with your child, bolster sibling relationships and support your child's friendships.
▶ **Behaviour:** what you can do to minimise children acting up and to promote socially minded behaviour.
▶ **Physical health:** how to improve your child's sleep, ensure they willingly get enough exercise, and help them to develop a healthy relationship with food and with their body.
▶ **Learning and play:** how to support your child in the areas of screens, outdoor play, learning and life skills.
▶ **Happiness and well-being:** how to promote your child's mental health, resilience and self-esteem.

This second part presents the research in each of these areas and translates it into evidence-based suggestions. These offer a variety of avenues you can try based on your knowledge of what's likely to work for your child, your family and your life. Part Two also presents troubleshooting sections for each area, looking at what you can do if your child is being bullied, feeling anxious or having regular meltdowns.

The Epilogue provides a summary of the book's most important points. It recaps the main advice for parents and their children, according to the evidence, and discusses how parents can apply the different ideas to their daily lives.

There are two key points when reading this book:

▶ **It doesn't need to be read from start to finish.** You can dip into the sections you find most relevant to your own situation.
▶ **It's not a blueprint.** There is no such thing as a perfect parent, and there's no universal recipe for parenting. The evidence base is not there to provide a series of instructions, but instead is a constellation of ideas from which you can create your own path.

Full references are available online at www.matildagosling.com/parenting.

Parenting styles: warmth and control

I've included a brief introduction to parenting styles, as these are often used in research studies to explore what creates the best outcomes for children in specific areas such as behaviour or health. The most popular way of classifying parenting styles is to divide them into categories based on warmth and control.[1]

1. PARENTING STYLES

	LOW WARMTH	HIGH WARMTH
LOW CONTROL	Neglectful parenting ★☆☆	Permissive parenting ★★☆
HIGH CONTROL	Authoritarian parenting ★★☆	Authoritative parenting ★★★

▶ **Authoritative parenting.** This is the gold standard across the research literature. Authoritative parents treat their children with warmth while also setting clear boundaries. Imagine a parent who's affectionate, creates routines and isn't afraid to say no to their child. This parent listens carefully to their child and is flexible enough to change direction when something's not working.

▶ **Permissive parenting.** Permissive parents are warm, with low levels of control. This is the parent (and we all know one, or are one) who gives masses of affection and little in the way of hard edges. The child of permissive parents is the one who stays up late and gets to raid the snack cupboard with abandon.

▶ **Authoritarian parenting.** Authoritarian parents are cold, with high levels of control. This kind of parenting was probably more common in our own childhoods, and even more widespread among our grandparents' generation. The authoritarian parent provides much fodder for children's literature – the classic idea of a distant figure exacting high standards of behaviour and compliance from their slightly fearful but internally rebellious child.

▶ **Neglectful parenting.** Neglectful parents, who show neither warmth nor control, have children with the worst outcomes of all. Rest assured that if you're reading this book, you're unlikely to be this kind of parent.

What does it mean to be warm and to exert healthy control? In practice, warmth can be physical, shown to your child through kisses, hugs and other warm gestures. It can also be shown in what you say, such as telling your child why you like the snail picture they drew or showing interest in their new-found dragon obsession. Warmth can also be measured by its absence: when children feel rejected by their parents' hostility or indifference, or when they feel unloved or unappreciated.

While warmth is easy to define, control is trickier. There's an important difference between healthy boundaries relating to behaviour and trying to control what children think or feel, or the decisions they make. You might show healthy control to a child who's screaming at you by making it clear they need to express their anger without yelling. Unhealthy control might be expressed to the same child by telling them they're wrong for feeling angry or showing them through your body language that you think they're wrong. The 'control' part of the grid above relates to the healthy form of control. Ideas about how you can do this are explored in Chapter 4.

This illustration shows how authoritative parenting is linked to children's relationships, their health, learning and play, behaviour, and happiness and well-being. Each area connects to many others, and pulling one thread of parenting may have knock-on effects elsewhere. In other cases, several threads may need teasing at once to make a positive difference to your child.

2. CONNECTIONS BETWEEN AUTHORITATIVE PARENTING AND CHILDREN'S OUTCOMES

RELATIONSHIPS	BEHAVIOUR	PHYSICAL HEALTH	LEARNING AND PLAY	HAPPINESS AND WELL-BEING
▲ Parent–child relationship	▲ General behaviour	▲ Exercise	▲ Academic achievement	▲ Well-being & mental health
▲ Sibling relationships	▲ Socially minded behaviour	▼ Being overweight		▼ Perfectionism
▲ Friendships	▼ Aggression	▼ Taking up smoking		▲ Self-esteem
▼ Being bullied				

Authoritative parents, those who successfully combine warmth and healthy control, are more likely than other parents to have children with good mental health and high self-esteem. Their children are less likely to suffer from perfectionism, have behavioural problems or act aggressively. Children with authoritative parents are more likely to act in a socially minded way and to do better at school. They have a more secure relationship with their parents, better relationships with their siblings and find it easier to make friends. They're less likely to be bullied. These children are more likely to exercise and to be a healthy weight, and are less likely to take up smoking when they get older.[2]

It is helpful to keep this warmth-and-control framework in mind when you read the rest of the book, but it's not worth getting too distracted by it. It's more useful to think about what works in practice. How can you show warmth to your child on days you might be struggling? How can you set healthy boundaries while avoiding controlling your child in ways that might be less helpful for them? These questions, and many more, are explored in the chapters that follow.

Influences on parenting styles

Parents affect their children not just by their parenting styles but also by who they are. If you're naturally pessimistic, your child is more likely to become Eeyore than Tigger. And parenting styles aren't always as much of a choice as they might appear. For example, parents who find it hard to control their emotions are more likely to be authoritarian with their children – it's tricky to be warm with your child if you're drowning in your own feelings. How much stress parents are under also has a direct effect on their parenting style. It's easier to be a 'good' parent if you've had lots of sleep, you're not worried about money, you live in a safe area and you don't have multiple demands on your time.

Just as parenting styles can affect children and how they sit within the world, children themselves can influence the parenting they receive. Being warm and responsive can be instinctive when you have a child who wants hugs and to snuggle in a chair with stories, but it's taxing when you have one who's raging at you for cutting their sandwiches into the wrong shape. That's not to say that how you act as a parent can't make a child less likely to scream at you, but children have different temperaments. It's much harder to parent well when you don't have an easy child. A child's agreeableness can also fluctuate with their mood, of course. As any parent knows, the same child can morph from angelic cuddler to vengeful havoc monster in seconds.

Individual parenting decisions can only do so much. Outcomes for children are dictated by their local area, the society in which they live, and national economic and social policy. Do children have local green spaces they can reach easily? Are they able to breathe reasonably clean air? Do parents get paid enough to allow their children to be brought up with good food, access to toys and things to help them learn, sufficient space within the home and parents who aren't worn down by financial stress? These questions are beyond this book's scope, but it's important to be clear that parents aren't single-handedly responsible for their children's health and well-being. Parents can only do as much as the system around them permits.

A note on 'good enough' parenting

One of the most stressful things about being a parent, at least in my experience, is thinking about the things that are lacking or being done badly. I think about the club my older daughter's desperate to attend but can't, because her parents are both working and it's too far for her to walk. I think about the fact that both my kids eat too much sugar, which we have somehow achieved at the same time as over-controlling what they eat. I think about long days and evenings and tiredness and me reacting badly to yet another fight between the two of them. I think that I don't play enough with my children. I think about the time on the way back from school when I'm hurrying home to work, and my daughter sits under a tree and refuses to move because I haven't gone back to school to get the book she left behind. The only thing I can think of at that moment is to threaten not taking her to see her best friend the next day.

But show me the perfect parent, and I'll show you a perfect child. They don't exist. Donald Winnicott was an early parenting theorist who came up with the idea of the 'good enough' parent. (More accurately, he came up with the idea of the good enough 'mother', although we'll forgive him that, as he was doing most of his writing in the middle of the last century.) He theorised that there's value in children not having somebody who's available and responds immediately all the time. Children need to learn to tolerate frustration. Making mistakes gives us the opportunity to repair them and to model for our children how to do this.[3] The key is to try to limit these mistakes, as far as possible, and to make sure our children aren't overwhelmed by them.

This idea is different from the rest of the book, as it's based on logic and experts' views, not on the results of stacks of research reports. The reason for this is simple. There's no easy way to test outcomes for bad parents versus good enough parents versus perfect parents in a research setting, and it's hard to test something with a group of people who can be found as often as werewolves and unicorns.

I think this is probably my most important point. Amid mountains of data and suggested approaches, it's vital to say that no parent should try to hold themselves up to impossible, or even exacting, standards. Some ideas in this book will be helpful, some ideas won't – no family or child is the same, after all – and you'll only be able to put some of the more successful ideas into practice some of the time. And that's OK.

PART ONE

Cross-cutting parenting approaches

CHAPTER 1

YOU

Balancing parenthood and general life can wear down the most patient of parents, of which I'm certainly not one. We all have competing pressures. By the end of a typical week, I might have taken one child to the optician to replace a lost pair of glasses, dropped off a forgotten musical instrument at another child's school, booked dentist appointments, done four or five drop-offs and pickups at different clubs or friends' houses, cooked multiple meals, put on a mystifying amount of laundry, paid several bills and worked a full week. The gruelling nature of the list probably sounds familiar to you even if the items on it vary. Patience and calm are the aims; irritability and fatigue are often the reality.

But research points to a need to prioritise parents' own well-being. Decent parenting depends on the parent – how you feel has a massive impact on your child. While life can get in the way of a full night's sleep, eating well, speaking to friends and doing activities that make us happy, these things help us be kind and loving with our children. It's a predicament that requires hard choices. When my children were small, I eventually overrode a sense of guilt so I could exercise in my lunch break instead of finishing work as early as I could to spend time with them. I think it was the right decision (I was much nicer to be around).

This chapter looks at what you can do for yourself that will also help your child. So much of what we're told we need to do for ourselves requires time, but it's not always possible to wring more hours from a busy day. Some suggestions in this chapter can be done with minimal time input, such as redirecting your energy away from intensive parenting and reframing negative thoughts. And when all else fails, you have the e-nanny. Screens aren't necessarily a bad thing if the content is good quality and you're a better parent because you've had some time to yourself.

Look after yourself and support your well-being

Research shows that children are better off when their parents are OK. Unless you're already in the best mental shape of your life, it means either reducing stress or finding ways to manage its impact. This can seem daunting when sources of stress stem not only from general life but also from the fact of being a parent. Routine childcare is more stressful than interactive childcare – preparing meals and getting children to go to bed is probably going to have more of a negative impact on you than playing games together. Mothers tend to find childcare more stressful than fathers do, possibly because they often pick more of it up and are more likely to combine it with other domestic tasks.[1]

Stress can have its uses if it prompts us to balance our well-being scales a little better, while in other cases, a cue may come from an outside source. My own realisation that I needed to tip the scales more favourably came after I was referred by my doctor for a short period of counselling. This was meant to help me deal with the intense sadness I felt at my dad's terminal cancer diagnosis, but it reminded me that there were many other areas of my life in which I could look after myself more. The downsides to stress, though, tend to outweigh any utility. Sometimes it's possible to get into a negative spiral of stress within a family. The stress of being a parent makes children more likely to act up, which then causes further pressure for the parent.

Many sources of stress can't be magically eliminated. If you have a child with autism spectrum disorder or developmental delay, you're more likely to experience stress than other parents. If you've previously experienced postnatal depression or you have an ill child, your stress levels are also likely to be higher. Your well-being can be affected by financial problems, relationship difficulties or whether you live in a country with supportive family policies. Much of my own stress when my children were very small was internally driven – a creeping sense of ineptitude and an inability to vault over the high bars I'd set myself – but that didn't make it less real or more controllable.[2]

All parents experience at least some stress during their children's early lives. Our frequent lack of influence over its causes makes it important to find other ways to promote well-being. Better well-being can also help protect your child from some of these uncontrollable sources of stress. Even if parents work unusual hours or shift patterns, children are less likely to be affected if their parents are happy and healthy. And while children are affected by their parents' state of mind, sometimes it's the children who influence how their parents feel. Parents are less stressed when they have a good relationship with their child, and I've run out of fingers and toes to count the number of times my excellent mood has been punctured by a small child who just wants to complain about everything.

What can we do to reduce stress and increase well-being when there's often little give in our lives? Many things don't need another adult, money or lots of available time, of course. They can be done while your child is asleep or otherwise distracted; screen time can be invaluable in clawing you back some much-needed headspace. You might want to listen to music or a podcast, read a book, have a hot shower, stretch, lift some heavy weights or chat to a friend. Whatever it is that soothes you, your child will benefit from you being more at ease. Even the ideas with the strongest evidence base are unlikely to work for everybody, though, so don't worry if you try something and it's not a success. I've tried mindfulness. It's never going to help me. However, high-quality research throws up a lot of great ideas, so there should be something in the next few paragraphs that chimes with you.

Physical activity is linked to better well-being, but it can be hard to build structured exercise into full days. Workarounds include taking your child to school or clubs on foot, getting off the bus a stop early, or carrying heavy shopping bags home. Small bursts of movement throughout the day can keep your metabolism high. These can be as effective, or even more effective, as doing the same amount of exercise in a single session.[3] If you have stairs and you're at home, you could walk up and down them a few times once an hour, or do some hourly squats or press-ups. (You may be in the 'don't tell me to move' camp. 'People will detest you for writing this paragraph,' said my partner. I blame the research.)

Reinterpreting how you think about events that upset you is another way to improve mental health.[4] 'Cognitive reappraisal' involves finding alternative, more positive explanations for a situation. If a friend cancels dinner with you, you might focus on how overstretched they are instead of worrying they don't like you enough to prioritise you. If you cancel a trip because you become ill, you might think about now having time to watch a TV programme you've been wanting to see or to catch up on sleep. This approach is most useful in situations over which you don't have control. If you can change a negative situation, you should do so. Your mental health benefits more by changing something awful (or even merely irritating) than it does by accepting it.

Better sleep improves well-being. Tired parents are less likely to be confident about their abilities than those who are better rested, and this lack of confidence leads them to parent less well. The amount of sleep you get may be out of your control, of course. If it's not, you could try tested strategies like avoiding screens and bright lights near bedtime, reducing the amount of alcohol you drink, going to bed and getting up at the same time every day – including at weekends, however unpleasant that feels – and following a bedtime routine. If you've lain awake for more than twenty minutes, it's recommended you get up for a bit so your brain doesn't start to associate lying in bed with not sleeping.[5] I've found that it's not tempting to do this at 3 a.m. on a cold winter's night.

Paying attention to the present moment, also known as mindfulness, can reduce parental stress and improve outcomes for children. Kids of mindful parents have better mental health and are less likely to act up.[6] You could try an app offering mindfulness meditations, do regular body scans (moving up from your toes to your head to notice how different parts of your body feel) or perhaps pay regular attention to your senses, noticing what you can see, hear, feel, taste and smell at different moments during the day. To show that research findings do not apply to every person, I get spikes of adrenaline when I try to be mindful. For me, paying attention to the present moment reminds me of the things taking time to be mindful has prevented me from doing.

Research also tells us to avoid intensive parenting if we want decent levels of well-being.[7] Parents who invest the most time in providing emotional support for their children report worse mental health. This may be because their own needs aren't met if they have little time available for anything beyond their children. Intensive parents have certain beliefs: they're the more capable parent, happiness comes mainly from being a parent, parents should always provide stimulation for their children, parenting's hard (they may have got that bit right), and parents' own needs are secondary to the needs of their children. It's worth questioning these beliefs if any of them sound familiar to you.

One aspect of intensive parenting can support parents' own mental health. This is the investment of thought and effort: doing some research to support your child's education, perhaps, or finding out-of-school clubs that match their interests. My younger daughter likes hanging upside down like a monkey. It took years of doing nothing, followed by a four-year waiting list, to discover that she would get enormous pleasure out of an aerial circus class. A little more dedicated research earlier on might have got us there sooner.

Time spent with your children – chatting to them, playing games together or watching a film, perhaps – can boost well-being. For many parents, this is the most enjoyable part of their day. At the same time, don't beat yourself up if this isn't among your top activities. Your children need your input, but it doesn't mean you're an awful parent if you'd rather be working or running or hiding in a corner with a book.

Wider social support is another key ingredient in parental well-being. For those who don't have close family or friends nearby, options include local community groups or parenting networks. Online communities might help for those with nothing physically near them (though you need to be careful not to compare yourself with other parents on social media. Mumsnet can be invaluable, but it's not real life).

If your child's other parent lives with you and you're doing more than your fair share of childcare, your well-being is likely to be supported by finding better ways of distributing responsibilities. Stress is higher for parents when their partners are less involved than they'd like them to be. I've seen marriages end over less. And if you're in a less-than-happy relationship, it could probably do with some attention. A strong relationship with your partner means that any feelings of misery and insecurity in other areas of your life are less likely to affect your child. Ideas on how to strengthen your relationship are given in the next chapter. If it's your work, not your relationship, that's making you miserable, and your job allows for it, you could request flexible working. This has been shown to reduce stress for women and for single parents in particular.[8]

Strategies to support children's behaviour represent another potential stake in your happiness palisade. Parents are more content when their children behave well, just as parents' well-being influences how children behave. I'm happier when my children are chatting away about their day than when they're scrapping about who got the biggest square of chocolate, and they're more likely to be in a chatty-not-fighty mood if I'm outwardly happier. (You might well say 'Dealing with behaviour is all very well in theory, but how do I stop my child from daubing my cat with purple poster paint?' Ideas about behaviour are covered later in the book, so you may need to accept your unusually coloured mog until you get that far.)

It's important to go easy on yourself when you're hurting, when you believe you've failed to do something, or when you don't meet the standards you've set for yourself. Being understanding and warm towards yourself is key. Self-compassion helps to improve well-being by reducing any guilt and shame you feel as a parent. If you want to know more about how to be self-compassionate (which is an extremely difficult thing to do if you have a history of being self-critical), it's worth looking online for the work of Dr Kristin Neff. She offers good, practical advice in this area, and makes the point that we can all learn to be self-compassionate because we do it for other people.

One simple way to be more compassionate towards yourself is to ask the question 'What do I need?' and go from there. The answer to this doesn't need to be about big things like money or relationships. It could be about what you need *right now*, like a stretch or some breathing exercises, a cup of tea or to give yourself five minutes away from your child while you leave them in a safe space. Ask this question of yourself regularly and respond to the needs you identify.

Expert advice tells us we should consider our own needs, not just those of our children. If you find it hard to make time for yourself, a first step is to list a few things that are important to you – time with friends, a hobby, some exercise. The next step is to schedule time for these things, using another parent or childcare as needed, or doing them while your child is occupied by something else. A Duplo set or *Minecraft*, depending on your child's age, are your friends here. Even taking ten minutes a day for yourself can be a good start if you haven't allowed yourself any time so far. It's good to be open with your child about giving yourself time; if you're clear about the need to care for yourself, they'll be more likely to feel able to do the same for themselves.

Personal well-being is only one tool in an arsenal of things you can do as a parent to help your child (and this arsenal is large enough to fill a book!), so don't panic if none of these suggestions sounds right for you. If you're concerned about your well-being and don't know how to improve it, there are plenty of sections later in this book that can help insulate your child from any negative impacts. But if you're feeling very anxious or low, it might be an idea to get some support from your doctor or mental health services.

Be aware of and manage your emotions

Some researchers believe there are six major emotions – happiness, anger, sadness, disgust, surprise and fear. Others think there are twenty-seven; more subtle variations might include joy, contentment, envy and rage. Still others have counted many more, creating envy in me of what must be their sophisticated emotional landscape. Healthy management of emotions is rightly seen as something we need to help our children to develop, but it's just as much a thorny issue for parents. My child's unlikely to learn patience if she witnesses me railing at traffic or twitching to get on with my day while she ambles over a meal.

When parents show unhealthy anger or express other negative emotions in response to bad behaviour, children behave even worse in future. An angry response to siblings bickering at the dinner table upsets children and makes them more likely to behave that way again, or even to fight with each other more. Positive behaviour is linked to parents reacting well to how their children express their feelings and being able to discuss them: 'It's been a long day. How about we reset? How are you both feeling?' is more likely to get a positive result than 'Oh, for goodness' sake, will you two just stop it?'

Managing emotions in a healthy way means taking a moment to think about how to react to a particular feeling – should I shout at my child for dropping the contents of her cereal bowl on the floor and making me late, or should I ask her to help me clean it up? It also involves being aware of how you are feeling, changing the way you think about things when your previous way of thinking is unhelpful to you, and being self-compassionate about feeling angry or scared. If you're feeling on edge because your gas bill has arrived and it's not going to be easy to pay it, you might pause to recognise that it's a tough situation, and that it's not surprising you're feeling upset. This recognition may help you avoid transferring the stress onto your child.

Being aware of your emotions is the first step in supporting your child to be emotionally aware (something covered later in the book). This awareness may be as simple as linking physical feelings to emotional states. When you feel angry, you might notice that your face is hot and you feel light-headed; when you feel worried, it might be hard to breathe in deeply and you may have a tight sensation across the top of your stomach. The second step, if you sometimes feel overwhelmed by your feelings, is to find ways to manage them healthily.

High-quality research suggests that healthy management of emotions means taking time to consider your thoughts and feelings, rather than avoiding them.[9] People who try to suppress what they think or feel tend to focus on their thoughts and feelings more than they would have done otherwise. If somebody says 'Don't think of the Eiffel Tower in a thunderstorm,' it's hard not to imagine it. The same is true if you tell yourself to get over your feelings. You might want to find alternative explanations for things that would normally make you feel sad, angry, frustrated or otherwise negative as part of this process. Cognitive reappraisal, which I talked about earlier in this chapter, can help you feel better. Again, it's most useful in situations over which you have no control.

Distraction is another tool when you find yourself endlessly focused on a particular feeling or event. This is different from suppression; you're not exactly trying to ignore what you feel, but instead you're giving yourself a break when you can't stop thinking about something. Interminable rumination is a track my mind slips into with ease when something is wrong. Distraction can be achieved through a hobby (for me, running, painting or cooking a hellishly complex meal can give me a break, however brief) or even something as simple as turning on the TV, listening to the radio or reading a story to your child. Distraction is also a good way to improve your mood.

Mindfulness practice also turns up in the research relating to emotions. Emotions tend to be healthier, with more good feelings and fewer bad ones, if you focus on the moment at least once a day. Another research-based suggestion is to make sure, within reason, that you show your feelings to your child. Parents who feel they need to conceal sadness, anger and hurt from their children are less able to help their children manage their own emotions. A friend of mine not only shows her difficult feelings but explains her moods to her young child – perhaps saying she's grumpy as she's feeling premenstrual. This helps her child realise that her mother's moods are not her fault. Parents and children are in a worse mood and get on less well when parents hide their difficult feelings, according to the research. If you are feeling uncontrollable anger or raging sadness and your child is present, then it is best to step away.[10]

Showing your feelings to your child can be tricky if you're not used to it. You could use a template to make it easier: 'I feel... when... because...' You could say 'I feel happy when you hug me, because I love you,' or 'I feel sad when I can't see Grandad very often, because he's so important to me.' You could also make time towards the end of the day, perhaps at dinner, to talk about how everybody's day was and how they're feeling. Part of this conversation means sharing your own experiences and emotions – obviously making sure the things you say take account of your child's age and stage of development and aren't likely to cause stress. You might say, 'I had lunch with [best friend's name] and it made me happy,' or 'I got stuck in a lift, and I was so bored and uncomfortable.' It is best to avoid thoughts about how frustrated your child made you feel when they smeared jam over the freshly painted walls.

My own model for this is a counsellor friend with a much better-cultivated set of emotional resources than I have. She talks about her feelings with her children lightly, perhaps sharing her worries because she has to give a big presentation at work. Her children respond positively and as a result are comfortable exploring their own feelings with her. Jam-based exploits aside, there will be times when it's important to show your child you feel angry, sad or afraid. This is probably harder than signalling your joy when your football team has won a key match or you've had a promotion. Showing negative feelings should be done in an age-appropriate way, ensuring your child doesn't believe they're to blame for the way you're feeling. And touching on difficult adult feelings is different from exploring them in depth. The former is probably healthier from your child's perspective.

A further point is to use 'I feel', not 'I am', when describing feelings. 'I feel cross' suggests a passing state, while 'I am cross' suggests you identify with the feeling. Using language to imply impermanence allows people some distance from their fear or fury. This sense of transience can help children understand emotions better and avoid becoming weighed down by them. You can use language in this way when talking to your child about how they feel as well: 'It seems you're feeling sad tonight.'

Part of healthily managing your emotions is being emotionally available for your child. In the research literature, emotional availability is based on four main elements.[11] The first of these is *parental sensitivity*, which involves picking up on your child's emotions and expressing your own genuinely. Sensitive parents respond quickly to their children's signals, are flexible according to their needs and can mend things when there's conflict. You might show sensitivity if you notice your child is withdrawn and you sit with them quietly until they feel comfortable enough to talk about what's bothering them.

The second element is *structuring*. This means helping your child explore and learn in a way that suits them, while also promoting their independence. It means giving your child clues – but not too many – about things they don't know yet, being clear about any rules relating to learning and showing your child what expectations you have of them. You might, for example, choose to structure some maths for them. If your child has started subtracting numbers to two decimal places at school, you could ask how much change they'll have from their £3 pocket money if they decide to buy the £1.75 toy they want.

Element three is *non-intrusiveness*. Being non-intrusive means trusting your child to be able to find solutions to problems and make decisions, and being present for them when they need you. It's a fine balance. Non-intrusiveness also involves trying not to be overprotective or interfering. If your child tells you about a problem they're having with a friend, you might ask them what they want to do about it rather than offering a solution.

The final element is *non-hostility*. This is probably the most straightforward part of emotional availability, and it's self-explanatory. Instead of being hostile, emotionally available parents are pleasant and patient. (I want to like this idea, but I resent the concept of parents who can respond to a child-led coup with endless equanimity.) These parents are assertive when needed, and they're able to show anger in an appropriate and controlled way. A non-hostile response to being shouted at by your child might be to say that you're happy to discuss the reasons they feel upset when they're ready to talk to you calmly.

Make time to reflect on your childhood experiences

When American author and shame researcher Brené Brown did a TEDx Talk on vulnerability, she described going into therapy. She said to her therapist: 'Here's the thing: no family stuff, no childhood shit. I just need some strategies.' But family and childhood always matter. Her therapy turned, she said, into 'a year-long street fight. It was a slugfest. Vulnerability pushed; I pushed back. I lost the fight but probably won my life back.' Her advice was to embrace vulnerability – to recognise that showing other people we're vulnerable allows us to connect with them better. Part of this means teaching our children that they're imperfect, like us, but that they belong and they're loved despite – or because of – these imperfections and vulnerabilities.[12]

Childhood experiences affect our own vulnerabilities and, by extension, the way we act with and feel about our own children. If your mother was frequently angry with you, you may be quick to feel fury with your own child. If your brain turns into molten lava when your child makes a cheeky comment, it may be because you weren't allowed to do the same when you were younger. Being aware of important history that might affect your approach to bringing up your children can help you to be a more effective, sensitive parent. When your child says or does something that reminds you of a traumatic event from your childhood, this awareness also makes you less likely to freeze in the moment or to want to get away.

If you give no thought to your childhood and how you were raised, negative aspects of your experience are likely to repeat themselves in your parenting. Even if you had a really hard time as a child, making sense of those experiences can help protect the next generation from feeling their effects. You can divert the force of nature that is history repeating itself.

Childhood experiences can be at the heart of parents' frustrations with their children. It's important to admit to ourselves when we find our children's behaviour aggravating. It's possible to feel deep love while recognising that, right now, little Betsy's acting like a total bloody nightmare and you need to reset. Pretending otherwise isn't going to solve the issue. Instead, those difficult feelings can be managed without thinking your child is at fault for causing them. It's important to work out why the pressing of a seemingly innocuous button can incite anything from minor irritation through to blinding rage or sorrow. This process helps us avoid acting on these feelings. It's not the negative feelings themselves that are able to cause harm, but what we do with them.

This recommendation doesn't apply only to people who experienced huge trauma, though. Everyone had some degree of childhood difficulty or even minor inconvenience that still resonates today. As one early researcher and psychoanalyst in this area, Selma Fraiberg, so beautifully put it: 'In every nursery there are ghosts… Even among families where the love bonds are stable and strong, the intruders from the parental past may break through the magic circle in an unguarded moment, and a parent and his child may find themselves re-enacting a moment or a scene from another time with another set of characters.'[13]

You'll probably also see echoes of your childhood playing out in things that are an ocean away from anything difficult or traumatic. I have a messy parting because my mum always combed my hair apart in a straight line. My daughter combs herself a straight parting because mine is always messy. There's a pleasing symmetry in this.

So what can we do with this knowledge that the shadows of our childhoods fall on our own children, and that we need to consider the shape of these shadows to help us be better parents? High-quality research tells us to watch out for hostility and harsh discipline if we had a difficult time as children. Parents who have had tough childhoods are more likely to shout at or be coercive with their children and to discipline them harshly, all of which can increase behavioural problems.[14] I'll outline ideas on how to steer away from these approaches later in the book.

It's important to get a sense of your child's thoughts, which may be hard for you to do (and about which you may be less curious) if you had a painful childhood.[15] When parents can focus on what their children are thinking, these children are better able to learn about themselves and society. This learning, in turn, supports their development. Being curious about your child's thoughts and getting a more accurate sense of them may be as simple as asking questions when you're unsure, or as complicated as reading around on childhood development and mental states.

Being aware of the emotional impact of traumatic, abusive or otherwise shattering childhood experiences is also crucial. It'll help you keep a healthy perspective – one in which you're aware of things that might trigger difficult feelings and memories while also being able to meet your child's needs. But you should always be aware of your own levels of comfort and seek professional help if thinking about your childhood is having a negative impact on your mental health.

If you had a difficult relationship with your parents, it may be helpful to write a list covering your similarities and differences to them. The list might include what you liked about how they brought you up, how your own approach to parenting chimes with and differs from theirs, and thoughts about who and how you want to be in future. A journal is another tool you can use to log difficult feelings that come up for you when you're with your child. Writing down when you feel particularly upset or angry can help you spot patterns and work out what might be driving these feelings. As part of this process, you could think about what your child does that drives the strongest reactions in you, and what happened to you as a child when you acted in the same way.

There's value in thinking about areas of parenting that you find almost irrationally upsetting, as you may be able to find clues as to why that is. My own children laugh at how enraged I get if anybody, including them, uses my towel. I thought it was just a quirk until I gave it some proper time and consideration, and realised that towels and similar items represent boundaries. When I was a child, my family prioritised closeness over boundaries, so now I fiercely protect the things I believe I shouldn't need to share with anybody else – towels, pillows and socks. This realisation doesn't mean I'll lend my children a pair of socks. I won't. My socks are mine. But it does mean that I sometimes remember to check my reaction if I spot a pair of smaller feet clad in them.

When you feel angry in the moment, you can give yourself space by telling your child you need time to think about what's happened. If you have a lot of anger relating to your own childhood that's spilling over onto your child, and you can afford it or can get referred by your doctor, you could look into getting support through some kind of talking therapy. If this isn't an option for you, writing exercises can be helpful – setting aside regular time to write about what happened and how it made you feel, or writing letters (ones you never share) to the people who hurt you. Writing can be a powerful tool in helping us to process difficult things that happened in the past.

Try to create boundaries between work and home

If you work, you'll be familiar with how tough it can be to balance work and family life. Boundaries can be incredibly hard to put up and maintain, and may require a huge amount of emotional investment. Guilt is often wrapped up in this, especially if your child plaintively tells you that she believes your work is more important to you than she is (a helpful critique made by Daughter Number Two, who knows precisely how to target my vulnerabilities). If this happens to you, it's worth avoiding lengthy explanations. Instead, you could try reflecting back what they're trying to say to you, perhaps offering a remedy: 'It sounds like you don't think I'm around enough right now. Maybe we could do something about it at the weekend?'

Setting hard edges between home and work can have negative repercussions if the reason for constructing them is for the benefit of employers rather than parents or their families. Some employees (research shows that it's usually women) feel they must show themselves as being flawless, dependable workers who don't let family commitments get in the way of doing their job.[16] They believe, often with justification, that they must present an ultra-reliable version of themselves to the world to protect their jobs and opportunities for promotion. This is draining, and it's an area over which individuals have only limited control, especially if they're in low-paid or insecure work. Legal employment protections haven't caught up with the way that people are working now. There's an absence of legal protection over the right to an uninterrupted home life – and, if you're a shift worker or on a zero-hours contract, certainty over when you'll be working. It's down to the decency of individual employers as to whether you get the support in this area that, in an ideal world, you would be offered.

There are things you can do, though. One of these is to consider your mood when you finish working. If you're feeling negative about work, your mood can affect the quality of your relationship with your child. It may be particularly important to consider mood if you're working from home, as you don't have as much time to turn it around as you do if you have a journey to spend resetting. Parents whose work commitments conflict with their family obligations are more likely to be harsh with their children, with a knock-on impact on their children's well-being. And while the number of hours parents work doesn't affect the quality of their relationship with their children, tiredness from work does.[17]

Mood is a hard thing to control, and negative feelings about work may need to be closed down to prevent you carrying your stress into time with your family. One thing that may help you create a sense of separation is to have or create a 'boundary marker' between home and work. This might take the form of a journey, if you travel to work. You could do something during this time that you wouldn't do anywhere else, like listening to a podcast or reading a book, to help mark it as a separate space or decompression zone.

It's also important to create a mental separation between work and home, and to focus on the value of doing so. You might choose to find ways to distract yourself from thoughts about work if you're contemplating it in your downtime. I've found it helpful to write a list of tasks and a note of any work-related worries just before I leave my desk, as there are fewer things to scream 'Don't forget me!' in my ear when I'm brushing my teeth or reading my daughter stories. People who are keen to keep work and home life separate are more likely to be psychologically detached from work when they're away from it.

Working from home makes the boundaries between home and work particularly porous. I started working from home at the beginning of the pandemic. My children were old enough to have a reasonable degree of self-sufficiency, but my day was still punctuated by urgent information bulletins that we were out of milk, the dog had stolen a shoe, a bank statement had fallen through the letterbox, a scab had started bleeding or there was extreme hunger that needed immediate sating. At one point, deep in the pandemic – with two homeschooling children and both adults working in separate makeshift corners – I found myself howling: 'There's another parent in the house! Leave me alone!'

A first step may be to develop confidence in your abilities to be able to balance work and family demands. One study found that those who feel confident in this area (for example, believing they can give enough attention to things they find important at work and at home) experience less conflict between work and family.[18] Taking regular breaks from work is also helpful for those who work from home. This can make dealing with any interruptions less stressful, as you get breaks from being interrupted as well as a breather from the work itself. I have an alert on my watch that vibrates gently once an hour if I've been sitting down. In theory, I stand up, stretch and perhaps do a few plank walkouts or some lunges. In reality, I'm usually deeply absorbed in whatever I'm doing and promise myself I'll do these things the next time my watch reminds me.

Another suggestion is to create a separate workspace, if you have the physical room to do so.[19] It's easier to maintain boundaries if you're not working where you sleep or cook. You may need to get inventive if space is lacking. When my first daughter was young, I worked from home with her once a week. Our flat was small. My solution to her lack of space to play and my lack of ability to work was to rejig her playpen so I was sitting inside it. She had the run of the room, but she couldn't access my precious laptop through the bars. It was my own miniature workhouse.

It's worth being clear with your child when it's OK to interrupt your work and when they must not, except, perhaps, if they're bleeding or on fire. You might say that if you're on a call when they want to talk to you, they need to wait until you finish. You could come up with a joint signal together – perhaps a thumbs up – to show you know they want your attention, and you'll give it to them as soon as you're able to do so.

Boundary markers aren't just the preserve of those who travel to work. You could create a short routine to act as a boundary marker once you've finished at your desk and before you rejoin your family. This might be a five-minute physical stretch or a set of breathing exercises. If there's another adult in the house or your child isn't at home with you, you could go out for a short walk to mark the end of the working day. I often mark the boundary between work and home by watering the houseplants I haven't yet managed to kill.

A final point is to avoid checking email or answering the phone once you're done for the day. And yes, as someone who works from home, I know how hard this is to do in practice. Clear boundaries can make it easier to keep away from after-hours contact – keeping work emails off your personal phone, shutting down your computer at the end of the day and being clear with colleagues that they can expect responses from you within working hours only. You may, however, have a job where you need to be available for calls outside normal working hours. My very organised half-sister has a system for this, telling colleagues she has a hierarchy of post-work contact. Emails will be answered when she's next at work, texts will be dealt with as soon as possible but may not be handled straight away, and phone calls will receive urgent attention. This way, she can leave her phone within earshot but doesn't need to have it close enough that it might disturb her conversations with her family.

If you're unable to maintain boundaries between work and home for any reason, it's paramount to find other ways to protect your well-being. You might seek help from friends and family, and build in time – however limited – to do things that allow you to comb out any mental knots.

Be confident in your abilities as a parent (and, if you lack confidence, read books like this one)

Parenting 'self-efficacy' is what the research literature terms confidence in parenting skills. Confident parents are less likely to use harsh, permissive or inconsistent discipline with their children. They experience less parenting stress, and their children have better outcomes. It's arguable that parents feel more confident when they have good mental health, excellent social support, and money to buy good-quality food and stimulating resources for their children. These things also benefit children directly. That said, there's a case to be made that parenting confidence is important in its own right.[20]

Imagine a situation in which things have been tough at home for a few months, you're worried you're not doing a good job as a parent and your stress levels are high. Your patience levels are probably thinner than when you're feeling better about things. If your child aggravates you now, you're more likely to shout or be irritable. On the other hand, if you believe you're flourishing within this odd constellation of behaviours and emotions known as parenting, and you're happy and relaxed as a result, you're probably more likely to respond well to a child who is miserable or cross.

Parenting confidence depends not just on individual parents, but also on circumstances and what's happening in the world. It also depends on how much social support parents have. The self-efficacy of new parents fell during Covid-19 lockdowns.[21] And parents who have recently moved to a new country often see their parenting confidence eroded in line with a loss in easily accessible support from friends and family. It also depends on their children – parents tend to have more confidence when they have healthy children with easy temperaments. It's also fair to say that confidence ebbs and flows. Sometimes I believe I've mostly cracked it. Other times, when a screaming child has fled the room or told me that I've never once, not in her whole lifetime, thought about her feelings, the wind is knocked from my sails.

While parenting confidence can be affected by situations out of your control, there are still several things you can do to increase it. The first is gaining knowledge. Knowledge is the currency of parenting self-efficacy. Through it, you accumulate a better understanding of child development. By reading this book or others on parenting, you have the potential to increase your confidence in your abilities, and, hopefully, improve outcomes for your children.

You can avoid drowning under the weight of this knowledge by telling yourself that the most important things are warmth and boundaries; everything else follows from these. There's also an element of the emperor's new clothes here. A feeling of confidence, whether or not it's justified, seems linked to positive outcomes for children. It's also good for you as a parent. If you feel confident in your abilities to bring up your child, you're likely to be happier with the decisions you make. And confidence isn't necessarily about new knowledge. It may also stem from reassurance that your instincts are sound. In the words of author Alberto Manguel, 'Maybe this is why we read, and why in moments of darkness we return to books: to find words for what we already know.'[22]

Research suggests that confidence can also be bolstered by knowing the parenting difficulties you experience are normal. Parents across the world experience day-to-day challenges. If you're struggling with your child's behaviour, health, mood or well-being, or your relationship with them, you're not alone. Parenting programmes that encourage parents to share daily hassles with each other are successful in increasing self-efficacy. It's easier to feel confident in your abilities if you know everyone else struggles too.[23]

It can also help to think about your strengths and how you can apply these more as a parent.[24] If you're visually creative, you could do lots of crafty things with your child. If you're good at scheduling regular exercise for yourself, you could model healthy habits and perhaps play sport with them. If you're good at cooking or baking, you could teach your child to do these too. Confidence increases when parents apply their own strengths to cultivating their children's. Sleep is also important. Well-rested parents have more confidence in their abilities, in turn making them better parents.

If you live with your partner or the other parent is involved in your child's life in any way, it's important to try not to undermine each other, and be nice to each other. Partners who undermine each other are less confident as parents, so it's worth trying to back each other up. Making consistent efforts to have positive interactions with your partner is linked to more confident parenting.[25] This may be because confidence levels go up when people feel both supported and able to support others. It's also going to be destabilising for your child if you both have dramatically different ideas about how to bring them up.

You can't support each other on everything, but it's most important to do so when setting limits. If you find it hard to agree with each other's approach to parenting, you could each choose your two or three most important priorities in terms of raising your child. Timekeeping is high on my own list: the thought of being late makes the circuits misfire in the rational parts of my brain, which I blame on my dad's historical eagerness to be at the station at least ninety minutes before any train was due to leave. My partner is keener on table manners, and needs me to back him up, however relaxed I feel about the issue, if we see our daughter scooping peas into her mouth with her hands.

If you understand which elements are the most important to your partner and vice versa, it's easier to back each other up than if you're trying to support each other on a never-ending slate of priorities. As for the rest, instead of having fixed ideas – even evidence-based ones – about how to parent, it's probably worth approaching this as a conversation. What does your partner think are the most important red lines for parenting? How do these compare with your own? Where can you find common ground, and how can you both compromise on the things that sit outside this?

Expert advice, finally, suggests you have every reason to be confident. While others might have general knowledge about parenting and education, you are genuinely the expert on your child. Nobody else in the world – except, perhaps, the child's other parent, depending on your circumstances – understands your child as well as you do. You're also the only person who can read through the list of evidence-based ideas in each section of this book and have a sense of what's likely to be best for them. Other people may know the research, but you know your child.

CHAPTER CHECKLIST

Key recommendations

- ▶ Look after yourself and support your well-being.
- ▶ Be aware of and manage your emotions.
- ▶ Make time to reflect on your childhood experiences.
- ▶ Try to create boundaries between work and home.
- ▶ Be confident in your abilities as a parent (and, if you lack confidence, read books like this one).

Some of the ideas below may help you put these recommendations into practice.

High-quality research

- ▶ **Look after your body.** Move more and get more sleep, if you can.
- ▶ **And look after your mind.** Don't try to suppress your thoughts or feelings. Try mindfulness. See if you can find alternative explanations for things that might normally make you feel sad, angry, frustrated or otherwise negative. Try distraction when you find yourself endlessly focused on a particular feeling or event. See if there are ways of increasing the social support available to you.
- ▶ **Recognise how normal it is to find parenting challenging.** It's incredibly common to experience difficulties, and it's useful to know this.
- ▶ **Take in some broad-brush parenting recommendations to improve your well-being.** Work on feeling more confident in your abilities as a parent, which can help to alleviate feelings of depression. Avoid 'intensive parenting'. Watch out for hostility and harsh discipline, which can make you feel worse (and aren't brilliant for your child either).
- ▶ **Use family time to boost how you feel.** Make the most of time spent together as a family, as well as playing with and chatting to your child.
- ▶ **Try to reset your mood when you finish work.** Low mood when you finish work, as well as work-related tiredness, can affect how you feel and your relationship with your child.

Moderate-quality research

▶ **Be self-compassionate.** If you had a difficult childhood, it's especially important to keep in mind what you've been through.

▶ **Be open with thoughts and feelings.** Try to get a better sense of what your child may be thinking, and don't (within reason) hide your feelings from your child.

▶ **Make your work work for you.** If your workplace allows it, request flexible working. Create a mental separation between work and home, and focus on the value of doing so. If you travel to work, use the journey to mark the boundary between home and work on the way in, and work and home on the way back.

▶ **If you have a partner, make sure the partnership works for you too.** If your relationship isn't making you happy, consider whether there may be ways to improve it (see Chapter 2). If you're doing more than your fair share of childcare, try to work out better ways of dividing responsibility. Try not to undermine each other. Be nice to each other.

▶ **Use parenting techniques to your advantage.** Think about your strengths, and how you can apply those more as a parent. If your child's behaviour is an issue, work with them to improve it (see Chapter 6).

▶ **Avoid comparisons.** Don't compare yourself with other parents, in particular on social media.

Anecdotal research/expert advice

▶ **Carefully frame the language you use.** Use 'I feel', not 'I am', when describing feelings.

▶ **Use writing to your advantage.** If you had a difficult relationship with your parents, consider writing a list that covers your similarities and differences to them. Think about keeping a journal covering difficult feelings that come up for you when you're with your child.

▶ **Don't be a martyr.** Consider your own needs, not just your children's.

▶ **Recognise your expertise.** You have every reason to be confident about your abilities as a parent: you are the authority on your own child.

Troubleshooting: working from home

Create a separate workspace if you have physical room to do so. Be clear with your child when it's OK to interrupt your work and when they must not. Take regular breaks from work. Try to develop confidence in your abilities to balance work and family demands. Don't check email or answer the phone once you're done for the day.

CHAPTER 2

HOME LIFE

Like most couples, my partner and I have had periods of simmering unspoken rage that flash into the odd argument, usually driven by some tedious, eternal to-do list. I want it done so I can relax. My partner thinks it'll never get done, so we may as well ignore it and enjoy life. We probably both have a point. (That's not true. I'm right.) But any periods of bubbling acrimony make it hard to concentrate on anything else. During these moments, I have a ticker tape of furious mutterings running through my mind, making it hard for my children to break through.

Your child's outcomes depend on your family and home. Arguments breed arguments, and relationship stress leads to unhealthy conflict between parents and their children. Good parenting can be elusive when there's a toxic atmosphere at home, but a calm environment offers children stability. Being organised makes things less stressful for children – I've seen myself how the heat is dialled up if we can't find my daughter's school shoes when she was meant to leave five minutes ago or we've run out of things to put in her packed lunch that she deems non-disgusting. This is where that to-do list comes in handy, you see? It's definitely not my inability to back down or admit defeat that's the real issue here.

The available evidence suggests that reducing unhealthy conflict, if there's a lot of it in your family, is the most important part of this chapter. This conflict might be between you and your partner, you and your child, your partner and your child, or between your children. Perhaps your family is generally argumentative. (Tick.) You may feel you don't want to reduce conflict if it's in the healthy zone – if people are expressing their needs assertively and they're able to maintain affection while disagreeing. But if it's corrosive and making people unhappy, some of the ideas here may help.

Try to reduce levels of unhealthy family conflict

Conflict can teach children how to assert their needs, and it can help family members negotiate day-to-day issues – who does which jobs, who gets priority over the remote control, how to stop 103 sheets of loo paper being used for every poo. Healthy conflict in a family is about calm discussion of disagreements, while showing others you support them and care about them.

Young children develop better social and emotional skills when they have parents who are good at conflict.[1] A skilful parent might be able to explain why they're asking their child to do something they clearly don't want to, help them find healthy ways of expressing their anger, and teach them to compromise where needed. Healthy conflict can have long-term benefits, including emotional security, in those who experience it. When children negotiate with their parents to resolve conflict, they learn something valuable they can later apply with their friends and reflect back to their parents. Through this process, my own children have learned the ability to defeat me and my partner with deadly logic. This is a brilliant outcome if they ever want to become lawyers, and a terrible one at 3 p.m. on a Sunday when I just want them to walk the bloody dog.

Family conflict, when it's less healthy, isn't fun for anyone. It has all kinds of negative consequences for both children and their parents. Conflict becomes destructive when people get defensive, insults are thrown, family members are hostile with each other or they sulk. When it's between parents, conflict can be particularly damaging – children may blame themselves or feel rejected. They may also feel sad, angry, scared or insecure. Conflict can even cause harm when children aren't around to witness it. It's hard to be responsive and warm with your child if you're mulling over a massive row you had with your partner or feeling anxious due to constant friction. When parents feel irritable, conflict is more frequent, and frequent conflict leads to irritable parents.

Sometimes, parents focus anger or criticism on their children as a way of distracting themselves from tensions with their partners. Parents fighting with each other may spend less time with their children. In some cases, on the other hand, parents' relationships with their children improve when they're fighting with their partners. This can happen when parents try to build a closer relationship with their child to compensate for the less satisfactory one they're enduring with their partner, or, more healthily, when they've recognised that parenting responsibilities don't disappear when other aspects of their lives are tricky.

The impact of conflict on children depends on how secure they feel and how well they can handle emotional disruption. A key point, and one I find reassuring when I hear my kids yelling at each other yet again over some infraction, is that conflict is incredibly common. One estimate suggests that toddlers argue with their parents around seven times an hour.[2] If you feel embattled, it may be reassuring to know that so, too, are most other parents.

Ideas for reducing unhealthy conflict between you and your child, or between your children, are covered in Chapter 5, so this section focuses on conflict with your partner. Frequent arguing with a partner can be reduced through more general improvements in your relationship – something covered in the next section – so this part has been kept brief.

Emotionally focused couples' therapy has been shown to reduce conflict and to increase relationship satisfaction. A less financially taxing option, however, is to take steps to disagree with each other constructively. This means discussing things calmly, and showing each other support and affection. Constructive disagreement entails avoiding insults, hostility and defensiveness. And if your temptation, like mine, is to shut down or sulk after a row, it means overriding this impulse and engaging with your partner. Constructive conflict between partners is linked to happier relationships, improved parenting and better-adjusted children.[3]

Sometimes you might find yourselves disagreeing over a particular issue. Common ones in my home are the right setting for the thermostat (I believe in multiple layers of clothing; my partner believes my perspective is skewed because I 'grew up in a shed on an island in the middle of the North Sea') and how long it's acceptable to leave the washing-up undone. You might try a ten-step programme to resolve this type of conflict:[4]

1. Agree when and where you'll discuss this issue.
2. Define it with each other – what exactly is the problem?
3. Work out how each of you contributes to the dispute. (If the cause of arguments is that one partner is messy, it's not just the messiness that's an issue. It's also the other partner's intolerance of that mess.)
4. Remember times you've tried unsuccessfully to resolve this in the past.
5. Work together to list all the possible solutions.
6. Talk about these solutions, and what the benefits and challenges are.
7. Choose one solution to try.
8. Work out and agree how each of you will contribute to this solution.
9. Plan another meeting.
10. Give each other recognition for any contributions you make towards this solution.

Alcohol can make people feel worse about conflict with their partners, and can also lead them to take a more negative view of their partners' feelings.[5] If you think this might be true for you, you could try to reduce your alcohol intake.

You might occasionally find yourself in a rocky patch with your partner, or your children may be fighting with each other no matter what you do. At these moments, having a strong relationship with your child can help protect them from the negative effects of conflict (see

Chapter 5). Being emotionally available for your child can also help them navigate some of the challenges that come from living in a home in which there's lots of conflict.

If you're separated from your partner, a process called 'mentalising' can help reduce conflict. This involves thinking about your own mental state and those of your ex-partner and child, removing (if you can, and assuming there is no abusive behaviour) any assumptions that your ex-partner's behaviour is malign. Instead, consider what might be driving their behaviour – for example, fear they may not be able to spend as much time as they'd like with their child, hurt relating to the end of your relationship, or loneliness. Your own behaviour might be driven by similar feelings. If you've had a difficult break-up and this approach feels too charitable towards your ex-partner, remember that the purpose is to help with parenting. It's important to keep your child's needs and feelings in mind. The process of mentalising won't necessarily reduce your feelings of anger, but it does seem to reduce how much anger is shown. This in turn reduces conflict levels. Mediation can also help reduce conflict in couples who have split up.

There is lots in the research literature about parental separation damaging children. It's not living in a single-parent household that causes harm, though – it's the conflict, at least in part because it makes children fear being abandoned. One study took conflict out of the equation by comparing single-parent families with two-parent families. All families involved in the study had chosen to become pregnant using sperm donation. The single-parent families had chosen this family set-up from the start; there had been no relationship breakdown. The study found no differences in either parenting quality or child adjustment between single-parent and two-parent families. Conflict between parents and their children was actually lower in single-parent households.[6]

In other words, there's no need to feel guilty about the end of a relationship or to worry about its effect on your child, so long as you can minimise conflict. If fighting is inevitable, you can protect your child by building a strong relationship with them and being emotionally available.

If you live with your partner, try to support each other and build your relationship

Relationships with partners are hard to get right, and yet they're crucial for your child's mental health and their connections with other people. Building a strong relationship, or getting over the inevitable bumps in the road, isn't as simple as just getting on better with each other. The myriad potential infringements on your relationship include pressures of finances, work and family admin. If you have a partner with whom things aren't entirely right, you may want – and need – far more than a few paragraphs in a parenting book can offer you. On the other hand, a summary of research in this area might be useful.

The quality of parents' relationships has far-reaching effects for their children. A struggling relationship casts a long shadow. It affects the atmosphere at home, how much (or how little) parents are able to show their happiness, how grumpy they are, how distracted they are, how much children are exposed to (and may later copy) arguments between parents, and how safe and secure they feel.

If you have a good relationship with your partner, it allows you to model healthy ways of solving conflict. 'I don't have enough time to exercise, and it's important to me. Can you help me find a way to carve out some time?' may be more likely to help a child solve conflict with a friend or sibling than if they hear 'I'm fed up with being the one to pick everything up. I don't even have enough time to exercise. You need to do your fair share.' And if you're able to create an atmosphere at home with lots of positive emotions, negative feelings may have less room to flourish.

Just as the quality of your relationship with your partner affects your child, your child affects your relationship too. A relationship can be put under severe pressure by a child's mental health problems, or a child who has regular episodes of screaming, or even something as simple as disagreement over the best way to solve some of these issues. And in a piece of research that will surprise nobody who's been a parent of a small child, parents' relationships are more likely to be strained if their children are sleeping badly.[7]

While supporting your partner across lots of areas is important, bolstering each other's parenting confidence is especially so. When parents don't feel confident, they can be less engaged with their children, act more harshly and be less consistent. These factors in turn negatively affect their children's behaviour. My partner is lavish with his compliments, boosting how I feel and helping me be more confident as a parent. I find giving compliments much harder. They don't trip naturally off my tongue, however much I might feel the sentiment behind them. But time and experience have taught me the value of being generous with words. It's not enough to feel or think things. Nobody can read minds.

Marriage and relationship education programmes have long-term, positive effects on couples' communication skills. Couples' groups can have a lasting impact on how well partners get on with each other, as well as how satisfied they are with their relationships. You don't necessarily need to find an in-person group – relationship education DVDs also have positive effects on relationships. And if DVDs work, we can reasonably assume that good-quality online courses or YouTube videos would work, too.[8]

You could also try specific exercises to help build your relationship with each other. One suggested approach is a 'wish list' exercise, through which you and your partner each share three things you'd like the other to do more often – for instance, that you'd like them to ask about your day more, you'd like more backup on parenting decisions and that you'd like to share the school runs more equitably.[9] It's important to demonstrate you understand what they're saying before you give your answer. Active listening is key here: showing your partner you understand what they're asking of you, even if you don't agree with it.

Another avenue is to develop some goals together. The process of doing this can help you feel close and communicate better with each other. Goals could relate to your family, your relationship or yourself. The research literature describes how this works in couples' therapy. Each partner develops two or three goals individually as homework, then the therapist supports them to share these in turn, focusing on where their goals are similar and how they differ.[10] You could try doing this exercise yourselves, working out how you can help each other achieve these goals (assuming they don't conflict with each other). Again, active listening is important here. It's important to take time to show you understand what your partner wants and to discuss any steps you need to take together to realise these goals.

Individual writing tasks can be useful too. One study showed that getting people to take a third-party perspective can help keep relationships healthy by reducing the amount of conflict-related distress people feel. This task requires you to think about a particular difference of opinion you've had with your partner from the perspective of a neutral observer, trying to find the positives that might come out of it; to think about the barriers to taking this neutral perspective, especially in the heat of an argument; and to consider how to take such a perspective in future. Using these prompts, you only need to write for a few minutes, and repeat it every few months.[11]

Taking an example that almost never happens (or at least no more than twice a week), I might think about a simmering dispute over laundry. I've put on a laundry load the previous evening, and in the morning – after I have started work, and before my partner has done the same – it sits there in the machine, stewing. My initial perspective is that I put on the laundry in my leisure time, and it's only fair that my partner hangs it out in his. In my neutral-observer perspective, I might note that I haven't told him it needs hanging out, and that he's trying to fit walking the dog, making my daughter's packed lunch and eating breakfast into the same fragments of time.

If I'm thinking about the positives that might come from this neutral-observer perspective, I could think that he'd probably be willing, the next time it happens, to get out of bed a few minutes earlier to hang it out, assuming I've let him know there's a load in the machine. I could also consider my own propensity to scan the horizon for jobs, and question whether it's reasonable to expect my partner to do the same – and whether it might be healthier for me to avoid constantly flicking through my mental smorgasbord of possible tasks. One of the major benefits of this task is that, unlike couples' counselling, it doesn't require the involvement of your partner, so if you aren't ready to face issues together, there's still action you can take.

You might occasionally want to reflect honestly on whether you're expecting more from your partner than is reasonable, based on what you put into the relationship (or vice versa). Many people imagine a relationship should meet a variety of needs – for example, offering an opportunity for personal growth and self-expression – while not investing the time and energy required to develop the deep insight into each other's lives and minds, and the related bonding, that would be required.[12]

If you're expecting too much, you could make the most of what's already available to you in the relationship – like if your partner's brilliant at practical support. You could reframe the relationship in your mind, perhaps by doing the writing exercise mentioned above. You could also make more time for each other, both alone and with other people. Alternatively, you could try to get from somewhere else what you're currently missing in your relationship: you could talk about your existential fears with a friend, for instance, if this kind of discussion is not one of your partner's strengths. My own partner knows to go elsewhere if he wants company to watch men's football, see a play or listen to Leonard Cohen.

Communication is key, as is paying attention to your partner's attempts to connect with you. These may be minor (saying, 'Hey, guess what happened today?' or reaching out a hand). You've probably felt the frustration of trying to talk to someone who's distracted by something on their phone. Couples who respond well to each other's attempts to connect are more likely to be together several years later.[13] Similarly, it's good to give each other your full attention when talking to each other. It's easy to be distracted by the washing-up or the pieces of Lego under your foot, but people feel happier in their relationships when they are mindful of bringing their attention to interacting with their partners.

Couples can get into positive cycles where individuals are assertive about their needs (such as making sure household tasks are fairly divided) and ensure that any important issues are tackled head-on. These positive cycles increase their self-confidence. They can also find themselves in a negative spiral in which one partner believes the other is being too dominant about what they need, leading the partner who feels less dominant to avoid dealing with relationship issues.[14]

Sometimes people might ignore elephants in the room due to cowardice or convenience. I have been known, in previous relationships, to ignore issues to the point of only mentioning them in the 'this relationship isn't working for me and I'd like it to be over now' chat. Fortunately for my partner, I'm slightly more mature these days.

Better sleep in children is linked to happier relationships.[15] This is probably because parents feel better rested themselves. Of course, the causality might be the other way round: children may sleep better when their parents get on. Or both may be true. Either way, it may be worth trying to support your child's sleep, if it's an issue (see Chapter 7).

Finally, it's important to make time to have fun together. Spending free time with each other in a way that's enjoyable for you both – whether that's a game of Scrabble, watching a film, climbing a mountain, karaoke, dancing, Frisbee in the park or a swim in the river – is linked to people feeling happier and more stable in their relationships.[16]

Ensure a calm home environment and have routines

Have you ever been to visit other parents and been blindsided by how their homes compare with yours? They also have small children, yet not a thing's out of place, there's a jarring absence of sticky fingerprints forming an impenetrable two-foot-high line in the paintwork, they have a day bag permanently stocked with healthy snacks and water bottles in place of yesterday's detritus, they never forget a birthday and they make you feel as if you're constantly failing. These are the families who have kept the household chaos wolf from the door. I am not recommending you aspire to these heights. It's also important to model failure, which is one of my stronger parenting abilities.

Children do worse when they live in chaotic homes, or those that are unpredictable, rushed, noisy, crowded and disorganised, as do their parents.[17] Chaotic homes are the bright, clashing, unpredictable tones of Stravinsky set against the calm, rippling order of Chopin. Disorganisation and instability are the truly destructive elements of chaos. Of course, there are some harbingers of chaos over which parents have little or no control. Chaos is more likely in households in which there's less money and parents are working multiple low-paid jobs, and in families in which parents have fewer emotional resources to bring more order to home life – those who are physically unwell, for instance, or depressed.

Noise is one of the agents of chaos over which you may have more influence than others. The volume control can be turned down through less arguing, less music and TV, or less shouting across the home for people's attention when dinner's ready or you're putting on a wash (guilty as charged). There's no need to live silently, though. Liveliness and chatter are important too. It's worth thinking about small ways in which noise levels could be reduced, if you think your home is more raucous than most. It's also worth keeping the TV switched off if there's nobody actively watching it – not necessarily because of the noise, but because it disrupts relationships and is linked to children being more aggressive.[18]

It can be hard to work out how to be more organised in a way that suits your brain's preferred pathways. You might be somebody who likes spreadsheets and task manager apps, like me, or you might be somebody who runs screaming from the mention of a spreadsheet, like my partner. More universally helpful ideas include setting aside a weekly time to manage unread post and emails. This could include taking actions needed, such as putting non-uniform days in the diary, or putting in a calendar reminder for things you can't do at the time – say if paying bills needs to wait until the end of the month.

You could also try a general sort-out of rooms and drawers, and, if you have space, create a dedicated place for everything. I've found everything easier since labelling a load of small drawers – important documents, cables, tools, stationery and receipts. This also gives my friends something to laugh at. Recycling, donating or selling stuff you don't need or use can be helpful too. Sorting small areas at a time is more achievable than a single massive overhaul. Children can also be encouraged to help tidy away any mess they've made when they've finished playing. If you're someone who objects to repeating yourself hourly, look away. And if anybody reading this finds any research or tips that work on how to organise children's bedrooms in a way that enables them to stay that way, I'd be grateful to know.

I'm still at the 'anarchy and chaos three hours later' stage of this particular journey.

Chaos is inevitable for all families at least sometimes, such as when moving house or at times of family illness. For many people, it underpins daily life on a more permanent basis. It may be that you don't have the ability to make things less chaotic. Perhaps time and money are short, you're living in a crowded space or your partner leaves behind a wake of turmoil. There are still things you can do to reduce the impact on your child, including time in good-quality childcare, if it's available to you; less screen time (see Chapter 8); and helping your child manage their emotions better (see Chapter 4).

Routines can help offset some of the effects of chaos and support children to become better at regulating themselves. Suitable routines will obviously depend on your circumstances and preferences. They might include regular mealtimes, eating together as a family when possible; reading routines, such as reading a chapter of a book together before preparing dinner; bedtime routines, such as a bath and a back rub; weekend routines, such as pancakes for breakfast then a walk to the park; or routines for celebrating religious or cultural events, if these are relevant to your family.

These routines will reshape themselves as your family's needs change. My Saturday mornings no longer involve being woken at 6.30 a.m. with a demand for pancakes, but instead involve a protracted period of attempting to wake my child to get her to her beloved wind band in time. One day soon, I anticipate being able to drink a cup of coffee in absolute peace while teenagers slumber upstairs.

CHAPTER CHECKLIST

Key recommendations

- ▶ Try to reduce levels of unhealthy family conflict.
- ▶ If you live with your partner, try to support each other and build your relationship.
- ▶ Ensure a calm home environment and have routines.

Some of the ideas below may help you put these recommendations into practice.

High-quality research

- ▶ **If you have a partner, do some maintenance work with them.** Every few months, try a writing task that helps you to see relationship conflict from a different perspective (see page 46). Consider taking part in a marriage and relationship education programme, if any are available in your area, or emotionally focused couples' therapy if you're arguing a lot.
- ▶ **Make your home work for the people living in it.** Increase your use of routines. If you live in a noisy home, try to restore some quiet. Think about whether there are better ways of organising your home.

Moderate-quality research

- ▶ **Use some evidence-based approaches in your relationship.** Try to disagree constructively with your partner. This means discussing things calmly, and showing each other support and affection. Use your full attention when you're talking to each other. Try to ensure household tasks are divided fairly. If you're arguing a lot, be careful of alcohol. Make time to have fun together.

Anecdotal research/expert advice

▶ **Try some more advice-based approaches to bolster your relationship.** You could try a 'wish list' exercise, where you each share three things you'd like the other to do more often, prioritising active listening while the other shares their list. Develop some goals together. Be assertive about your needs. Don't avoid important issues in your relationship. Pay attention to your partner's attempts to connect with you. Check whether you're expecting more from your partner than is reasonable for what you put into the relationship, and vice versa. Try a ten-step programme to resolve conflict over particular issues (see page 42).

Troubleshooting: when household chaos is unavoidable

For young children, consider increasing the amount of time your child spends in childcare. If your child has a lot of screen time, think about reducing it, especially close to bedtime. Support your child to be able to manage their emotions better.

CHAPTER 3

BEING A PARENT: WHAT TO AVOID

At the birth of their first child, few parents would say they want to be hard, critical, shouty and controlling. And yet it's where many of us find ourselves when unglued by lack of sleep, uneasy about money and wrung out by tantrums.

Other, rarer parents are consistently like this. A girl at my primary school had a mum who would aggressively berate her at the school gate. This girl – I'll call her Louise – would lash out violently at the smallest provocation, and she'd fire off the sort of insults that would make my most filterless acquaintance hesitate. By the time she was nine, Louise had been caught smoking behind the bike sheds in the school playground, and most of her classmates had learned to give her a wide berth for their own protection. She eventually got suspended. I tell this story not to criticise Louise, though I loathed her at the time, but as an example of what happens to children when their parents are persistently vile to them.

There are few such clear-cut examples in parenting. Most of what we shouldn't do as parents is wrought in shades of grey. None of us is perfect, and few of us are like Louise's parents. We occupy the hinter-lands of imperfection and well-meaning endeavours. This chapter may be useful for the inevitable moments in which you find yourself slipping away from the parent you wanted to be when you first held your child.

I initially wanted to frame everything in this book positively. I think it's more helpful, in general, to offer constructive ideas than a lecture on what parents shouldn't be doing, but the research didn't support avoiding the flip side of this particular coin. The evidence base shows enough in the way of situations and actions to avoid – things that can be harmful to children across a range of outcomes – to warrant a dedicated chapter.

Some of the parental actions described in this chapter may cause children's behaviour to flare up. Imagine a five-year-old boy whose parents are generally calm and level-headed, but who sometimes shout at him and give him the occasional slap. He isn't sure when these things are going to happen. Will spilling his cereal make his parents angry, or will his messy bedroom cause them to punish him? The constant uncertainty about how his parents will react to everyday situations makes him anxious. His anxiety means he's less in control of his behaviour, so something small – being asked to clear his plate after dinner – can move him into 'fight or flight' mode instead of being able to respond calmly. This brings more punishment from his parents. The family is in a downward spiral.

The good news is that your children will probably be fine with the odd slip-up. It goes back to the point from the Introduction about being a 'good enough' parent. We're all fallible. I've criticised my own children too much, and it's a constant struggle to do this less. I almost always manage not to shout at them, but I've certainly shouted in the past. It's taken a lot of work to get to the point at which I can control my temper.

By keeping my voice level, I'm not confident I've drastically improved things for my children. My younger daughter cheerfully tells people: 'Mum never shouts, but she has this look when she's cross that's terrifying. It's worse than being shouted at.' But I'm hopefully good enough, despite getting it wrong some of the time. And I think that even the least fallible of my parent friends would say they occasionally do the things this chapter tells us we should avoid.

Don't spank your child or use any other physical punishment

For those of us brought up in the twentieth century, the occasional spank may have been a normal part of childhood. In the period since, evidence has become overwhelming that this kind of discipline is, at best, unhelpful. At worst, it's profoundly damaging.

Most evidence points to physical punishment harming children. Even 'mild' physical punishment has negative consequences. Children whose parents hit them experience poor outcomes, no matter what the reason for their punishment or the extent of it. Slapping a child on the hand to stop them reaching for another biscuit risks making their behaviour and mental health worse, as does more violently hitting a child for talking back. Children who behave badly because they've been spanked are at particular risk. They're more likely to be spanked again due to this behaviour, creating a vicious circle.[1]

Physical punishment teaches children it's acceptable to use violence to get what you want. It also makes them more likely to take a negative view of what others do. A child who's physically punished at home might believe they've been left out of a playground game deliberately, while another child in the same situation might think it accidental. This belief among children who are physically punished that other people's intentions are bad makes it more likely they'll respond inappropriately. In the playground scenario, a child who believes they've been left out of a game by accident might ask to join in, while one who thinks they've been left out on purpose might start a fight.

An early experiment, one unlikely to be cleared by any modern ethics committee, found that boys became more aggressive when playing with dolls after they'd watched a video of another boy being shaken and spanked.[2] Just witnessing this type of punishment was enough to affect children's behaviour. It's not too much of a stretch to see why being subject to physical punishment at home, which is far more intense than watching a video, can lead to a child becoming aggressive and disruptive.

Physical punishment also fails to teach children to internalise reasons for behaving in a particular way. Two children at nursery might have very different attitudes to sharing, based on whether they've been punished physically by their parents. One might be happy to let other children use his toys. He's been taught to share because it's kind, and because other children are more likely to share their own toys if he does the same. This child doesn't need his parents to be in the room to remember the reasons why it's good to share. Another child might have been taught to share because, if she doesn't, she'll get a swat on the arm. When she's in nursery and her parents aren't present, she's got no obvious reason to let other children join in her game of skittles. If children are only taught to behave well through punishment, they haven't learned how or why to behave well when there's no immediate threat of sanction.

Children's mental health is also affected by being physically punished. One explanation is that this type of punishment makes children angry. They have to suppress this anger because they're dependent on their parents for everything.[3] If you were a child who was regularly smacked, you might be hazily aware that it's not safe to feel angry in case your parents stop looking after you. You might find, though, that extinguishing these feelings makes you sad and anxious.

Another theory on the link with mental health is that the pain resulting from physical punishment is a source of toxic stress with long-term negative effects. Certainly, children report feeling more stress if they're physically punished by their parents, and there are higher levels of the stress hormone cortisol in their bloodstream. Stress responses in both children and adults are linked to several mental health issues, including anxiety and depression.[4]

If you find it's not as straightforward as simply deciding you won't physically punish your child, there are a few things you can do to make it less likely. One is looking after your own well-being (see Chapter 1). You're likely to be more patient when you're well rested, you've eaten well and you've spent time with people you care about. Ideas for healthily managing your anger are given later in this chapter. Another avenue is to get support from a local parenting programme such as Triple P, which is offered freely by many local authorities in the UK.

You'll be less likely to use physical punishment if you're successfully able to use alternative forms of discipline (see Chapter 6). It's also worth trying to cut down on alcohol if you drink it regularly, and to try strategies to reduce family conflict (see Chapter 2). Children are more likely to be physically punished when they live in a negative home environment, either because one person is hostile or because parents are fighting.

Try not to criticise your child

If I verbalised the voice in my head, my morning monologue would run something along these lines: 'Can you please remember to turn out the bathroom light and make sure you've hung up the bath mat when you've finished with it? I don't want soggy feet when I get out of the shower. I can't believe you've left the toothpaste lid off the tube again. Now there's toothpaste all over the sink. Why on earth is there a set of dominoes, a pair of knickers and some muddy socks on the floor? And – if you don't want me to resign from my role as your parent – will you replace the loo roll when you finish it?' Fortunately for them, I'm well practised at keeping this train of thought to myself, though aspects of it sometimes slip out. The toothpaste lid in particular shuts down the areas of my brain relating to rational thought.

There's a fine line between supporting children to be socialised and not subjecting them to constant criticism. It's hard to avoid being critical when you're getting them to put the milk back in the fridge, fart somewhere other than your lap and generally learn to behave like human beings who will one day need to live with relative strangers. But criticism of children can make them feel powerless, which might lead them either to comply unquestioningly out of fear or, eventually, to rebel. I don't think any of us would see an ideal in either the child who's gone off the rails or the one who follows every instruction without hesitation or deviation.

Being criticised can make people feel worse about themselves and may lead to changes in the brain. One study scanned brain activity while people heard themselves being criticised by their mothers. The brain patterns observed by the study's researchers indicated that criticism by parents may train neural pathways in a way that makes people more vulnerable to depression. Another study ran an experiment with children between the ages of seven and eleven to find out what happened to their brains when they either won a prize or lost out. The children played a guessing game with two doors. One door had a cash prize behind it and the other didn't. The children of parents who were more critical of them had more muted responses to both winning and losing.[5]

You're probably more critical if you were criticised as a child. Language like 'Oh, you're so lazy,' 'You're such a clumsy clot,' or 'Why can't you be more like your brother?' becomes normalised when you hear it day in, day out. It may be that you don't even hear yourself when you criticise others. Research shows that parents generally think they're more positive with their children than they are. One study found that most parents said they praised their children often and criticised them rarely, yet these parents actually criticised them three times as often as they praised them.[6] You could try tallying up (in your head, so your child doesn't think you have lost the plot) every time you say something positive and every time you say something negative or critical. You may be surprised by the high proportion of critical comments. This was certainly the case for me when I tried this experiment.

Criticism doesn't need to be handed down across the generations, though. Awareness is the first step. You can also try some of the slightly sparse ideas in this section; there's ringing silence in research articles on the question of how to guide behaviour without being critical. I've thought hard about how I can socialise my children and avoid constantly having to tidy up after them without a fair amount of criticism. I don't want to be the person who picks other people's socks off the sofa and damp towels off the floor.

While the research literature is vague in this area, advice from experts is a bit more useful. My reading of this advice is that there's a difference between criticising and asking your child to do something, or gently correcting their behaviour. This might be the difference between saying 'You've left your socks on the sofa again – this is the third time this week I've had to ask you to move them' and 'Please put your socks away.' You might even just say 'Socks.' This is sufficient in my house, as it's a daily event. Don't expect this stuff to lead to magical tidying abilities.

The other thing to try, if you find yourself being critical despite your best intentions, is increasing the number of positive things you say to your child. This can change the balance of praise and criticism, so any criticism has less of an impact. Professor John Gottman is a psychologist who studied relationships for more than twenty years, videotaping hundreds of couples' talks with each other. He coded both what couples said to each other and the emotions they showed in their expressions while talking. Gottman's analysis led him to suggest an ideal ratio of one negative comment to five positive ones when it comes to relationship success. In other words, relationships are more likely to succeed when at least five positive comments are given for every negative one. His work has since been widely applied to children and families. When parents are prompted to increase the number of positive comments they give to their children, the balance of positive to negative comments improves.[7]

Criticism certainly bites less if it's balanced with plenty of warmth, praise and humour. Warm ways to balance out any potential criticism include telling your child you love them, showing them affection with a hug or a touch on the shoulder, and mentioning how much you enjoy their company. You could also start looking out for your child's good behaviour. We don't spot what we're not seeking. If you comment on your child's good behaviour, their positive actions will be reinforced and there will be less for you to criticise. Saying 'well done' to a child for doing something kind for her sister makes it less likely she will thump said sister next time you leave the room, and it removes an opportunity for criticism. Humour-related strategies include exaggeration, funny stories, absurd statements, wordplay and – of course – talking about body parts or functions. Nothing beats a good poo joke when you're a scatologically minded preschooler.

Descriptive praise is also worth a shot. There's more detail on this in Chapter 6, as well as reasons why it's good to avoid praising children's personal qualities. Briefly, though, descriptive praise is about noticing children for their effort, not their achievement, and finding small details you really like in what they've done. My younger daughter is learning the saxophone. The sax is not a musical instrument that blends quietly into the background – not helped by the dog howling along, vaguely trying to hit the same notes, whenever he hears the first squeak of her reed starting to vibrate. But I can praise the small things. I can tell her what a good sound she's getting out of the instrument (it's a great sound, even if it bends my ears away from my head) and how much she's improved because of all her hard work. I just say it with a slightly ringing skull.

Don't shout at your child or be otherwise hard with them

Parents are hard with their children when they're physically or verbally aggressive, use strong discipline, or use force or threats to get their way. This hardness can range from mild to extreme, and most of us are occasionally guilty of acting at the less awful end of this spectrum. I've noticed I'm most likely to use threats in response to either full-throttled defiance or being screamed at ('No, I'm not going to tidy my room. No, I'm not going to pick up the water jug I've deliberately knocked over. No, I'm not going to apologise for kicking my sister'). My threats tend to relate to activities – a loss of screen time is something I use more than I like or intend. There's also the rock bottom of losing play time with a friend, which only gets wheeled out *in extremis* and when I'm not fully in control of what I'm saying.

I've pretty much trained myself not to do this, but not entirely. The threats are no good. I can tell myself and my child all I like that these threats are the result of logical consequences (see Chapter 6) – 'If you shout at people, they're less likely to want to do you favours like take you to see friends' – but it's a stretch. It's not just the threats themselves that are an issue, though. The language and tone parents use also matter. If your child has a tantrum in the supermarket, it might be easy for shaming phrases to slip out, such as 'Don't be a baby' or 'Your brother wouldn't behave like this, and he's younger than you.' Words that can seem relatively inconsequential to a parent may humiliate a child.

Further along the hard-parenting continuum, there are those who deliberately, ritually humiliate children and act with cruelty towards them. If you've got far enough into this book to read this section, you probably aren't consistently hostile in your parenting. But how many of us can say we always respond to our children with perfect equanimity? Hostility doesn't only exist in parents who are abjectly horrible to their children. We all have episodes of it in vexing or demanding moments.

When parents shout, it creates fear and distress, and children learn that yelling is an acceptable way to communicate. When parents try to get children to behave through threats or force, these children are more likely to try to avoid difficult thoughts and feelings. This kind of parenting can create negative cycles – it can cause children to feel sad, which can make parents even harder with them in future. Harsh language can also be interpreted by children as being hostile or rejecting, driving them to behave badly.

Being hard or hostile with children can make tough occasions worse. Hostility and anger breed the same in other people. When both parents and children are acting through this lens, they often try to punish each other. From the child's perspective, this might be 'I hate you,' 'You're horrible,' or 'Go away.' Reactions escalate quickly. It's a hard loop from which to escape, and one that's on us, as the literal grown-ups in the room, to work out.

A first step, if you find yourself parenting harshly, is to be aware of your risk factors. You're more likely to parent negatively if you had a difficult childhood, if you're easily overwhelmed by what you're feeling and if you find it hard to calm down. You're also more likely to shout when you feel stressed – perhaps you've had a bad day at work or you're worried about finances. You'll be better equipped to head off certain behaviours if you know you're currently experiencing something that makes you more at risk of responding harshly to your child.[8]

Getting more sleep (Chapter 1) and dealing with any relationship issues (Chapter 2) can help parents shift away from harsh parenting. Reading with your child can be beneficial, possibly because shared reading leads to a better parent–child relationship, meaning behaviour improves too.[9] This, in turn, makes it easier for parents to respond to them positively.

Thinking differently may also be useful. Reframing the language you use with yourself, from negative statements ('I'm not going to shout today') into positive ones ('I'm going to speak to my child calmly today'), can work well. You might also keep certain questions in mind when things get tricky, such as how you'd feel if somebody were to act with you the way you are acting with your child. You could ask yourself whether your child would describe your behaviour in a way that would make you happy, and whether you're likely to get a good response from your child from what you've chosen to do or say. I sometimes imagine how someone I care about would react if they were watching my life as a TV programme. Would they think I was doing an OK job as a parent? Or might they think I needed to dial up my patience levels a little?

How you think about and respond to negative events can shape how hard you are with your child. Minimising this kind of thing – telling yourself it doesn't matter that you lost your temper, as you can start again tomorrow, or suggesting to your child not to pay any attention to someone who has been mean to them – can have its uses. It can give your brain space to make sense of what's happened. But it also has downsides. It can mean you miss the subtle filaments forming the thread that instigated an argument between you and your child, or that your child's feelings go unnoticed.

When I collected my daughter from a friend's house one stormy winter's evening, she became angry and quarrelsome after I said no to three of her requests: she wanted some sweets, to change the car radio station and to be able to watch TV when we got home. I'd probably shut her down because I was frustrated at feeling like a taxi service when I had work to do. It transpired that she responded to my shutdown badly because she was in pain, and I hadn't paid her discomfort enough attention. She'd 'accidentally' tackled a boy she didn't like to the ground during tag rugby earlier that day, and she'd lost most of the skin off her knee in the process. I was grumpy, so she was grumpy, so I was grumpy. Minimising events and feelings can lead to tired and crabby children being ignored, making them more likely to act up. This in turn increases parents' own annoyance levels. It's this irritability that can lead to hostile parenting.

The opposite extreme, on the other hand, carries its own risks. Hyper-focusing on a problem can make it hard to respond effectively to children, meaning they're more likely to misbehave and your irritation levels will skyrocket – which again can lead to hostile parenting. It seems there's a sweet spot between minimising problems and focusing on them too much.

A key part of preventing shouting or harshness with children is finding healthier ways to express your anger. You can't switch anger off, and nor should you. Bottling up weighty emotions can be corrosive, and it might lead children to believe they need to swallow down their own feelings. It can also be good for your child to see how to be angry in a way that's constructive. And sometimes it's good for children to know you're upset. The aim is to shift how you express your anger so it's assertive, not aggressive (or indeed passive or passive-aggressive, both of which can be damaging in different ways). Being assertive when you feel angry is better for your child and more likely to get you what you need.

3. WAYS TO SHOW ANGER

Being aggressive	➤ Shouting at your child.
Being passive	➤ Sulking.
Being passive-aggressive	➤ Becoming irritable with your child rather than engaging directly with what has caused you anger.
Being assertive	➤ Calmly and confidently explaining what has caused you anger, while being open to your child's feelings.

When you experience anger in a healthy way, you feel it without being overwhelmed by it. You recognise it as a signal to work out what you need and want that you're not currently getting. You try to be self-compassionate when you feel angry and to communicate assertively what you feel. You also try to ensure that your anger doesn't make you or other people unhappy, but changes things positively instead. The key with assertive anger is to speak calmly and respectfully, explaining why you're upset in a way children can understand.

One place to start in reducing unhealthy expression of anger is to identify what sets you off. Most people have something that causes their fuse to start smouldering. I have many. It might be that your pathway to anger is shorter if your child is loud or doesn't do what you ask of them, or if you're exhausted. Perhaps you're triggered by things from your own past, such as your parents getting angry with you for similar behaviour.

A friend's temper used to be ignited by her daughter appearing to be deliberately slow when the two of them were trying to leave for nursery in the mornings. Her daughter was quick when they weren't in a hurry and sluggish when they were. My friend discovered that she might need to do something about her frustration levels at the point her daughter announced to her, crossly, 'I'm not a dickert.' She realised 'Stop being a dickhead' had slipped out and been overheard, and she might need to get her daughter out of bed a little earlier. Establishing what enrages you won't necessarily prevent it from doing so, but you can feel calmer by understanding it and putting in place strategies to deal with it effectively.

If you're not someone wound up by the entire concept of being told how to breathe (I can get so agitated by this that I hold my breath, which I don't recommend during childbirth), you could try concentrating on your breathing when you feel angry. Inhaling deeply through your nose can help calm your system down. Some experts recommend 'square breathing', through which you inhale for a count of four, hold for a count of four, exhale for a count of four, wait for a count of four, and repeat. Others suggest making sure your out-breath is longer than your in-breath – you might breathe in for a count of four and out for a count of eight. This can move your body from 'fight or flight' mode, which is the seat of anger and threat, into so-called 'rest and repair' mode.

You could also allow time to pass between an act that's made you angry and deciding what you'll do about it. You can be honest with your child about this, saying you need time to calm down or to think about what happened before you can talk about it with them. Stepping out of the room is fine if you're too upset to respond appropriately to a child when you feel angry.

One expert estimates it takes three months to train yourself to stop shouting.[10] Having accountability to the person most affected, assuming your child is old enough to understand, can help, perhaps through a reverse sticker chart. This time it's your child who decides whether you get a sticker at the end of the day for using a respectful voice rather than shouting. Committing to yourself, on top of the commitment to your child, can also be useful – for example, writing a Post-it note saying 'I will speak respectfully to [child's name]' and putting it somewhere you'll see it.

Don't try to control the way your child feels

Psychological control is where a parent tries, in a negative way, to influence how a child thinks or feels, perhaps through intrusive behaviour or by trying to make the child feel guilty. Psychological control, unwittingly or deliberately, can be about parents trying to keep children emotionally and physically close. It can be incredibly subtle, shown through an offhand remark or not looking at a child who's misbehaving.

It's important to distinguish psychological control from behavioural control. Behavioural control isn't about attempting to influence how children think or feel. Instead, it involves parents supervising and monitoring their children, and setting both rules and expectations. Behavioural control can have positive outcomes for children, while psychological control does not.

4. WHAT MIGHT PSYCHOLOGICAL CONTROL LOOK LIKE? [11]

Guilt induction	➤	'You're going to make me really disappointed if you do that.'
Contingent love or love withdrawal	➤	Not making eye contact with your child when they aren't behaving as you would like.
Instilling anxiety	➤	'If you don't come here right now, you're going to regret it.'
Invalidation of the child's perspective	➤	'Don't be silly – that's not something to get upset about.'

If you act in a controlling way, it's probably not obvious that you're doing it. You could try keeping this table in mind when you're having a few normal conversations with your child, to see if there are any elements that might apply.

When children have a psychologically controlling parent, they don't tend to believe they can influence what happens to them. This can make them feel anxious. They're also more likely to see situations as threatening when their parents are controlling. Perhaps a trip to see grandparents might seem fraught with danger to your child if they sense you're going to withhold affection if they don't behave in a particular way. Psychological control also makes children less able to develop a secure sense of self.[12]

When a friend of mine was young, her mother was warm and lovely in many ways, and controlling in others. This control reared its head in two ways. Her mother wouldn't look at her when she'd done something wrong, and she'd constantly, with the best of intentions, invalidate her feelings. She wasn't really scared – look! There was nothing to be afraid of. She didn't really dislike her grandad – he was a good person. She didn't really feel sick when she ate peppers – she was just being silly. This ceaseless erasure of her feelings led to her being unable to trust what she felt. Her mother was the adult, after all, and made it clear she knew best. To this day, my friend feels anxious in situations that require her to trust her own judgement in the face of disagreement by others. The effects of the psychological control she encountered as a child have been long-lasting.

I wanted to illustrate this section by drawing on a fairy tale or a well-known children's book. Literature for children is jam-packed with complicated adults, after all. But there's little in the way of subtlety or nuance in many of the best-known stories. The archetypal wicked stepmother instils anxiety and guilt, and the neglectful father puts the needs of his new wife above those of his children. But where is the all-too-human parent or step-parent who cuts down their child by looking away from them when they're whining or needy, or the one who makes the child doubt their own mind by telling them they're wrong in feeling the way they do?

There are certain risk factors for being psychologically controlling. You're more likely to be this way with your child if you have tendencies towards perfectionism and if you're particularly sensitive to hurt. I tick these boxes, so I have to check myself. Having separation anxiety in relation to your child is another risk factor, possibly because it makes you more afraid that your bond with your child will be damaged if you don't take steps to remain close to them. You may also feel sad and angry that you aren't able to stay close to your child as they grow. Perhaps we all experience this to some extent, but parents with separation anxiety feel this more than most.[13]

If failure is likely to dent your self-worth, you're more likely to try to protect your child from similar feelings by trying to control them, not realising it may well have the opposite effect. Think of the parent who encourages their child to study hard for their own reasons, not their child's: 'If you do well in this test, I'll be proud of you.' This language is easy to slip into, but a more successful and healthy strategy would be to encourage hard work so the child knows they've done their best and can feel proud of themselves. You're also more likely to be psychologically controlling if your own mother or father acted in the same way towards you when you were a child. Knowing your risk factors can help you guard against the risk being realised.

The main recommendation here is to avoid the main areas of psychological control. Two of these, I think, are most likely to slip under a parent's radar. The first is making your child feel guilty, as getting a child to feel remorseful can seem a temptingly straightforward way to encourage good behaviour. I've often heard parents use phrases like 'Please don't make me get upset with you.' The second is invalidating your child's perspective. If your child thinks you're being unfair and you don't believe that's true, it may feel easier to dismiss what they say. 'I'm not being unfair' can be a more instinctive response than 'I understand you think I'm being unfair. It's hard when we don't agree with other people's decisions.'

There are two other main elements of psychological control. These are making your child feel anxious by threatening them, and withdrawing attention or affection when your child doesn't do or say what you'd like. This is one that needs a bit of subtle interpretation. It's fine to remove the oxygen of attention if your child is shouting at you, as this avoids reinforcing the behaviour. It's more pernicious to refuse to look at your child when they've told you they have a bad school report.

It is critical to get your own needs met if you have tendencies towards psychological control. This is no doubt a recommendation that's harder to put into place than some of the others – after all, if this were easy for you, you'd probably be doing it already. It's vital, though, to prioritise yourself and your well-being. Many parents think they're being selfish if they consider their own needs, while the reality is that children need their parents to be healthy, happy and fulfilled too.

If you don't like children showing negative emotions such as sadness and anger, it may be useful to read articles or books on the value of them being able to do so. Parents who take a dim view of their children's negative feelings are more likely to use psychological control.[14] Chapter 4 covers some introductory reading on why children need to be able to express a range of emotions.

One conundrum is how to be clear with a child what the impact of their actions may be, while avoiding making them feel guilty – for example, when they say something unkind. The research falls short here, probably because it's aimed more at testing big ideas than it is at developing granular advice for parents. Based on the reading I've done and trying to think logically, it's probably fair to say there's a difference between being clear about the impact of certain actions and labouring the point. 'I don't like it when you shout at me – please use words to explain how you feel' is very different from saying 'You've made me feel really upset by shouting at me. I don't understand why you keep doing this. It's hurtful.'

If your partner is psychologically controlling and you want to try to protect your child from its effects, you can work on building the quality of your own relationship with your child (see Chapter 5).[15]

Avoid being overly permissive

Permissive parents don't set too many rules and expectations when it comes to their children, and they tend to avoid discipline. It's this absence of being demanding that sets them apart from quintessential authoritative parents. Both types of parents are child-centred, responsive and warm, but while authoritative parents are demanding of their children, permissive parents are not.

It is possible to be permissive only some of the time. My authoritative mask slips when I'm on holiday or with parents who are more permissive than me – who, after all, wants to be the parent who forbids another packet of sweets being opened or makes the dreaded mention of bedtime? Despite my best intentions and leaving the rule-enacting as late as I can stand to, I remain the strictest parent. All that happens in this situation is that my rules are temporarily relaxed, and I try (and fail) to sit it out until someone else calls time. I'm still the first person to hail an end to screens, ice cream or being awake. I get to feel stressed about sugar levels and insufficient sleep, and my kids still resent me. It's not exactly a win–win.

The children of permissive parents are less emotionally intelligent, on average, than other children.[16] This may be because they're less likely to experience emotional challenges than the children of authoritative parents. Imagine a child who's given pretty much everything he wants. He can't have limitless cash or bunk off school, but he gets to go to bed when he wants, watch TV whenever he likes and set the emotional tone of mealtimes. He's rarely told no and, as a result, he doesn't have to learn how to interpret what his parents are thinking or feeling when he asks something of them. He's not challenged to understand why someone might take a different position from him, because his standpoint is the one that takes centre stage.

This lack of practice in understanding other people's body language and intentions can make it harder for this child to untangle what others may be feeling. Alternatively, it's possible that a laissez-faire approach to parenting extends into other areas of child development, and that permissive parents may be less likely to support their children directly with emotional growth. A parent whose permissiveness stems from wanting their child to be in the driving seat of their own development might spend less time helping them label and understand emotions.

There's also a link between permissive parenting and poor behaviour in children, possibly due to reinforcement – children behave worse when their past misbehaviour has been reinforced in some way.[17] If a child kicks a sibling in the shin, removing the child from the room is a logical follow-on from that behaviour. It provides an incentive not to promote shin-kicking to the position of favoured pastime. If a parent ignores this behaviour, though (as permissive parents are more likely to do), there's no real incentive for it not to happen again. Sometimes the reinforcement may even be positive rather than neutral. If the child who has kicked is given a lollipop or a tablet as a distraction, there's every incentive to move Shin-Kicking up to Number One Activity, or even to see what happens if Hair-Pulling or Arm-Scratching are tried out as alternatives.

The main recommendation for being less permissive is simple. It's to set out – and stick to – appropriate rules and boundaries for your child. Thoughts on how to establish boundaries are available in Chapter 4. The other thing that might be worth a try is some 'mindful parenting'. If the term causes you an initial eye-roll (it did me), then wait. There's a lot of research currently taking place around this practice. It's not just about being fully present with your child, but also about practising compassion, kindness and acceptance with yourself and them. One study has found that parents who adopt a mindful parenting approach are more likely to be authoritative and less likely to be permissive with their children.[18]

As with some other areas of parenting, culture is important. I've chosen to focus principally on studies looking at Anglophone societies as that's where I'm based, and if I were to look more broadly, this book might distend itself into a series of encyclopaedias. And it's worth reiterating that not all findings will apply everywhere. In Spain, for example, some research shows better outcomes for the children of permissive parents than for authoritative ones.[19]

Avoid 'helicopter parenting'

Helicopter parents hover over their children. We all do this sometimes – when our children are feeling anxious or, more likely, when we're feeling anxious ourselves. Intriguingly, authoritative parents, who otherwise tend to see the best outcomes for their children, are more likely than other parents to advocate helicopter-parenting practices, which have negative links with children's behaviour, relationships and well-being.[20] This suggests a tipping point at which closeness and protectiveness start to slip into something less helpful.

When I was a new parent and before I'd started digging too far into the research, I pragmatically managed to avoid helicopter parenting through giving primacy to convenience. Essentially, I took parenting shortcuts or, in a more brutal interpretation, succumbed to laziness. It seemed far less effort to hunker down at the edge of the playground than it did to shadow my children, though that didn't stop me hovering at the bottom of the climbing frame ready to catch them if they'd scaled a height that made me dizzy. It was easy to tell myself I was fostering independence by letting them play solo while I made dinner or finished writing a report. Occasionally, this strategy would go wrong. I still have bad dreams about the time I left my elder daughter alone to make cupcakes. It was during the pandemic, I had work to do, and she was bored. It took days to remove the two-millimetre-thick layer of icing that coated every surface, there was a sludgy mix of food colouring in every cup we owned, and our feet stuck to the floor every time we tried to walk across it. In a mystery yet to be unravelled, there was icing on the ceiling.

On balance, I think my laziness/convenience strategy has paid off, and luckily for me, the research supports it. When we're helicoptering, we might think we're caring for our children by keeping them safe, but taking a step back and leaving children room to take decisions and make mistakes is, according to much of the research literature, more likely to be useful for them. Overprotectiveness can result in children internalising their parents' worries, seeing themselves as unable to control events and lacking an ability to assess risk properly. It can lead to them reacting against their parents as they get older and finding their own (risky) ways to work out their limits.[21] Evaluating which activities are going to lead to a skinned knee in a playground seem, to me, less perilous than encountering the extreme ends of the risk bell curve at a teenage party.

The children of helicopter parents can find it harder to respond appropriately to other people's signals as they get older.[22] This may be because they are used to their parents responding to other people on their behalf. Consider a small child whose grandparents have come to stay and ask her what her favourite things are to eat. If her parents are helicopters, they might respond: 'Oh, she loves tacos. And her favourite dessert is mango ice cream.' If they're not helicopters, they may let her answer for herself.

A child who is used to answering questions from other adults gets a chance to practise communicating with people slightly less familiar to them. This equips them to read other people's body language and interpret what they're saying when their parents aren't around to do this for them. On the other hand, a child whose parents field questions for them hasn't had the chance to develop these skills, and may struggle to respond in an appropriate way once their parents aren't in the room.

While helicopter parenting is linked to many poor outcomes for children, including mental health, there may be a limited, positive link with physical health.[23] But this may well be because the studies on health don't look at long-term risk (see my point about skinned knees and teenage parties). If you feel that the benefits to physical health from helicopter parenting outweigh any detriment to mental health and the other areas highlighted, though, skip to the next section.

The parents I've known with helicoptering tendencies seem to do this instinctively. It may be a hard pattern to break, especially if you're anxious. I used to know one mum who gasped and ran to her children every time they did anything unexpected (which was a lot. They were kids). I don't think she could have overridden this instinct, at least not without help and support, any more easily than she could have stopped comforting them when they were hurt.

But while a certain amount of helicoptering can be explained by parents' anxiety and personal situations, research points to something going on at a societal level. One way of looking at overprotective parenting is to measure how many hours per week parents spend looking after their children. It's not a perfect measure – after all, parents who spend more time with their children could be doing it with a light touch and no hovering – but it's one of the best we have. The amount of time parents spend looking after their children has gone up in the United Kingdom, the United States and Canada since the late 1980s and early 1990s. It's also gone up in the Netherlands, Italy and Spain, and not just by a little bit.[24]

So what's going on? One team of scholars has argued that it's to do with rising economic inequality and the fact that while holders of graduate and postgraduate degrees used to earn a similar amount, those with postgraduate qualifications now earn around a third more than their graduate peers.[25] In a less equal society, parents want their children to be among the lucky ones who earn well, and the more children end up studying, the more they'll eventually earn. If parents protect their children and are closely involved with their education, giving them as many opportunities as possible, these children may stand a greater chance when they're exposed to the maelstrom of paid work.

This is an interesting perspective, though if there's research on the direct effects of helicopter parenting on income and job prospects, I haven't found it. You'd need an excellent long-running data set to be able to do such an analysis. That doesn't mean it's not plausible, but something else might be underlying all these changes. It may equally be that parents think that even the slightest chance of pay-off is worth being a helicopter parent – in which case, fair enough.

If you find yourself unwillingly flying within a formation of heli-copters, a good starting point is to address the root cause of any anxiety you may be feeling. Anxious parents are more likely to be overprotective of their children; separation anxiety is a particular risk factor.[26] Anxiety is a massive thing to try to fix. I say this as somebody still trying to deal with my own. There are some ideas that might help in the sections on supporting your own well-being in Chapter 1, and some tips on supporting children with anxiety in Chapter 9 that you might be able to borrow for yourself. If your anxiety is severe, your first port of call should be your doctor.

You're understandably more likely to be overprotective if your child was slightly premature. Figuring out why you might be making particular choices can help you make different ones. It can also help to think about the impact on you of this energy sink. There's a huge time and energy cost of intensive parenting. If there's social pressure on you to be a helicopter parent – 'But they might fall! They need you to be with them!' – it's worth thinking about whether you would make the same choice without that pressure, particularly in light of research that suggests investing all this time and energy may not be great for your child's relationships and mental health.[27]

Comparing the risks you were allowed to take as a child with those you allow your own child may also shift your thinking away from overprotectiveness.[28] It may also bring into sharp relief the way the world has shape-shifted in the intervening period. It's a cliché to talk about children having more freedom to play in the halcyon days of adults' own childhoods, but there's often a bedrock of truth under-lying such platitudes. Parents' concerns about safety have increased, meaning they allow their children to do less than they were allowed to do themselves. Reading about risks can be helpful in developing your own risk assessment when it comes to your child. It makes sense to be protective where risks are significant, and less so when they are vanishingly small. National studies have shown that children are safer today, on average, than ever before.

Some parents may worry about how they can balance keeping their children safe with an anti-helicopter approach. This dilemma can only be solved by individual parents in terms of how they assess and tolerate risk, and what their own children are like. I have one child who can glance at a map and know exactly where to go, and another who may have walked the same path fifty times but ambles off in the wrong direction if she's the one walking in front. Child Number One was given an instant pass to walk to school by herself as soon as the school allowed it; Child Number Two was given a term and a half to practise, with me or her dad walking close enough to check direction and road sense but far enough away to let her lead the way. (We also got Child Number Two some glasses at around the same time. I suspect being able to see properly may have helped the situation.)

We each make our own assessment of risk based on what's right for our own families and situations. I think the key, though, if we have overprotective tendencies, is to be curious – which risks are real and genuine, meaning that we need to protect our children, and which risks are minimal and can be approached a little more lightly?

CHAPTER CHECKLIST

Key recommendations

▶ Don't spank your child or use any other physical punishment.
▶ Try not to criticise your child.
▶ Don't shout at your child or be otherwise hard with them.
▶ Don't try to control the way your child feels.
▶ Avoid being overly permissive.
▶ Avoid 'helicopter parenting'.

Some of the ideas below may help you put these recommendations into practice.

High-quality research

▶ **Find more constructive ways of parenting, if you find yourself slipping into any of the behaviours described in this chapter.** Set out – and stick to – appropriate rules and boundaries for your child. Consistently use alternative, non-punishing forms of discipline. Read together regularly. Try to avoid the main areas of psychological control: (1) making your child feel guilty about their thoughts or behaviour, for instance by highlighting the impact on you as a parent of what they've done or said, (2) withdrawing attention or affection when your child doesn't do or say what you'd like, (3) making your child feel anxious by threatening them, and (4) invalidating their feelings, for example by dismissing what they've said.

▶ **Develop self-awareness in some key areas.** Be aware of your risk factors for parenting negatively – if you had a difficult childhood or if your parents were controlling with you – and use this knowledge to steer your parenting. If you find yourself responding to your child's behaviour in a way you don't like, see if there are any local parenting programmes available to you, such as Triple P.

▶ **As with Chapter 1, look after yourself.** Your well-being is critical. If you're anxious, find support. If you argue a lot with your partner, consider whether there might be a way to tone down this conflict (see Chapter 2). If you drink alcohol regularly, consider trying to cut down or quit.

Moderate-quality research

- **Get your needs met.** And if it's possible, get more sleep.
- **Expand your thinking.** If you don't like children showing negative emotions such as sadness or anger, consider reading around about the value of them being able to do so.
- **Deal with anger and criticism appropriately.** Find healthy ways of expressing your anger with your child, such as stating calmly why you are angry and what you would like to happen differently. Know that you're probably monumentally underestimating how much you really criticise your child, and take steps to reduce it. Try to parent mindfully. Increase the number of positive things you say to your child.

Anecdotal research/expert advice

- **Think about emotional investment and risk.** If you're an intensive parent, investing endless emotional support and time into your child, think of the impact on you of this energy sink. Read around on risk to get an understanding of acceptable versus unacceptable risks for your child, and think about the risks it was acceptable for you to take in your own childhood.
- **Change what you won't do into what you will do.** Try converting your intentions not to parent in a harsh way into positive statements about what you will do: 'I'm going to speak calmly to my child today.'
- **Find a balance between dismissing problems and giving them too much attention.** Try not to ignore or minimise negative events, but don't go to the opposite extreme and focus too much on a problem.
- **Be curious.** Look out for your child's good behaviour. Keep certain questions in mind when you feel upset with your child, such as how you would feel if somebody were to act with you the way you are acting with your child.

Troubleshooting: reducing unhealthy anger in front of your child

Identify what sets you off. Concentrate on your breathing when you feel angry. Allow time to pass between an act that's made you angry and deciding what you'll do about it. Create accountability through a reverse sticker chart.

CHAPTER 4

BEING A PARENT: THINGS THAT WORK

Before I had children, I didn't think being a parent was going to be equivalent to sailing on calm seas, but I did imagine it'd be pretty straightforward. I'd love them, make sure they had food in their bellies and books to read, and I'd trust my instincts. What more could there be?

It'll be clear to anyone reading this that I hadn't previously spent much time hanging out with the average two-year-old. They're complicated beings. There's the stuff that all two-year-olds do – they break down sobbing because their orange socks are in the wash, and they resist sleep as if their bed is full of ten-foot anacondas. There are also the peculiarities that are unique to your child and to which you need to find a solution. For me, it was the violence of an almost-three-year-old as she realised she wasn't going to be an only child for much longer, and the question of how to clean up a pot of nappy cream that's been smeared over every surface in a bedroom, including the child in question (answer: you can't).

There are steps you can take, though, to head off many problems (at least those that don't involve oil-based ointments), and this chapter looks at some of them. Many of the headline recommendations are self-evident, but they become useful in the detail of how to put them into practice. It's one thing to know you need to be responsive to your child. It's another thing to know how to do this when there are fifteen other things clamouring for your attention, you're out of coffee and a wasp has flown into the kitchen.

You don't need to be perfect. You don't have to follow every idea set out here. You just need to be a good enough parent, and one with the internal resources and confidence to be OK in yourself while doing it.

Be warm with and responsive to your child

There's a risk that recommending warmth and responsiveness is a truism equivalent to saying 'Be nice to your child.' For many people, it's obvious. But for me, at least, it was reassuring to see that the available research backs up warm parenting. This is the state towards which people and parenting books have gravitated in recent years, leaving traditional, strict parenting on the horizon. Much advice to parents is faddy. (If you're sceptical, check out how recommendations have changed on sleep, routines and feeding for very young children.) But the advice to be warm and responsive is solid, with reams of high-quality research to back it up.

Children benefit in all sorts of ways when parents show them huge warmth and care. As well as striking links with positive outcomes – including in health, behaviour and well-being – warmth and positive parenting can safeguard against negative influences. A secure, nurturing relationship with a parent can help protect children against the changes to their brain they might otherwise experience from poverty-related stress.[1]

As with all research, there are imperfections in the data and in the way it's been put together. While a lot of the studies underpinning this section use the term 'warmth', it is clear when you drill down into the indicators they use that there are a few other things they measure alongside how warm parents are. What about an absence of hostility and aggression, indifference and neglect, and parents' rejection of their children? Some of the extensive links with positive outcomes for children are probably due to being warm while avoiding some of the behaviours described in the previous chapter.

Being warm with and responsive to your child is easy advice to follow when you're happy and your child's being lovely. My personal barrier here is that I find it hard to be warm when I'm annoyed. Irritated silence becomes my default if a child yells at me that her sports kit is still in the wash and she needs it, or I've been asked 'Why can't we just have Heinz?' when I've made tomato soup from scratch. One thing that's helped me is seeing that being warm heads off a lot of the behaviours that might otherwise wind me up.

One of the key elements of being a warm parent is to say nice things to your child, and to make it easy – if you can – for your child to confide in you. One way of helping your child feel comfortable confiding in you is to validate their feelings. This can be done by articulating back to them what they're trying to say to you about what they feel, without denying, dismissing, contradicting or minimising it. You don't have to agree with what they say, but they need to see that you've heard and acknowledged it.

Later in the chapter you'll find more on validating children's feelings, but to give a brief example, I was told firmly by one daughter that 'school is stupid'. I fought down my strong instinct to explain all the reasons why I think education is brilliant. Instead, I said I didn't agree with her, but completely understood why she thought that, and let her know I'd felt the same when I was her age. I'm not saying this to be smug. I would definitely have listed the top twenty-five reasons why school is a Good Thing before I had dug deep into the research, and my children would have cried with boredom while remaining unvalidated. Also, when you're a child, school sometimes sucks.

There are other ways of making your child comfortable confiding in you. One is to pay attention to them when they're speaking – fully, and not at the same time as trying to read an email. (This suggestion clearly depends on context. If my child comes in when I'm working and expects an instant response while I'm mid-thought or mid-call, she'll be disappointed.) Another is to avoid giving them advice when they have a problem. You could try asking questions instead. If a child tells you their best friend has been mean to them, instead of suggesting that they should talk to their friend about it or avoid them for a while, you could ask 'What would you like to do about it?' Finally, you can avoid judgement, criticism or shame when responding to your child. It's easy to respond to a story of havoc-making at school with a cry of 'Why on earth did you do that?' or 'That wasn't a very nice thing to do.' Instead, you might be curious about what happened and what might help them avoid a similar situation in future.

Another element of warm parenting is making your child feel wanted or needed. You can do this, at the risk of stating the obvious, by spending time with them. It's hard for a child to feel wanted if they're constantly left to their own devices. Dedicated time together might manifest itself as shared meals in the evenings, playing games together, or taking a walk somewhere your child has chosen. It can be particularly helpful if you make it clear you won't answer your phone during this time. Even five minutes of individual positive attention every day can be a place to start, which sounds like a comically small amount when written down, but it can be hard to carve out even this if you and your child are both busy.

Asking for help from your child is another way to invite them to believe you need them. This needs to be age-appropriate – while asking them to help paint the front room and dust the light fittings might make your to-do list shorter, it's probably going to be better for you both to ask for their help in getting lunch together. (My child was determined to paint walls. I let her. There are still pale green footprints on the carpet.) Hugs, kisses and touch are valuable too. My children are now old enough that they often twist away from hugs, but I can get across the same message by occasionally touching them on their shoulder or their head when I'm talking to them, or by holding a foot when we're watching a film together.

When you have the time and ability to do so, you can increase your warmth by joining in with the activities your child suggests, such as building a Lego tower or baking. My heart sinks when my children suggest playing Cluedo for the 783rd time but, if we do so, they'll be more willing and happier than if we do something I suggest. One day, they will learn the pleasures of an obscure French world-pillaging board game called Richesses du Monde, but that day has not yet arrived.

Active listening is another important aspect of warm parenting. It involves paraphrasing or reframing what your child has told you, both to confirm to the child you're listening and to check you've understood them correctly. If your child tells you they have a tummy ache and they hate school, you might respond, 'It sounds like school's making you feel unhappy at the moment. Is that right?' Or if they tell you about a new game they've been playing with a friend, you might say 'It sounds like [game name] is fun. Can you tell me a bit more about it?'

You might also want to reframe any negative language you use about your child (even if it's just the language you use in your head), to make it more positive. For instance, you could choose to see your perpetually talkative child as someone who's eager to communicate and good at doing so, or you could see a child who's constantly searching for attention as one who needs a chance to connect with you a little better. There was a point at which I had to make myself stop describing one child's incessant chatter as Radio [Her Name], both to myself and to my partner, and to consider instead how much she had to say about the world. Reframing language in this way can make you more accepting of your child and more responsive towards them.

It can be helpful to keep certain points in mind when talking to your child: are you treating them with respect, properly listening to them and validating what they say, and setting boundaries which help them to learn rather than to resent you? Acknowledging your own mistakes and saying sorry, where necessary, are also important.

If you know you say no a lot more than you say yes, or if you need to re-establish trust with your child, you could try spending a week prioritising positive responses. This doesn't need to mean saying yes to everything. Instead, you could offer your child options: 'Would you prefer to eat that tasty thing after lunch or after dinner?' or 'We can't do a sleepover tonight, but tomorrow or Tuesday would work – which would you prefer?' It's hard to focus on being more positive over a long period of time, particularly if you're trying to weave in lots of other ideas and advice. Focusing on it for a week is a bit easier, and the habits may last. This exercise may place an uneasy spotlight on how often you say no.

For my part, I know my children are easier to be around and act out less when I'm warm with them. If I respond badly to a fib or a trashed bedroom, we get into a negative spiral of irritation and rotten behaviour. If I can respond calmly and warmly, with clear limits, things tend to improve. This has been a worthwhile but bruising learning curve.

Be consistent

Being consistent in the way you treat your child means they know what to expect from you. You might remove your child from the room every time they act violently towards another child, or calmly ask them to speak to you in a normal voice each time they scream at you. Consistency might involve ensuring that children eventually carry out the task they've been asked to do, such as tidying their bedroom or setting the table for dinner. It might mean dependable routines – having a bedtime story each night or brushing teeth straight after breakfast.

Consistency around limits (such as around bedtimes or behaviour) is likely to be most critical for your child – for example, reinforcing the message to a yelling child that you won't be shouted at and that you'll be ready to talk to them when they're able to speak calmly. There's more later in this chapter about limits and boundaries. Having consistent limits will give children a feeling of safety and a secure platform from which they can learn and explore. It's likely to be less important for your child to have the same straw every time they have a drink, a consistent place setting at the table or an identical packed lunch every day. When it comes to a packed lunch, it's much better for their taste buds and gut health to have a variety, even if your own ear health may be at risk through ongoing complaints about novelty.

It is also important for a child to have consistency from the adults in their life.[2] It's confusing for a child if one parent says they can do something and the other parent says they can't, or if parents have different expectations. If your partner says your child can watch TV for an hour and you make them turn it off after twenty minutes, your child is left unable to rely on the messages they are receiving. Inconsistency, in my experience, can also lead to children making requests of the more lenient parent to maximise their chances of success. 'I asked Dad if I could watch TV. I knew you'd say no.' Children are nothing if not shrewd.

There's not much in the research literature about how to back up your partner, though, if you have radically different approaches to bringing up your child. And sometimes the advice on consistency conflicts with other fundamental tenets of parenting. I know two parents who naturally take a different approach to discipline. One of them hates shouting and thinks it's bad for the kids; the other thinks it's fine to show anger by shouting in certain, very limited circumstances. The one who hates shouting certainly isn't going to follow her partner's approach to show consistency, and she's left between a rock and a hard place when her children talk to her about how upsetting they find being shouted at. Does she validate their feelings, damaging how her children view their dad in the process as well as undermining parental consistency, or does she explain to them why he might be upset, potentially justifying his approach while undermining her children's own assessment of what's happened and how they should be treated?

I don't know the answer. Nor does the research. We probably need to accept that some decisions will always have trade-offs. In the meantime, some smaller steps towards family consistency, such as sitting down with your partner to talk through the pros and cons of different approaches, might help. It could also be beneficial to identify what the two of you can agree on. This is usually more substantial than the areas of disagreement, even if it doesn't feel that way at the beginning.

The section in Chapter 1 on parenting confidence contains some suggestions that might be useful in terms of cooperating well with your partner. You'll never be consistent about everything, so choosing the two or three most important issues for each of you – and agreeing to back each other up on these – can be helpful. In particular, a joint approach to discipline will help your child more than if you have different rules and tipping points. If you're not able to sort it out between you, a trained therapist may help, if you can afford one.

It's also important to discuss and agree how to approach behaviour and limits with other carers, if there are any. These might be grandparents, nursery staff or babysitters. The challenge with this, in my experience, is that it may not feel appropriate to request a particular approach if someone is doing you a childcare favour. Another is that non-parent carers won't always listen. A friend's parents-in-law are incredibly warm and kind with their grandsons but, despite the entreaties of my friend and her partner, they won't ever say no. This has led to some interesting behaviour on the boys' part when they've spent any extended time with their grandparents, particularly when they were younger. The behavioural legacy has simmered down with age. Now, everyone just assumes they will get a free pass with the oldest generation.

Being consistent shouldn't be confused with being rigid. Rules and consequences can be changed when the situation changes or if it's clear something isn't working. Being flexible with children increases their own ability to be flexible. If changes are made, it's vital to have a conversation with children so they understand the reasons behind them. A conversation also gives your child a chance to put across their point of view on family rules.

My partner and I have needed to amend our rule that our children keep their rooms manageable, as the tidy gene has yet to express itself in our younger daughter. My own 'requires order amid chaos' gene didn't switch itself on until I was well into my mid twenties, so we could be waiting a while. Whenever I help my daughter sort out her bedroom and label drawers so she knows where to put things away, I tell her that this time she needs to do a little bit of tidying each day so it stays that way. And every time, I give in a few weeks later. I could decide to let her room stay in hurricane mode, knowing that, if she cares enough, she'll learn how to tidy it for herself. I also need to be pragmatic. It affects me, not just her, if she doesn't have enough clean knickers to last the week or we can't find her homework book.

There isn't much in the way of evidence-based pointers to increase consistency, as it's fundamentally a straightforward concept. If the way you treat your child fluctuates with your mood, they don't know what to expect from you. And if you have a rule that your child lays the table for dinner every night, but you only enforce this two thirds of the time, you're likely to get more complaints about that 66.6% than you would if you enforced it almost every night.

Beyond this, it's about balancing consistency with pragmatic flexibility. You could have a bedtime of 8 p.m. that's stuck to the majority of the time but that can be moved later if, say, there are friends staying, or it's the weekend and you're having a family film night. Having a predictable approach most of the time is a more realistic ambition than consistent consistency.

Help your child manage their emotions

My natural reactions when somebody is furious with me are to respond in kind or to get away as fast as I can. There's a reason I like running. But neither of these reactions is helpful when it comes to raising children. I've had to learn how to contain my children's feelings and help them believe it's safe to have them, even if I sometimes ask them to express those feelings in a different way.

Children need to recognise when they feel sad, frustrated, lonely or angry.[3] They also need to know that what they feel is valid and acceptable to you. Validating emotions – recognising and being clear you accept them – can help your child manage them better. This may be because they feel soothed by this validation, or it may be that it causes them to have a different relationship with these emotions, perhaps no longer feeling ashamed of them or feeling more in control.

Knowing what we feel can be incredibly useful. Anger can tell us that something is unfair, and it can help us assert ourselves to other people. Fear can make us cautious around something that might otherwise hurt us. Sadness can show us what we care about. If children are taught that feelings like anger are inappropriate, they may not be able to stand up for themselves. If they believe showing anger to other people is forbidden, they may even blame themselves for situations outside their control. If a child feels angry that a trip has been cancelled due to illness, and they're not permitted to show this anger, they may focus on what they perceive to be the wrongness of their feelings, not on the upset of losing a longed-for treat. Telling or showing children they're wrong to have feelings – even ones with which you vehemently disagree – can make them doubt themselves and their instincts.

When children are supported to understand and manage their feelings, they develop words to describe them. Being able to communicate feelings verbally makes it less likely children will feel the need to convey them through actions. If a child can tell you they're angry because you didn't notice when they tried to speak to you, they're less likely to grab your attention by hurling their cereal bowl to the floor. Communicating feelings in a way that's met well also encourages children to do the same again in future. If you respond with empathy when your child tells you how angry they are with a sibling, they may be more likely to tell you later on when something bigger has upset them. Children's behaviour is affected more by parents helping them with their negative emotions than by focusing on their positive ones. There's not a lot of constructive input a parent can give when a child is feeling happy – you can simply enjoy the glorious moment – but you can give a lot of support to children who are sad, scared or seething.

It's fine to be angry. It's only how children (or adults) behave as a result of that anger that might need addressing, not the feeling itself. There's no need for any of us to stand like a Charlie Brown cartoon in front of a raging child, skin and hair being blown backwards by the force of their emotions. Instead, we can help children label those feelings and find healthy ways to express them without hurting others.

Being emotionally responsive to children is an important part of helping them learn how to manage their feelings. This means becoming aware of your child's emotions, seeing the potential for your child to learn about their feelings or for you to find a way to be close to them through how they feel, and then either showing the child that you see their emotion as valid or that you empathise with it. You can also show your child it's OK to be vulnerable. Where feelings are linked to a problem, emotional responsiveness also means supporting the child to solve it. Asking questions that help children solve problems themselves, rather than rushing in with a solution, can be particularly helpful.

If my child's looking sad, I might show that I've noticed, leaving it open to her to say more if she wishes. If my child agrees that she's feeling sad, I might say 'I'm sorry you're feeling that way. Is it OK if I sit with you for a while?' If my child tells me she's sad because her best friend's ill and they can't see each other, I might ask her what she'd like to do once her friend is better. Children may not be able to explain why they are feeling a certain way, but having an adult they trust recognise how they're feeling – 'You seem sad this evening' – can make them feel more able to talk. Even if you're not sure you're right about how they're feeling, it's worth making a stab at it. Your child will correct you if you're wrong.

Being careful not to dismiss children's feelings is part of emotional responsiveness. This sounds reasonable and obvious in theory, although in practice it's incredibly easy to dismiss what a child feels, especially if this way of parenting has been ingrained in us throughout our own childhoods. But when children are told they're being silly when they're scared of a spider or that they don't really hate the sibling who has just spilled water over their careful drawing of a helicopter, it risks making them think they're mistaken about their feelings or wrong to have them. Acknowledging feelings makes it easier for children to move on.

5. EXAMPLES OF DISMISSING AND ACCEPTING YOUR CHILD'S FEELINGS

CHILD	DISMISSING PARENT	ACCEPTING PARENT
'I hate fish fingers.'	'You love fish fingers. It's your favourite dinner.'	'You loved them last week, but I hear that you're not so keen on them today.'
'I don't want to go to school today. I hate it.'	'Don't be silly. School's brilliant.'	'It seems that you're finding school tough at the moment.'
'Mum's always so horrible.'	'No, she's not. Don't say things like that.'	'It sounds like you're feeling upset with Mum. Do you want to talk about it?'

One way to listen empathically and non-judgementally is to reflect to your child what they are feeling when they're upset. You don't have to agree with what they're saying – just say what you have understood them to be thinking and feeling, as with the examples in the right-hand column of the table above.

Teaching your child about emotions is important too. This can be done by talking about your own feelings in an age-appropriate way that doesn't require your child to provide you with comfort or other support. If you're reading a story with your child, you could talk with them about how the characters might be feeling. If you witness another child melting down at a bus stop, you might have a chat (carefully out of earshot of their parents) about what the child might be feeling.

---

6. TECHNIQUES TO HELP YOUR CHILD LEARN ABOUT EMOTIONS

Link emotions to things your child has experienced ➤	'This person looks excited, a bit like you were on the morning we went on holiday.'
Talk about your own emotions ➤	'I felt really sad that I couldn't be there for your assembly.'
Suggest ideas about other people's emotions ➤	'Maybe she was quiet because she was feeling upset.'
Give labels to emotions ➤	'She looks happy.'

Anger may be a particularly hard emotion for parents to manage, and understanding the underlying emotions can help parents select the most appropriate response. Anger can be set off by other negative feelings like rejection, fear and envy; if you think about what lies behind your own anger, you'll probably find the same. I might get angry when I'm on my bike and I get cut up by a car, as I'm afraid of getting knocked down; when my wonderful friend has to cancel yet another coffee date, as I feel rejected; and when I put on the fifth load of laundry in a row, as I feel envious that my partner's benefiting from time not spent loading the washing machine.

Children may be irritable or angry when they're not getting what they want or need. They want chocolate now, not later. They want to read their book now, not tidy their bedroom. They want their parents to listen to them. They may feel anxious or threatened. It's also useful to know what's considered to be developmentally appropriate in the realm of children, anger and tantrums. One study found that one-year-olds had an average of eight to nine tantrums every week. By the age of four, this fell to between five and six.[4]

An angry child may need your help to escape from the epicentre of their rage. You could ask them to use a mental image of something happy as a means of distraction. If they loved a trip you took to the seaside, you might ask what they remember about that day and what they most enjoyed about it. Any attempts to distract your child, though, should recognise that you're not trying to deny their feelings or avoid them. You can move back to chatting about why your child is feeling angry once they're slightly calmer.

Comfort is another helpful strategy. When parents comfort an angry child, the child is more likely to talk about their anger in a constructive way.[5] The type of comfort that might work depends on your child's personality and age. You might blow some bubbles together, hug your child, sing some songs together, give them some putty to play with or do some deep breathing together. I had the Calm app on my phone for a while, and one of my daughters used to enjoy listening to the music for kids or the sleep stories when she was upset. You could also use your understanding of your child to consider any immediate needs that might be affecting their mood. Sometimes a child may need nothing more than a snack – or several, if my children are anything to go by.

More general approaches you can take between episodes of anger to make things generally calmer include identifying the triggers for tantrums or other angry episodes. These triggers may include sudden changes of plan, noise or being asked to share or to get ready for bed. Understanding the triggers means parents can work with their children to find out how to make these less of a flashpoint. One of my daughters tends to get cross when she's asked to do more than one or two things at once – a peaceful morning is not made by asking her in the same breath to brush her teeth and her hair, and to change her shirt to one that is clean. Asking for the same things in stages works much better for her and therefore for me.

You could also find out which activities have a calming effect on your child, creating space for these activities on a regular basis. Calming activities vary from child to child. They might include art, music or exercise. Candlelit baths and time curled up with a book go down well with my children. These activities can help your child reset and be less stressed, reducing the chance that feelings of stress will later be condensed into anger.

Children who are quick to anger may need support to develop an ability to be flexible and adaptable, and to tolerate frustration. These children may need help developing skills to manage their emotions, get on with other people, understand other people's points of view and wait for something they would otherwise – if everything else were equal and you were considering their immediate gratification rather than their long-term development – be given immediately. Children may even simply need recognition from their parents that they struggle in these areas.

In many cases, parents may need to be patient. When very reactive children find themselves in conflict with parents or other authority figures, their high emotional state may leave them less able to learn from these experiences than calmer children. Children who are angry or reactive don't all respond to the same approaches. It's worth parents trialling some of the different suggestions in this section and seeing what works best for your child.

You should consult your child's doctor if they're frequently angry. A medical check can rule out physical reasons for high or persistent levels of anger, such as allergies, diabetes or attention-deficit hyperactivity disorder. Anger management programmes can also be worth exploring. These programmes can have positive effects on children's anger levels when they're designed to support them to develop coping skills, emotional awareness, self-control and problem-solving skills, and when they teach them relaxation techniques.

In some cases, though, the issue may lie (whisper it) with you and your ability to handle your child's feelings. If you find it tricky, you could try reframing their difficult emotions as a chance to become closer to each other or to teach them something. One of my daughters started complaining of a sore tummy at bedtime. I initially saw it as a sleep-delaying tactic to go with various others she wheels out on rotation: she's thirsty, she needs a piece of fruit, she needs a hug, she needs more stories, her bedroom's too cold, her bedroom's too hot or her mattress is too lumpy (perhaps someone hid a pea underneath it). Then I started to realise that she often mentioned her stomach when she'd lost her temper earlier or when she was worried about something. This was familiar to me. I'm Chidi from *The Good Place* whenever anything goes wrong: 'My stomach hurts.' We had a gentle chat about how difficult feelings can sometimes show themselves as physical symptoms. She was sceptical. Even if she didn't believe me, I was supporting her feelings better with this kind of chat than I was with an internal diatribe that she was still not in her bloody bed.

If you don't like the way your child's talking to you, you can make it clear that they should express their feelings in a different way. Adele Faber and Elaine Mazlish, who wrote the ever-popular *How to Talk So Kids Will Listen and Listen So Kids Will Talk*, suggest using the following words: 'I didn't like what I just heard. If you're angry about something, tell it to me in another way. Then maybe I can be helpful.'[6] Internally reframing your child's feelings – seeing them as a natural consequence of circumstances or their stage of development, rather than stemming from a character flaw – can help you respond constructively.

When children behave badly, avoiding a spiral of negativity is crucial. Showing increasingly negative responses to poor behaviour makes children less able to manage their emotions and more likely to behave worse in future.[7] If your child deliberately splashes bath water at you and your response is to shout, it may make your child anxious about when you might shout again. This anxiety can make it harder for them to behave in a way you might like or expect. You then get angry at this increasingly bad behaviour. It's better to cut off this spiral before it begins.

Positive strategies, such as being playful, may also be worth a shot here. Playful parents are more likely to have children who can handle emotions well. Increasing the time you spend talking about happiness and joy can also be helpful – young children who live in families who frequently express positive emotions are better able to soothe themselves when they're upset.[8]

Unless you want your child to run your household, which probably wouldn't be great for either of you, being emotionally responsive to your child should be done alongside setting limits. The next section on guidance and boundaries gives some ideas on how to do this.

Offer your child both guidance and boundaries

I have two university friends who somehow escaped the mortal blow that the end of finals usually lands on student relationships. They met at a rowing dinner, stayed awake that night to watch the dawn rise over the city, and have remained together through three and a half doctorates (they're overachievers) and two children. As well as Ultimate Frisbee, running and creating new scientific knowledge, their skills include the gentle, firm way that they speak to their kids when there has been any kind of upset.

It is a masterclass in communication. They bend down to eye level, touch the shoulder of the child in question and speak in a low voice. This means two things. Their children know they're not being shouted at, and they're not embarrassed or shamed if this happens in front of other people. The words vary, depending on the situation, but it's usually some variation on questions about why something has happened, clear explanations about what needs to happen now and why, and language that makes their children know they're loved.

Guidance and encouragement should be given to children alongside clear limits. This has been shown to increase children's ability to observe requests made by parents and to deal with unpleasant emotions in a positive way, which is sometimes referred to as self-regulation.[9] Guidance includes explanations, demonstrations, and clear and consistent messaging. I'm guiding my child when I explain why sharing toys helps other children feel good – as well as making others more likely to share their toys with her – and when I praise her for sharing. I'm giving her boundaries or limits when I teach her that she mustn't taunt her sister (this is a work in progress) or that it's better to speak during a pause in conversation than when somebody else is in mid flow.

Giving children guidance helps them develop an understanding of parents' expectations. Boundaries help children understand how responsibilities are divided between them and their parents. They also enable children to develop a sense of right and wrong, to cultivate a clear sense of who they are, and to feel confident, safe and secure. Putting boundaries in place can help children develop a healthy self-image through a belief that they're able to manage their emotions. Boundaries can also help children make healthy choices – in the school canteen, for example.

Setting boundaries isn't merely about saying what children can and can't do. It's about teaching children they can do things for themselves – with help, where needed, from their parents. Early childhood expert Janet Gonzalez-Mena developed a clever analogy to describe why boundaries are important for children: if you're driving at night over a bridge with no edges, you'll drive over it cautiously, whereas if the bridge has railings or walls, you can pick up speed and cross it with confidence.[10]

Limits create predictability and certainty, while a lack of certainty can make children feel worried and unsafe. A day is predictable if a child knows its shape. They know breakfast will happen before school or nursery, that a shower happens every day or after sport, and that they have a defined bedtime. Limits also ensure that children aren't left with too many decisions or choices. They know that they don't get chocolate at 5 a.m., and that coming into your bedroom to convince you they should isn't going to be met with enthusiasm. A lack of limits means the day is unpredictable and therefore stressful.

7. HOW TO SET RULES AND EXPECTATIONS

Explain what the consequences of certain behaviour will be ➤	'If you don't wear your coat, you'll get cold.' (If your child is as stubborn as mine, though, they will just let themselves freeze.)
Ask your child to talk about the consequences of certain actions ➤	'What do you think the dog might do if you keep pulling his tail?'
Discuss the reasons for rules ➤	'We say no screens at the dinner table as it's a chance for us to spend time talking with each other.'
Have a pre-emptive chat about expectations ➤	'When Billy comes round, I'd really like you to show me how well you can share.'
Discuss what's happened with your child when behaviour has gone awry ➤	'Do you think you kicked the chair over because you were feeling upset about something else?'

The table here gives some ideas about how to set rules and expectations with your child. Expectations should be appropriate for a child's age and level of development. It might be unreasonable to expect a child of two to share a toy, and it's probably asking too much of a ten-year-old to clear up an entire meal.

Boundaries should be reasonable and consistent. I fight constantly against my instinct to have rules about everything. Boundaries should also be about the parent, where possible, not the child. A smidgen of honesty can be a good thing here, and your child may appreciate it. Do you want your beloved to stop yo-yoing in and out of their bedroom because you want them to get a good night's sleep, or because you'd like some adult conversation and to catch up on *MasterChef*? Language relating to boundaries should be neutral, avoiding hard instructions or criticism. 'I don't want you to use my notebook. I need it for work,' is probably a more useful framing than 'Stop tearing pages out of my notebook and scribbling in it.'

Striking a balance between being overly responsive and too light-touch is likely to be important when a child tests boundaries. Your anger, or even a torrent of words, can bring too much attention to a particular negative action. This attention makes it more likely the child will, in future, refuse to go to bed, raid the fridge just before dinner time or persecute the dog. Equally, if you mostly ignore a child who's trying to test boundaries, you may not be showing enough authority. A short, simple statement is generally most effective: 'I won't let you hurt your brother' when you've blocked an action or 'I don't want you to hurt your brother' when the action has already occurred.

It's worth approaching the word 'maybe' with caution when a child has asked for something. If a child, particularly an anxious one, has the possibility on the horizon of an ice cream or a play date with a friend, a lack of certainty may lead them to focus on it exclusively. This risks them not being able to enjoy themselves, even when they're doing something fun. You can tell if your child needs clear answers by the number of questions they ask about something to which you have given a 'maybe' response. If I'm distracted and say 'perhaps' or 'we'll see' when my younger daughter asks if she can bake biscuits later, my moment of preoccupation is repaid by the thirty-three times she asks me if it's going to happen. Anxious children and those who require certainty are likely to need a 'yes', a 'no' or a 'contingent yes' – for example, 'You can have screens once your bedroom is tidy.'

One of the biggest parental challenges is sticking to any limits you've set. If this doesn't happen, children may believe they have more power than their parents. This makes them feel unsafe. Children are also much more likely to test limits that haven't been enforced consistently. In the discipline section within Chapter 6, you'll find more ideas about how to set reasonable limits with your child and what to do when limit-setting goes wrong.

Boundaries should be in place for adults in the family, too. These include protecting children from adult responsibilities. Children shouldn't have to provide emotional support to their parents, nor play a major role in physical care. Teaching children to develop their own boundaries – such as around bodily autonomy – is also vital. This means, for example, not tickling them if they have asked you not to. You could spend some time talking to your child to help them work out what they think is acceptable and when they need to make a boundary clear. They might be fine with hugs from you but find a grandparent's enthusiastic cuddles make them feel stifled. They might not want a sibling to go into their room without permission. They might not want to play games with other children that make them feel uncomfortable or unsafe. They need to know they can say no, take themselves away from a situation or get a grown-up.

One of my daughters went through an interminable two years of not wanting to be kissed. In her first year at primary school, she'd become a little too enthusiastic about one of the older kids. The school came down hard on her, telling her that displays of affection were inappropriate. She carried this message into the rest of her life. We had to respect her boundaries, while also making it clear that affection is a lovely thing, so long as both people involved are happy. It goes against every instinct not to kiss your child on the head while you're reading them a story, and it made us incredibly sad that she saw affection as bad. She's more tolerant of it these days, eye-rolls notwithstanding.

If it's hard knowing where to start with helping children to set their own boundaries, you could watch out for someone setting a boundary – or failing to set a boundary – in a book or a TV programme, and chat to your child about it. It's also good to show children how to set boundaries by doing it yourself. I have set many in front of my children, only to watch them crumble as they steal my favourite top, use up my Christmas shower gel and hurl themselves onto my back when I've asked them not to. But at least I've shown them how to draw a line in the sand, even if they've worked out how to cross it.

Give your child room to make choices and have autonomy

Next time you feel a sense of curiosity materialising in your brain, you could try a little experiment over the course of three days. (It might need to be spread over two weekends if you work during the week.) You can experiment with anything with which it's possible to have a wide range of choices or none at all. The example I'll choose is an afternoon snack. On one day, you might give limitless choices. 'What would you like to eat?' On another, you might offer a banana. On a third, you might offer a defined choice. 'Would you prefer a banana or cheese and biscuits?' You can then assess whether these different approaches have affected your child's mood. Granted, the order in which you ask these questions is likely to matter. Giving zero choice the day after limitless options may turn your child into a mutinous monster.

Most children prefer to be given choices.[11] Having room to make decisions, while being given clear limits and boundaries, has multiple benefits. Options shouldn't be open-ended or overwhelming, but tailored to your child's level of development and the kinds of things in which they like to have a say.

Choices should also be practical and feasible for you as a parent. Asking what children would like for breakfast, effectively giving them limitless possibilities, increases the chance they'll ask for something you don't have, or don't have the time or motivation to make. This may cause unhappiness or arguments. Offering them realistic options reduces this risk. 'Would you like Weetabix or toast for breakfast?' 'Would you like honey or lemon and sugar on your pancakes?' And you don't need to make your life more difficult by asking your child if they'd prefer a home-made unicorn cake or a ten-tier rainbow cake for their birthday, unless baking is your jam. I once made a similar error, only to be informed that my 'unicorn' looked like a lopsided donkey wearing an ice-cream cone. It was a fair assessment.

Over the course of a day, there are many opportunities to give options. You might offer your child choices about what they'd like to wear, eat, play or have as a bedtime story. If there are things that aren't optional, you could also offer choices in the timing or method – does your child want to put their shoes on now or after they've brushed their hair? Would they prefer to do teeth and pyjamas before bedtime stories or afterwards? Would they prefer a bath or a shower? I haven't worked out what to do with the latter question when 'Neither!' is hollered by a rapidly retreating child.

As well as offering children choices within limits, they can (where reasonable) have an input into decisions made about them. You might factor in your child's preference about which secondary school they attend, for example, while balancing it with other important factors such as school quality and how far away it is. Big family decisions, though, are likely to be overwhelming for your child. There's also a potential for things to go wrong – you don't want your child feeling responsible if they've decided you'll go camping and you arrive to find it may as well be monsoon season. There's value in canvassing children's opinions on family decisions and making them feel included. But the final decision is yours.

You might also find ways of giving them smaller, appropriate choices relating to a bigger family decision. If you're moving house and you have no preference on which bedroom becomes yours, you might offer your child the choice. We did this when we last moved. The short-term response, after the initial excitement, was suboptimal. 'I hate this room. I hate this house. I want my old room back.' However, it was sadness at the loss of my child's familiar space that she'd known since birth. By the time a few months had passed, she was quietly content in her middle bedroom with its secret cupboard-hideout-dragon zone.

This section is about autonomy as well as choice. Autonomy is about independence and having choices, but it's broader than those things. There's some overlap with other areas in this book, including explaining things clearly and ensuring that language isn't controlling. You might explain to your child why certain things are not allowed or why you want them to do something (like telling them you want them to take a coat on a walk because it's about to rain, and you don't want them to get drenched). Being open to your child having different opinions, thoughts and feelings to you is part of autonomy, too – like asking questions about why your child dislikes a family member who's dear to you rather than explaining why they're wrong to feel like this. Autonomy also includes adults acknowledging a child's negative feelings.

Letting children feel challenged, and not immediately jumping in to help, is another aspect of autonomy. You might let your child know you recognise that buttoning a shirt can be tricky if they are struggling, rather than leaping forwards to do it for them. This acknowledgement can give children the courage they need to do something by themselves. It also shows them that if they don't manage, it was because the job was a thorny one. If they do manage, they can be proud of having achieved something difficult.

But there's no point in letting your child struggle with something you know is far beyond them. Undermining their confidence is not the objective here. Just beyond a child's reach, there's a sweet spot for learning, and you can offer them your support and encouragement to get to this point. They might be trying to draw something using perspective, for example. Rather than showing them how to do it, you could suggest they use a pencil to see how big the same object looks when it's close compared with how small it looks when it's far away. You could then suggest using what they've learned to determine what size they draw things in their picture.

There's another category of activity: things they're capable of doing alone. If they're keen, you should let them. If they need encouragement, you can offer it. It may well be something requiring patience, a quality in short supply in many children, in which case particular encouragement may be needed: 'It's a tricky job, but I know you're able to do it.'

Encouraging your child to do things for reasons they themselves value – not because of other people's opinions about what matters, or because you've coerced or bribed them like a suggestible politician – can also support their autonomy.[12] If your child keeps losing their favourite toys, you might casually encourage a tidy bedroom so they know where to find the things they love. This is an area in which parents can struggle. It's easy for controlling language to slip in when there's half an hour left to get homework finished or their bedroom has become a contender for an episode of *Hoarders*. And sometimes you may have to use external grounds as a basis for getting your child to do something: they may not fancy going to school today, but there are several excellent reasons why they must.

Some children see the word no as an invasion of their autonomy. This doesn't necessarily mean saying yes to children, but instead is about finding other ways of phrasing the idea. When they ask if they can have a biscuit, you could say you're having lunch in half an hour, or that they can have a biscuit after dinner. When they ask if they can have a sleepover tonight, you could say that you'd love it if they could, but tomorrow is a school day; or that tomorrow night would work better. Accepting feelings is another useful approach: 'I can see how much you want to stay up with us instead of going to bed.'

As with the section on guidance and boundaries, respecting children's bodily autonomy is important. This means trying to avoid constantly sorting out their hair, their clothes or that patch on their neck of what could equally well be mud or chocolate. And it's worth making sure your own needs are being met. Parents are more likely to support their children's autonomy if they're getting their own emotional and physical needs met (see Chapter 1).

Supporting children's autonomy is likely to work better for some children and families than it is others. And there's such a thing as too much autonomy. Before my younger daughter had any sense of how to find things, we went camping. We'd leave her and her sister playing in the campsite's well-supervised play area. My small daughter would eventually get bored, decide to come back to the tent and sprint in whichever direction her nose was pointing. We got slightly more responsible the second (or perhaps third) time an irate camper from the far corner of the campsite returned her to us.

Giving children autonomy within a structure of boundaries and limits is key. You're not telling your ten-year-old they can do anything they want after school, but you are letting them invite their friend to come round to play. You're not telling your four-year-old they can have screens whenever they want, but you are offering them a choice of watching a TV programme before or after dinner, and letting them choose what they want to watch (if it is, in your view, suitable for them). You're not letting your two-year-old go to the playground wearing a pair of knickers on their head and slippers on their feet, but you're letting them choose between the dragon sweatshirt and the dinosaur hoodie. If you're allowing choice and autonomy within age-appropriate boundaries, you can't go far wrong.

CHAPTER CHECKLIST

Key recommendations

► Be warm with and responsive to your child.
► Be consistent.
► Help your child manage their emotions.
► Offer your child both guidance and boundaries.
► Give your child room to make choices and have autonomy.

Some of the ideas below may help you put these recommendations into practice.

High-quality research

► **Set healthy boundaries, acknowledge feelings and avoid control.** Offer choices within limits, explain your reasons for any limits or boundaries, acknowledge your child's feelings and avoid psychological control. Specific ways of doing these things include:
  • taking into account your child's point of view when making significant decisions about them;
  • allowing your child to make choices within certain limits;
  • explaining to your child why certain things are not allowed or why you want them to do something; and
  • being open to your child having different opinions, thoughts and feelings to yours own.

► **Be warm and centre what your child wants, when reasonable.** Say nice things about your child to them. Make it easy, if you can, for your child to confide in you. Try to make your child feel wanted and needed. When you have the time and ability, join in with the activities your child suggests, such as building a Lego tower or baking. Try 'active listening' with your child.

Moderate-quality research

- **Be clear that feelings matter.** Show your child what you're feeling, validate and respond to what your child is feeling, and teach them about emotions. Try a range of different strategies to do this, including showing them that it's OK to be vulnerable.
- **Help your child be driven to do things using their internal motivation** by encouraging them to do things for reasons they value, not for external reasons. (This may not work when you're encouraging them to load the dishwasher.)
- **Dig in when things get tricky.** When your child protests, be prepared to see through any agreed consequences for certain behaviour. If you find it difficult to handle feelings like anger or sadness in your child, try to reframe this as a chance to become closer to your child or to teach them something. Back up your child's other parent where possible. When your child behaves badly, try not to get into a spiral of negativity.
- **Find the good.** Be playful with your child. Work as a family on increasing how much you speak about things like happiness and joy.

Anecdotal research/expert advice

- **Reflect.** Keep certain points in mind when talking to your child: are you treating them with respect, properly listening to them and validating what they say, and setting boundaries that help them learn rather than resent you?
- **Align with other key adults in your child's life.** Discuss and agree with other carers how to approach behaviour, boundaries, discipline and other relevant areas.
- **Aim for balance.** Try to find a centre ground in which you're neither too responsive nor too light-touch when a child tests boundaries. Make boundaries about yourself, where possible, not your child ('I don't like cleaning toothpaste off the sink'). Make sure any choices you offer are realistic.
- **Respond to requests carefully.** It may be better to give certainty than to say 'maybe', depending on your child's temperament, and check how often you say no. If you say no a lot more than you say yes, or

if you need to re-establish trust with your child, try spending a week prioritising giving positive responses.

▶ **Know that boundaries work both ways.** If your child is struggling to do something like buttoning a shirt, don't jump in to help. Instead, show you recognise it can be tricky. Respect your child's bodily autonomy. Ensure boundaries are in place for adults in the family, too.

▶ **Prioritise what your child is feeling over the reasons why they're feeling it.** Listen to your child with empathy and try to do this in a non-critical way, even when they're saying things that might upset you. Instead of asking your child questions when they're looking upset, try to acknowledge what they feel. At the same time, you don't need to absorb endless negativity; if you don't like how your child is talking to you, make it clear to them that they should express their feelings in a different way.

▶ **Be positive.** Try to have dedicated time with your child in a way that helps them feel special and appreciated, even if it's just five minutes of dedicated attention each day. Reframe any negative language you use about your child (even the language in your head) to make it more positive.

Troubleshooting: helping an angry child

Identify the triggers for tantrums or other angry episodes. Find out which activities have a calming effect on your child, and create regular space for these activities. When your child gets angry, use your understanding of them to consider any immediate needs that might be affecting their mood. Try using distraction, while not avoiding or denying how they feel, and provide comfort as needed. Help your child use constructive and safe responses to feelings of anger (see Chapter 6).

PART TWO

Focused parenting approaches

CHAPTER 5

RELATIONSHIPS

I had an unusual upbringing. I grew up on a small, estuary-bound island in Essex called Osea. It's now a luxury holiday resort. Back then, it was a working farm, where cottages were rented out to people like my parents who sought an alternative way of life. We harvested samphire from the saltings and mussels from the mudflats, my mum grew most of the vegetables we ate and my dad brewed his own beer. The island was tidal. You could access it by 'road' – a Roman causeway consisting of flattened rocks laid on a bed of mud – for around four hours, twice a day. The rest of the time, there were two options: stay put or find a boat. Most uncommonly, I was the only child on the island. There was the occasional holiday-home visitor, and my half-sisters would sometimes visit from London. Most of the time, though, it was just me.

There were benefits. I was excellent at making adult conversation. I had freedom to roam – I wandered the island's woods, fields and beaches without anyone needing to worry about me. My imagination had space to evolve. Living on Osea taught me independence and resilience. What it didn't teach me, however, was how to form easy relationships with other children. I thought there was something wrong with me until I went to university and realised that my endless hours chatting to adults had prepared me brilliantly for being a grown-up. They just weren't that useful for being a child.

Childhood and adult relationships need different skills. My children are better than I was at friendships. They're in an entirely different league, in fact. Early adult relationships might come slightly harder to them when they get to that point, but hopefully they'll be robust enough by then to withstand any rough edges being smoothed away. In the meantime, my hope for them is that they have a secure relationship with me and their dad, good friendships, and that they don't kill each other on the way.

Humans are social animals: our connections with others are critical to all sorts of areas of development, as well as to our health and happiness. During the pandemic, some of these connections – both our own and our children's – had periods of rupture, and we may not understand the implications of this for some time. However, we can still do many things to strengthen the links with other people that we know are essential. This chapter looks at evidence-based ideas on how you can support your child's relationships. It looks at your own relationship with your child, your child's friendships, sibling relationships and, finally, what you can do if you find out your child's being bullied.

Your relationship with your child

Having a good relationship with your child improves things for them in the moment. It also provides you with a protective shield when the rockiness of the adolescent years emerges on the horizon. The links between a secure parent–child relationship and positive outcomes for children are enormous, and there are other benefits. You'll no doubt feel happier when your relationship with your child's going well. Home life will probably be more straightforward, too.

Children can be buffered from some heavy things when they have a good connection with their parents. The difference between my parents' relationships with their own parents is a case in point. My mum's father was a crotchety character who was traumatised by war. He spent much of her childhood ricocheting between drinking binges and time in mental health facilities. They didn't have a relationship so much as an ongoing locking of horns. My grandfather would lay down the law and my mother would defy him. She left home as soon as she was old enough to get a job. My dad, on the other hand, was incredibly close to his parents. They had their flaws – don't we all? – but they created a childhood filled with fun, laughter and fierce, considered debate around the dinner table. Their relationship was sufficiently sturdy that even the rupture of being sent away to boarding school aged eight didn't diminish his memories of them.

A good relationship means different things to different people. One description of a good parent–child relationship is that the child enjoys spending time with the parent, and feels both valued and accepted by them.[1] Children have a healthy emotional bond with their parents when they feel secure and believe their parents will be responsive to their needs. But a good relationship doesn't mean an absence of conflict. Conflict is healthy and normal. Learning how to manage conflict appropriately with your child can improve your relationship and support their development. Sometimes, though, there's too much conflict, or it's corrosive. Ideas on how to smooth any spikiness are covered in the following section.

Often your relationship with your child will be affected by things outside the family. Pressures of schoolwork, for example, are a major cause of arguments between children and their parents. Your relationship with your child can be affected by how complex your job is and how much you feel challenged by it, how tired you are and how much money you have – it's easier to communicate well with children if you have a financial buffer. I know, for my part, that my relationship with my children feels easier during periods of low stress and when I don't feel subject to a maelstrom of other pressures on my time. (It's also better when I don't find the lid missing from the toothpaste tube every bloody time I brush my teeth.)[2]

One way to improve your relationship with your child is to focus on what they're doing well, and to ignore most of the things you're less keen on. Parents coached in this approach get on better with their children, with a side helping of better behaviour. They also tend to develop a better relationship with their children when they're able to understand what's going on in their children's minds and when they consider what thoughts and feelings may be leading their children to behave in certain ways. If my child temporarily refuses to turn off the TV when asked, I could see it as acting up, or I could choose to see it in the context that she's someone who needs plenty of warning before anything happens, which in this scenario I haven't given her.[3]

Dedicated play times and ensuring plenty of stimulation for your child can improve your relationship with each other, even if it's just thirty minutes playing together once a week.[4] Depending on your child's age, you might do trips to the park, baking, water play (in the bath or shower if you don't have outside space), painting or dancing. When my own children were small, they were endlessly entertained by me blowing bubbles for them to catch and pretending to be a horse while they rode around on my back. These days, it's more *Minecraft*, Monopoly and time with mates.

Play is helpful in engaging children who are withdrawn or untalkative.[5] I sometimes run focus groups with children as part of my day job, and I can confirm that play – often in the form of silly activities – is an excellent way of getting a reticent child to open up. You can also take your child into nature, whether that's a local city park or a nearby wilderness. Being outside in nature with your child can help you connect better with each other (though I've found this to be less true in the driving rain).

You could also try a weekly family meeting as a way of building connection, perhaps weaving in a board game or a film with time to talk as a family. It's worth setting meetings in stone to make sure they happen. A Sunday evening might be good, when other stuff's less likely to get in the way. Dr Lisa Damour, a psychologist specialising in teenagers, recommends getting a regular weekly night in the diary for another reason – if you put it in place early, before your child's close to hitting the threshold of their teens, it's a habit by the time they might otherwise push back against it.[6]

Some important aspects of your relationship are forged in the way you speak to each other and in the silent communication that fills the spaces between words. Focusing fully on your child when talking together is a good place to start, as is making sure there's plenty of opportunity for touch between you. Coming down to a child's level makes it easier to maintain eye contact with them and reduces the chance they'll feel intimidated. Listening to your child is done, ideally, by letting them lead the conversation, not asking too many questions and avoiding making demands of them while they're talking. If my child wants to chat about a TV programme I haven't seen, I'm better off following her lead than I am trying to change the subject to something on which I can have some kind of useful input.

Your relationship with your child can also be supported by having compassion for what your child is feeling, as well as for yourself, and avoiding judgement if possible.[7] If I have a deadline to hit and friends coming for dinner, and my child has seen the empty, gleaming kitchen as the perfect opportunity to establish a slime factory, I might snap at her. While this snapping will have been suboptimal, I can reassure myself that my short temper was understandable, given that I can't bring myself to deliver work late and I hate being surrounded by mess. I can also recognise that my child will have been hurt by my reaction, and that I need to repair any damage. Finally, I can work out how to avoid a similar situation in future – not inviting friends round on the night of a deadline, perhaps, or making it clear to my children when messy play is not going to be helpful to me.

When your child is feeling sad or upset, it's better to reflect back to them what they are feeling than it is to rationalise or deny how they feel. This approach, covered earlier in the section on supporting your child with their emotions (Chapter 3), can help your relationship. If your child says they're feeling lonely when they're surrounded by family and friends, you might say 'That's a really hard thing to be feeling' rather than an instinctive 'You can't be lonely. You have lots of company.' It's good, too, to avoid critical or otherwise negative comments when you can. If your child's acting in a way you don't like, these comments can be replaced with constructive statements that let children know what's expected in a direct and specific way: 'Don't hit your sister,' not 'You're such a thug. You're always hitting your sister.'

Supporting your child to develop a healthy level of independence from you – not too little and not too much – can also be useful. The development of healthy independence relates to some of the key ideas covered in Chapters 3 and 4: being warm with and responsive to your child, offering them both guidance and boundaries, giving them autonomy and room to make choices, and avoiding being a helicopter parent. These sections all have lots of ideas about how to put these things into practice. It's a balancing act. You want to be close to your child and for them to feel you have their back in all matters, while allowing them the freedom to explore and make decisions for themselves within the boundaries of what's safe and sensible. It is particularly important to ensure you don't overstep boundaries, such as pushing your child for information or looking through their things. Older children who think their parents are invading their privacy become more secretive as a result.[8]

I have always erred on the side of independence for my children, though experience has taught me that more in the way of limits on safety might be prudent. When my younger daughter was three, her scooter – then her preferred means of transport – meant she could keep up with the adults' pace when we went out for a walk. She was a menace with it. She'd duck and weave and zoom, alarming pedestrians and terrifying dogs. One harrowing day, when we were walking with friends along the seafront in Hove, I realised she'd scooted out of sight. This cued a terrifying half hour of running up and down the promenade, accosting other walkers to ask if they'd seen her. We found her curled up on a bench looking out to sea, hidden from the main pathway, as my partner was asking the coastguard to check the water. At that point, we became slightly better at putting clear limits on the independence we were trying to foster. (And yes, I've noticed that losing my youngest is a running theme of this book.)

It's a rare parent who never has any conflict with their child. Sometimes, your immediate issue may be how to take the heat out of conflicts, rather than how to build your relationship better. Building your relationship will help reduce conflict, but you will doubtless have periods in which some additional strategies are necessary (even more so as your child starts to morph into a teenager, but that's another book).

Being aware of what underlies conflict for your child can help you, as the adult, to manage it more effectively. Parents are likely to believe that children feel angry during an argument, but in reality children are most likely to feel sad.[9] Children usually feel sad if they've been denied affection or interaction, or if they've been punished. They're most likely to feel angry if something that belongs to them has been taken away or if they want something different from what the parent wants. A compromise is most likely when both parents and children make it clear they feel sad during an argument – it prompts everyone to want to rebuild positive trust and moves the conversation away from blame.

Parents who think about what they want for their child and for their relationship with each other during arguments (as opposed to their own personal goals) are more likely to solve conflict constructively, and to be warm and cooperative with their children.[10] I might have child-centred goals in mind if I want to make my child happy and help her get on in life, or I might consider relationship goals if I want to teach her compromise and build a loving and trusting relationship. On the other hand, parent-centred goals might be the order of the day if I want to feel less uncomfortable and to get my child to comply with what I've asked of her.

Being affectionate may be helpful when it comes to conflict. There's less conflict between parents and children when they're more affectionate with each other and more when they're stand-offish.[11] Of course, being affectionate leads to less conflict – although it's easier to be affectionate with your child when you're not constantly fighting with them. De-stressing (easier said than done) is another thing that may reduce conflict between you and your child. There are some ideas to support your well-being in Chapter 1, and these may also help lower your stress levels.

You can sometimes head off potential conflict by being curious when your child asks something of you to which you might instinctively say no. You can listen and show you've understood what they've said before you respond, perhaps by asking questions. Showing curiosity about why they want to do something or what they're feeling can make them more likely to listen to what you have to say. And if you are upset about something your child has done, you may be able to head off conflict by using sentences that begin with 'I', not 'you'. 'I don't want you to leave your coat on the floor because it gets in the way' is probably going to go down better, and be more likely to precipitate change, than 'You always throw your coat on the floor.'

Not all conflict can be avoided, though, and nor should it. If you approach conflict in the way you'd like your child to approach it too – assuming your preferred model isn't of the pistols-at-dawn variety – you'll give them a healthy framework to approach disagreements with other people as they get older. Children learn from their parents how to handle conflict.

The table here shows things it's worth avoiding during conflict. If you accuse, disagree with your child's interpretation of what has happened, counter-argue with them or dismiss them, you're likely to bring more heat than light to the discussion.

8. THINGS TO TRY TO AVOID DURING CONFLICT

Making accusations	➤	'You spilled milk and didn't bother clearing it up.'
Disagreeing	➤	'That's not what happened.'
Counter-arguing	➤	'That idea won't work.'
Dismissing	➤	'It doesn't matter what you think.'

It's not worth trying to rationalise with an angry child. They will probably feel even crosser, and it will make the problem worse. Children are pretty much incapable of reasoned thought when they're in the grip of strong emotions (so am I, frankly). Instead, you can take the oxygen out of an argument if you recognise and acknowledge a child's feelings. 'I know you want to finish your TV programme, but it's time to brush your teeth. You're disappointed that it's time for bed. I understand.'

It is also important to acknowledge that sometimes the conflict might result from you getting something wrong. Perhaps you've misinterpreted something your child has said, reacted badly to something they've done or made a poor judgement call. I've frequently done all these things. The key, if you've got it wrong, is to apologise. If you don't, your child may think that they've got it wrong – or even that they're fundamentally defective at their core. I've met people whose parents steadfastly held to the myth that they were always right, with the result that their adult children believe they're always wrong. It's more important for you to take steps to repair what's gone awry than it is to give your child the impression that you don't make mistakes.

If you're experiencing a lot of conflict together and your child is also acting up a lot, you might want to look at ways to support your child's behaviour. Conflict and behaviour are tightly intertwined – arguments between parents and their children can cause poor behaviour, just as poor behaviour can cause arguments. Ideas on behaviour are available in Chapter 6. Educating children about forgiveness can make them more likely to forgive, as well as to be less angry. I know many adults who might benefit from such an education, myself included. If things are difficult between you and your child, you could also tell them you're keen to improve your relationship and ask them for ideas on how you might do this. Many children like a direct approach.

Being realistic about age and stage of development is important when it comes to conflict. It's easy to overestimate your child's ability to take on board different perspectives, but young children aren't always able to integrate different points of view fully. You may be able to head off conflict with younger children by justifying why you have asked them to do something, or negotiating or compromising with them as needed. Justification might be saying something like 'You need to put on your wellies, otherwise you'll get soaking, freezing feet.' Negotiating or compromising might be saying that yes, your child can have TV, but only after you've all been out for a walk. Managing conflict with toddlers in this way is linked to their development of social and emotional skills.[12]

For older children, you could plan jointly how you're going to resolve similar conflicts in future. You might discuss how everyone can take turns better when talking to each other, which will make the conflict in question less likely to flare up in other areas. This kind of approach can involve suggesting a plan, asking others what ideas they might have, providing reasons why a suggested plan might work and asking your child whether they agree to the plan. You could also try working with your child, away from the heat of an argument, to understand each other's point of view. Understanding and appreciating other perspectives are central to constructive conflict. Your child may have more patience with your request to tidy up their toys if they understand you don't have the time or will to clear up their things yourself. You're more likely to be able to resolve conflict if you each think about how the other person's feeling, rather than who's right and who's wrong.

If you're worried your relationship with your child needs some remedial work, increasing the ratio of positive to negative interactions is one place to start. In Chapter 3, I mentioned a ratio of five positive interactions for every negative one to build a strong relationship. When relationships have deteriorated, it's easy to slip into a scenario where children are acting up because they're feeling unhappy, miserable parents are focused on misbehaviour at the expense of everything else and anything positive gets squeezed out of the equation. Actively building in more positive things – whether that's an invitation to read a favourite story, or noticing and commenting on what your child's doing well – gives a chance to redress this balance.

You can also keep gently suggesting joint activities. A child who doesn't want to engage is likely to say yes, eventually.

Friendships

Many parents instinctively steer clear of their children's friendships, but you can be a facilitator without being the engine driver. You can help your child lay the groundwork for friendships if they find them tricky, and make it easy for them to see their friends if your home set-up, transport and working patterns allow.

Most children experience friendship difficulties at some point in their childhood. For others, the fissure is bigger or lasts longer. My own experience colours my writing about this subject. From the age of eight until well after I started secondary school, I was lonely. I'd been abruptly moved up a year group in school, and the kids in my new class saw me as an upstart. Just as abruptly, I got moved back down the following year, by which time I was seen as an outsider by my original classmates too. I'm undone by the thought of a child on an empty bench, anxiously watching other children playing and counting down the minutes until the end of break time. That child was me, and I don't want any others to experience the same – and yet, of course, they do.

This is where parents come in. Kindness and care can't solve friendship issues, but they can assuage their impact. As a child, my friend Rowan came home in tears one day and told her dad she didn't have any friends. Her dad, who hadn't been raised to show much emotion, put his arms around her and said: 'I'm your friend.' Despite knowing his words wouldn't affect what was happening in the playground, Rowan felt soothed by them. Now a clinical psychologist, she takes a view that sometimes the small, simple gestures of love, without interrogation or problem-solving, are the best ways of helping children who are experiencing friendship difficulties. She comes back to this thought when an instinctive drive to problem-solve kicks in with her own children.

While parents might worry about shyness, research has shown that shy and withdrawn children are as likely as others to have best friends. Anxiety about making friends may be more likely to undermine their ability to do so. Children who want to make friends but feel anxious about it struggle much more than other children to make and maintain friendships. Their anxiety can interfere in their ability to interpret body language correctly and make them extremely concerned about what others are thinking. This, in turn, can prevent them opening up to others and developing the intimacy that comes from doing so.[13]

Having friends can protect children from being bullied. And friendships can protect kids who are being bullied from developing anxiety and depression, as their friends can help them cope and give them a sense of security. Friendships, or lack of them, can also influence how children interpret other people's words and actions. One of my daughters had periods of her early school life where she found it hard to make friends. A trace of meanness from another child was incapacitating. Once she'd found her friendship groove, however, she became more robust. She's mostly now able to flick away an unkind comment as a mark of utter absurdity on the part of the person uttering it.

Encouraging children to have high expectations of their friendships can inspire them to work harder at these friendships, making them more likely to succeed.[14] If you're worried your child is struggling to make friends or is going through a tricky patch, it may help to work on building their self-esteem – it's easier for children to make friends if they feel good about themselves (see Chapter 9). If your child sometimes acts aggressively, helping them temper any aggressive tendencies may also help them make friends (see Chapter 6).

You could also support your child to communicate well with other people. If your child is someone who regularly interrupts, you could practise taking turns to talk to each other. Children who have been rejected by other children can find conversation especially difficult.[15] They're more likely to try to talk over people and say something irrelevant to the conversation at hand. You may also want to look at your child's sleep (Chapter 7).

If your child is having a particularly hard time with friendships, you could enlist some subtle support from your child's teacher. I've known teachers shift seating plans behind the scenes to ensure that a lonely child is sat for a few weeks next to someone who will be kind, and to encourage children with shared interests to form a book club together or to play board games at lunchtime. Enrolling your child in a club related to something they love may also help them meet potential friends with shared interests.

A lack of friends may be nothing to do with your child and what they can or can't do, though. It could be luck (or a lack of it), or that your child has been marked as different in some way. Or perhaps it's a combination of factors. Reinforcing the message of luck and circumstance, and moving your child away from any sense of failure as a person, may be the best thing you can do for them. You could also focus on ensuring that everything's working for your child in other areas, so friendship issues don't loom as large. A child who feels loved, valued and competent is less likely to feel shattered by a lack of friends than one who does not, and a child who doesn't appear to need friends is more likely to attract them.

Sibling relationships

Fiction effortlessly paints the diversity of sibling relationships. You have the friendly teasing of the non-Percy Weasleys in Harry Potter, the enduring and inexplicable patience Charlie shows to Lola, the nastiness of Cinderella's stepsisters, the plucky mutual support rendered in Enid Blyton or Arthur Ransome, and the reluctant way Ruby tolerates her brother Max.

A more realistic assessment, though, is that diversity lies within sibling relationships, not only between them. It's not static. Sometimes it's gently fractious, sometimes it's playful, sometimes it's full of breathless excitement, sometimes siblings ignore each other and sometimes they get on so badly you almost wish you'd used a condom. The quality of relationships between siblings is measured in the research literature by three things: affection or warmth, rivalry or jealousy, and hostility. These areas can flare up and merge into each other moment to moment. I've watched my daughters grin at each other and then, when one of them thinks the other is getting something she isn't (access to more than 50% of the sofa being a current flashpoint), bellow with rage a minute later.

The arrival of a sibling can dramatically change family dynamics. The fact of a new brother or sister may affect existing children's sleep, lead to more tantrums and trigger other behaviour designed to get parents' attention. This is natural. If the people who made up your whole world suddenly became distracted by a squalling, helpless other being, you'd probably do the same. There may even be changes before the new child arrives, as the older brother or sister becomes increasingly aware that an unwelcome cuckoo is about to invade their cosy nest.

Children know how to wind up their brothers and sisters from an incredibly early age. By eighteen months, they're capable of deliberately showing a rubber spider to a sibling who's afraid of them.[16] Children fight more with each other when they're unadaptable, active or intense, or when their temperaments are very different from each other. Sibling fights are often a result of people being negative, or of other fights within the family – though parents fighting can sometimes have the opposite effect, bringing siblings closer together.

A focus on conflict between siblings may be less helpful than a focus on how to develop positive relationships between them. Positive relationships, as well as being utterly splendid, can make arguments less likely. If you think about your own relationships, you're probably better able to manage disagreements with the people with whom you get on well. For my part, I feel my hackles rise the instant there's a disagreement with someone with whom I already feel mildly annoyed.

When I started researching this part of the book, my children were not getting on at all well. 'I hate you!' was flung between bedrooms with alarming frequency. I mentioned to my older daughter that I'd started to research building relationships and reducing conflict between siblings. She asked me if I should really be writing about something that I didn't know how to do (a fair point, although that's what research is for). I said that I now had some ideas to try. 'Will they work?' she asked me, one eyebrow raised. 'Who knows? Let's see,' I said. They still fight regularly, but less frequently and with less intensity. Home life is happier as a result.

Having dedicated time alone with each child can be one way to help improve their relationship with each other, as it dampens the blaze of sibling rivalry. I find it's difficult to fit this time around everything else. I'd like to find some activities we can enjoy together (harder than it looks when my interests of art, cooking, running and growing chilli plants get evaluated as 'boring'. To be fair, I'd have said the same at their age. Hello, midlife). In the meantime, I've enacted a lazy version of this when I watch, on odd evenings where there's time, a different TV drama with each of them. We've covered moral philosophy, vampire lore and the science of cloning, so my official line is that this time is educational.

Encouraging children to have a balance of interests they share and ones they don't is another pathway towards more harmonious relationships. Shared interests can build bonds between siblings, while individual interests reduce any sense of direct competition between them. My children share a love of shooting each other with foam bullets, and they diverge when it comes to an appreciation of 1990s grunge music (elder) and stories involving blood (younger). Having separate interests also ensures dedicated time and attention from you as a parent.

A possibly obvious point is that fairness rules. Children who believe their parents are being unfair by treating them differently have worse sibling relationships than children who see parents as impartial.[17] Children might perceive fairness when they know a sibling's treated differently because they have special educational needs or a health issue. If there's no good reason to treat your children differently, it's best to avoid it altogether. Younger siblings tend to be particularly sensitive to differential treatment. We constantly have to reiterate to our younger daughter that there's a fairness that comes with age – her older sibling has a later bedtime and more TV options, which the younger one will also have, should she want them, when she's the same age as her sister is now.

I've found that children's opinions in this area are not always grounded in fact, though. I've had both my children complain to me in the same five minutes that it's not fair: I'm treating their sister better than I'm treating them. They might believe I've asked one of them to get water for everyone at dinner when I didn't ask the other last time, that one of them has been asked to clear away toys when the other hasn't, or that one of them has to feed the dog when the other always gets away with not doing it. These things are occasionally true. Mainly, though, it's perception, not reality. 'It's not fair – I did it last time' is an annoyingly common refrain.

A further point about fairness is that it's important to make sure the oldest sibling doesn't take on too much in the way of looking after any younger ones. Enmeshment happens when siblings are overly involved in each other's lives – such as when they take on caring duties that would normally be performed by a parent – and it can affect their later ability to adjust and to develop their own identities.[18]

If your children's behaviour is a concern, supporting them to improve it may have the side effect of helping them get on better (see Chapter 6). Better behaviour leads to improvements in sibling relationships – and better sibling relationships generate improvements in behaviour.[19]

No matter how hard you work to underpin the foundations of your children's relationship, though, fighting is pretty much inevitable. Sibling conflict can teach children a variety of skills, including problem-solving, negotiation and persuasion. It can also teach resilience and assertiveness. Conflicts are problematic when they become entrenched and they start to make those involved unhappy, including people standing on the edge – parents or other siblings. When my children's relationship was at its worst, it had a cascade effect on the rest of the family. Their fighting meant that their dad and I were both jittery. I suspect we reacted worse to our daughters' fights as a result, which made them unhappier. This made them fight more. If siblings are fighting in a destructive way, it's worth taking a step back to see how to break the cycle.

And while children are still young, at least, arguments between them shouldn't be ignored. Many parents have an instinct to steer clear of arguments, perhaps seeing it as good for children to learn to sort things out for themselves. Not intervening, however, is linked to more fighting, greater rivalry and worse mental health. Helping children to reason, to discuss their emotions and to understand the motivations of their siblings can support them to resolve conflict effectively. Failing to intervene means that siblings who fight a lot when they're young are likely to carry on doing so as they get older. It's only once children reach adolescence that the balance shifts in favour of not intervening. Parental intervention when children are older is linked to siblings being less close.[20]

Punishment and threats, like telling your children that they will be sent to their rooms if they don't stop fighting, make children more likely to fight with each other in future in a way they find difficult to sort out for themselves. Similarly, if you tell them to stop fighting for reasons relating to you – for example, you can't handle their constant bickering – any future fights are less likely to be easily sorted out. Instead, using language focused on your children is linked to more constructive ways of solving later conflicts. You could try saying something like 'I know you both want to find a way to fix this.' This kind of language obviously depends on your children. My own would respond to this phrase by spitting, in unison: 'No we don't.'

When arguments happen, mediation can be worth a try. This involves reasoning with children, discussing how they feel, and helping them understand what might be motivating their sibling to take a particular position or action. Mediation has been shown to help children between the ages of five and ten solve sibling conflict for themselves.[21] It also has benefits beyond resolving the immediate argument. Children whose parents help them with mediation are more likely to resolve conflicts constructively and to compromise.[22] Mediation can help repair relationships between siblings. A focus on understanding the other child's point of view may be a particularly useful element of mediation.

There are some practical steps for mediation:[23]

▶ Describe your own role in the process, while making it clear that it's your children's responsibility to find some way of settling the argument; agree ground rules; and get your children's consent for you to mediate. Ground rules could include not speaking when it's the other child's turn, avoiding blame, and staying seated throughout the mediation.

▶ Ask each child in turn to describe what happened and what the problems were for them, and recap each child's perspective for them once they've done this. Avoiding blame is important. Issues should be summarised in a neutral way that weaves together both perspectives. The children involved need to hear their own point of view reflected back to them.

▶ Ask each child to describe how they felt as a result of the argument, and why. During this stage, your aim is to try to get your children to appreciate the other's point of view and to feel empathy for each other. Each child should be asked to summarise how the other one feels about what happened.

▶ Help your children find some kind of resolution by asking them for solutions. These could either relate to what just happened, if it's otherwise likely to lead to further conflict, or to what could happen differently next time to avoid the argument. It is good to ask your children questions ('How do you think your brother would feel about that?') to make sure those solutions could work. Once agreement's been reached, children should be praised for their part in achieving resolution.

The mediation process can be helped by making sure children are calm before you start, perhaps breaking for a glass of water or taking some time in a different room to calm down. Asking children to focus on the word 'I', not 'you', can also be fruitful. 'I don't like it when my stuff is taken without my permission' is probably going to bring an end to hostilities more quickly than 'You're a thief and I hate you.'

Creative outlets for sibling hostility may be helpful. You might suggest, for younger children, that they show their angry feelings with a doll or draw a picture of their feelings. Older children could write a letter or keep a 'gripe' book in which they can each write down their feelings when they feel angry with the other one.

You can also teach your children to check what their sibling means by a particular comment or action, if they feel upset by it. Children may think their sibling is being malign even when the intention was to convey something neutral or positive. If children check their assumptions, an innocuous comment or deed won't escalate. It's not possible to misconstrue 'You're a smelly shitterooni,' though, as has been occasionally overhead when my daughters think I'm not listening. You might need to enact this guidance judiciously depending on the level of deliberate savagery in your household.

Teaching children perspective-taking, problem-solving and conflict management may reduce the short bursts of conflict that flare from pools of simmering resentment.[24] There are a few ways you can do this. If your children want different things, you can encourage them to give information calmly and to ask questions of their sibling. This will help them work out how to solve the problem in a way both will accept. You can also invite your children to talk to each other about their feelings on issues over which they might disagree. One of them might want to borrow the other's toys sometimes but feels they're always told no; the other might feel they don't want to lend their toys because they get damaged.

Encouraging the use of reasoning can be useful here. You might ask Child A to explain to Child B why they were upset the cherry yoghurt was finished before they had a chance to eat any, rather than shouting angrily that it's been finished. Siblings tend to copy each other when they're arguing or otherwise in conflict. If their sibling has used reasoning, they do the same, and if their sibling has acted aggressively, they too square up like a silverback gorilla. Reasoning helps children understand each other's perspectives and is more likely to end conflict.

More general family discussion of thoughts and feelings can be helpful, too. It supports children to understand how others feel and how those feelings might be different from their own. You can also teach your child how to turn down an offer of play from their sibling politely if they don't want to play, and chat to your children about when it might be right to get adults to help settle a dispute.

Role-playing some of these ideas with your child allows them to practise when they feel at ease. 'Overcorrection' is another role-play exercise. Children are asked to repeat the behaviour that has led to an argument, but this time in an appropriate way, perhaps exaggerating what happened. If an argument over who ate the last Jaffa Cake has descended into insult tennis, you might get them to role-play another way of ending the conflict. This process helps them learn better ways to engage with their brothers and sisters. Overcorrection can be as effective as time out (see Chapter 6) in reducing aggression between siblings.[25]

Positive feedback when they put these strategies into practice is also important – if you hear one of your children asking the other one to play and the other child responds 'Not right now, thanks, [name]. I'm a bit busy, but maybe later,' you might tell them how thoughtful they've been in their response, while quashing the instinct to tell them what an improvement it is on their usual snarls.

You may be appointed judge and high juror when it comes to disputes between and complaints about your children. When one child complains to you about the other, it's a good idea not to deny what they're saying or give them advice, but instead describe their feelings. If one child says 'Mum/Dad, she told me she hates me,' you might respond 'That hurt your feelings,' or 'You're really upset about that.' You could also try describing what your child wants to happen, even if there's no chance of it happening in reality. So when your child says, 'He borrowed my book and now the spine's bent,' you might say, 'You wish he'd look after your things better.'

By supporting children to create clear rules for managing conflict alongside teaching them how to negotiate effectively, you can help children plan for subsequent conflicts. It's important to focus on the future when doing this. Talking about past fights may reignite arguments. You could also teach your children how to express themselves better when they feel angry with their sibling, focusing on feelings and expectations rather than name-calling. 'I don't like that you finished the milk – I wanted you to leave some for me,' 'I'm upset that you broke my crayons,' 'I don't like it when you call me a brat,' 'I want you to ask before you use my things.'

If there's ongoing high tension, it may be a good idea to agree a set of family rules about how everyone should treat each other. This could take the form of a meeting in which everybody gets to put forward their ideas about common sources of arguments – perhaps sharing control of the television remote, borrowing or access to children's own toys and spaces, or where and how to draw a line between good-natured teasing and comments that are upsetting. Doing this together may make children more likely to remember and stick to what's agreed.

Finally, messages about fairness should be framed so children don't think they have to get exactly the same as their siblings. 'Everybody gets what they need in our house' is a message less likely to lead to conflict than 'Everything's fair in our house.' Another good message is that all members of the family get everything they need and some of what they want.

If siblings can make it through the inevitable conflict relatively unscathed, their relationship with each other can be protective. For example, sibling affection can help buffer children from the effects of stress.[26] I've watched two sisters I know support each other, as adults, through the fallout of their often difficult childhood. They call and send warm messages when the other one's going through a hard time – face-to-face seems to be less vital for them – and they've come out the other side stronger for it. Equally, I've seen siblings barely tolerate each other as adults and people using their friendship groups as sibling substitutes. If your child is the only one, there are other ways they can find protection.

Children who are bullied

It can be isolating, humiliating and even devastating to be bullied. Children can end up blaming themselves and feeling that they're not good enough. Bullying casts a long shadow. Parents' own experience with bullying when they were children, whether as a perpetrator, witness or victim, saturates their current view of bullying. This is true for me, as someone who was an easy target. I travelled to primary school from the island where I lived, turning up with muddy hems and speaking with an accent that marked me as different. I also had little idea how to interact with other children, what was in the charts or just how important it was to own a pair of Day-Glo socks. My experience of being bullied leads me to be hypervigilant when anyone is unkind to my own children.

Bullying isn't just about unkindness, however. It's also about power. My daughter can't bully me, no matter how many times she tries to stick her fingers in my ears or up my nostrils. Length of time is another factor – bullying isn't a one-off instance of teasing. It's sustained persecution with intent behind it. The bully deliberately wants to upset the victim or otherwise cause them harm. Bullying is most commonly related to children's appearance, and it can be physical, verbal or relational. Relational bullying is where threats to children's relationships or manipulation of those relationships cause deliberate hurt, such as when child B threatens to stop being child A's friend unless child A does what child B wants.

Most children are exposed to bullying behaviour at some level, but when it happens on a sustained basis, it can inflict real harm. Children who have been bullied are more likely than other children to develop physical and mental health problems, and these effects on well-being can last into adulthood.[27]

Bullying is also scarily common. Almost a quarter of six- to eleven-year-olds in the United States and around a fifth of ten- to eleven-year-olds in England experience bullying. Bullying may also take place between siblings or happen online – this can start earlier than parents might imagine. One American study, for example, found that online bullying was prevalent in schoolchildren between the ages of eight and eleven. Your child may be too young for a device but, once they start having access to the internet and the endless entertainment, knowledge and peril that lies within it, it's worth keeping a close eye on what they're accessing and setting early, unbreakable rules to keep them safe. These might include no screens in bedrooms, regular parental device checks and settings enabled so they can only talk online with existing contacts.[28]

A bullied child needs strong and secure relationships at home, and plenty of boosts to their self-esteem (see Chapter 9). It's all too easy for children to blame themselves when they are victims of bullying. Letting them know otherwise is vital. Your response to your child letting you know they are being bullied should include listening to them, encouraging them and checking in with them regularly. You should avoid scolding your child for telling tales as, according to children, this is the most harmful response adults can have.[29] Once you know your child is being bullied, you might want to spend some time thinking about and discussing next steps before taking any action. This could be with your child, but also away from them, perhaps getting some distance and perspective through an online parenting forum like Mumsnet.

In terms of practical strategies, you can recommend to your child – assuming they're in school – that they find an adult if they're being bullied, and to move around the school in groups if they have friends there. You might want to share strategies that other children have found to work. The four most successful strategies for children who have encountered bullying, according to a survey of almost 12,000 children, are to tell an adult at home (presumably you already know they are being bullied if you're having this conversation, so you could congratulate them on taking this first step), tell a friend, make a joke about it and to tell an adult at school. The least successful strategies, according to these children, are to pretend that the bullying doesn't bother them, to tell the other child or children to stop, or to do nothing.[30]

If your child wants to conform in the way they dress or speak, or the interests they have, it's worth not challenging this desire too much. Sometimes fitting in with other kids can be an easier path than blazing a trail of independence. I tried to adapt my accent to help me fit in when I was being bullied – I was 'posh' and my accent was mimicked when I said anything – but at home, my parents corrected the way I spoke. 'Matilda, the last letter of "what" is "t".' Eventually, I spoke in one voice at school and another at home. I could never get it right at either. My parents wouldn't have pursued this if I'd made it clear to them what the stakes were, but I didn't know how to do this. Conformity may be the most comfortable route for your child, whether or not you understand the reasons behind it.

You might want to support your child with social problem-solving skills, if these are something with which they struggle. Helping them develop these skills can make them less likely to be victimised. You could, for instance, encourage them to ask questions during a conversation. You could play board games with them to practise turn-taking and how to play well with somebody else. These things can be done subtly, without any suggestion your child needs improvement in any way or that the bullying may be their fault (which of course it isn't – you are simply supporting them to be less of a target). You could also practise assertiveness with your child. Children can become more assertive by practising at home what they want to say, acting calmly and confidently, with a straight back and no fidgeting, making eye contact, stating clearly and politely what they want, and making sure they don't apologise for saying what they need.

Exercise may help children deal with the effects of bullying. Bullied children who exercise every day, or almost every day, are less likely than other victims of bullying to feel sad. You may also want to explore the idea of forgiveness to help children cope. One study has found that forgiveness can help children feel less angry about their situation when they've been bullied. I'm cautious about this recommendation, though, as the study in question didn't explore whether it might be helpful for children to feel this anger as a way of resolving their feelings about the bullying.[31]

It may be that your child doesn't tell you when they're being bullied. While parents believe their children will let them know if other children are trying to damage their relationships or hurt them socially, one study showed this belief to be false.[32] This can make it hard to know when children are suffering. I remember not telling my parents I was being bullied because I was worried they'd think there was something wrong with me. I didn't want them to see me as the bullies did.

You can make it as safe as possible for your child to talk to you by being empathetic (which, to be clear, my parents did). If that doesn't work and you're concerned that your child is being victimised, you could watch out for sleeping problems, such as insomnia or nightmares; repetitive health problems, such as colds and sore throats; behaviour problems, including being aggressive; doing worse at school; and poor mental health.

If any of these are a concern, or if anything else is making you suspect that your child might be a victim of bullying, you should talk to your child's school, nursery or day care. And if you're worried your child might be the one doing the bullying, there's a dedicated section in Chapter 6 that should help.

CHAPTER CHECKLIST

High-quality research

▸ **Develop your understanding of your child, and help your child understand relationships.** Think about what your child is thinking and feeling. Teach your child perspective-taking, problem-solving and conflict management. Teach your child about forgiveness.

▸ **Be pragmatic.** When talking to or playing with your child, focus on what they're doing well and ignore most of their negative behaviour. Offer your child plenty of stimulation. If your child's behaviour is concerning you, find strategies to manage it. Support your child to act less aggressively, if this is a concern. Work on building your child's self-esteem (see Chapter 9).

Moderate-quality research

▸ **Be realistic about what your child can do and how they feel.** Don't overestimate your child's ability to take on board different perspectives. Be aware of the drivers of conflict in your child; parents are likely to think that children feel angry during an argument when they actually feel sad. Support your child to develop a healthy level of independence from you – not too little and not too much.

▸ **Help your child manage conflict well.** Justify why you've asked your child to do something, and negotiate or compromise where needed. If you and an older child have had an argument, plan jointly how you're going to resolve similar conflicts in future. When you and your child are arguing, consider what you want for your child as well as for your relationship with each other.

▸ **Work on your relationship with your child.** Set aside dedicated times to play with your child. Be affectionate. Don't overstep boundaries – for example, pushing your child for information or looking through their things.

▸ **Support your child in their relationships with others.** Help your child to develop high expectations of friendship and to communicate well with other people. If you have more than one child, make sure the older sibling doesn't need to take on too much in the way of looking after any younger ones. If your children fight with each other, intervene as needed in arguments while they're still young (this is less useful as they get older); encourage them to reason with each other when they disagree; and, if you're worried one of your children is bullying the other, try – if time and home circumstances allow – to spend more time with both.

▶ **Look after other aspects of your child's well-being that may influence their relationships.** Take your child into nature. Check your child is getting enough sleep (see Chapter 7).

Anecdotal research/expert advice

▶ **Focus.** When your child asks something of you, listen and show you've understood what they've said before you respond, perhaps by asking questions. Concentrate fully on your child when you're talking to each other, and come down to your child's level.

▶ **Maintain warmth.** Make sure there's plenty of opportunity for touch between you and your child. Try to balance giving your child autonomy (see Chapter 4) with being close to them, when work and other commitments allow. Avoid critical and negative comments.

▶ **Deal with sibling relationships appropriately.** If you have more than one child, try to have dedicated time alone with each of them, and if you treat your children differently, be fair about it. At the same time, make sure any messages about fairness are framed so children don't think they have to get exactly the same as their siblings. Encourage siblings to have a balance of interests they share and ones they don't. If one complains to you about the other, try not to deny what they're saying or give them advice, but instead describe their feelings. Find creative outlets for any sibling hostility, and make sure you don't centre your own wants or needs when telling them why they shouldn't fight. If your children feel upset by a sibling's particular comment or action, teach your children to check what the sibling means by it.

▶ **Plan.** Think about jointly creating a set of family rules about how everyone should treat each other. Try a weekly family meeting as a way of building connection. If you have more than one child, help them plan for future conflicts. If you have argued with your child, work with them, perhaps away from the heat of an argument, to understand each other's point of view. If things are difficult between you and your child, tell your child you're keen to improve your relationship and ask for ideas on how you do this.

▶ **Deal with conflict appropriately.** Approach conflict with your child, or conflict with somebody else your child sees, in the way you'd like your child to approach conflict. Reflect your child's feelings back to them when they're sad or upset; don't try to rationalise or deny how they feel. When your child is arguing with you, show you acknowledge their feelings while sticking to any boundaries you have given them. If you've got it wrong, apologise.

Troubleshooting: mediating a sibling fight

Make sure children are calm before you start, perhaps breaking for a glass of water or taking some time in a different room to calm down. Describe your own role in the process, while making it clear that it's your children's responsibility to find some way of settling the argument; agree ground rules; and get your children's consent for you to mediate. Ask children to focus on the word 'I', not 'you'. Ask each child in turn to describe what happened and what the problems were for them, and recap each child's perspective for them once they've done this. Ask each child to describe how they felt after the argument, and why. Help your children find some kind of resolution by asking them for solutions.

Troubleshooting: specific strategies for a child who is being bullied

Think about ways you can help your child develop social skills and support their relationships with other children. Create a supportive environment at home. Provide opportunities for your child to exercise. Share strategies with your child that other children have found helpful (see page 131). Listen to your child, encourage them and check in with them regularly. Explore the idea of forgiveness to help children cope. Avoid scolding your child for telling tales. Make it clear to your child that the bullying is not their fault. Spend time thinking about and discussing next steps once you know your child is being bullied. If your child is in school, recommend to them that they find an adult if they're being bullied, and advise them to move around the school in groups if they have friends there. Don't snub your child's desire for conformity. Practise assertiveness with your child.

CHAPTER 6

BEHAVIOUR

When I think about the word 'behaviour', a miniature cinema reel plays itself in front of my eyes containing the moments my children have shown me how marvellously misguided my assumption was that parenthood couldn't be that hard. I see a two-year-old in the middle of a supermarket aisle literally beating her fists on the floor while she screams. I see a door slammed in my face and hear the spitting of 'I hate you. You're the worst mother in the world.' I see a board game, three hours into play, being thrown into the air when a rule is rejected as unfair. I see one daughter put in a headlock and clouted by the other one.

There is another side to this. Behaviour isn't negative by definition – it includes all the good stuff too. A more balanced version of my cinema reel would show one of my daughters pottering off unbidden to teach herself another language on Duolingo so she can communicate with refugees. It would show a child stroking my arm as she falls asleep, a surprise birthday cake that's simultaneously the most revolting colour I've seen and my favourite thing ever, a painting of clouds and blue skies, irrepressible laughter during a game of chase, the unexpected gift of a hot drink and a comforting hand on a distressed animal.

This chapter covers discipline, general behaviour and promoting socially minded behaviour. There's a troubleshooting section for behavioural problems, including sulking, aggression and what to do if your child is bullying other children. I haven't included research or advice on behavioural conditions – it's important to get your child assessed by experts if these are a concern. Parents of children with these conditions are likely to experience particular strain and stress. If this is the case for you, be aware of it and, if you can, seek support for yourself from friends, family or external services.

Children act up all the time. Occasionally, though, their behaviour gets to the point where it's not doing them or their family any favours. There are good reasons to sort out children's poor behaviour. It's easier to be a good parent to a child who isn't pouring honey into your laptop case or using you as water pistol target practice. Children's behaviour can affect parents' relationships, just as the state of parents' relationships can influence how their children behave. When children act up to the point that family well-being is at risk, doing something about it can make everybody happier, including the child in question.

At the other end of the behaviour scale, it's not necessarily a good thing when children are incredibly compliant. It may mean they're scared. This was the case for a friend of mine growing up, who now takes great reassurance from the fact that her child feels able to rail against her occasionally. Immediate compliance can also make children less likely to behave well in the long term – they're so intent on making sure they follow the instructions they're given that they aren't able to consider the reasons they might have been asked to do something in the first place. This lack of reflection means it's hard to understand the rules by which we're all expected to behave.

Sometimes children's behaviour is natural and expected, and there's nothing fundamentally wrong that needs sorting out. If you've been the parent of a toddler, you may recognise a tantrum as you would recognise having noisy insides after eating a big plate of lentils – it's suboptimal, mildly embarrassing if you're in public, and as foreseeable as high tide. Even if you don't have any real behaviour concerns, many of the ideas in this chapter should be useful in helping your child develop securely and behave appropriately. In other cases, you may be genuinely worried about how your child is behaving and hoping to give them more targeted support.

Discipline and general behaviour

The word 'discipline' brings to my mind an old-fashioned view of children who get trained and socialised into appropriate behaviour. These are children who are seen and not heard, who get put over a parent's knee for a misdemeanour and who get served a cold, congealing dinner at every mealtime until it gets eaten – basically, everything the evidence shows doesn't work. The word is kinder and more encompassing than this, though. Discipline *is* about your child's behaviour, but is also about fostering their emotional maturity, their ability to consider what other people need, their assertiveness and their self-control. It relates to the teaching of knowledge and skills, and not, as is often understood, to punishment.

Effective discipline is consistent, fair and right for the child's temperament and stage of development. Toddlers don't have enough language to make instructions a reliable form of discipline, and individual children vary in when they're ready to do things. I remember trying to teach my then six-year-old that thoughts don't all need to be communicated at the volume of a jet plane taking flight, but she wasn't ready for that. Frankly, I'm starting to think nothing will ever be manifested in a normal speaking voice.

Effective discipline is also hard. A Swiss study of discipline found that mothers yelled as often as they used time out, despite them believing that yelling was among the least acceptable of discipline techniques. And, as referred to briefly in chapter 3, a study of families whose children were referred to mental health services in the United States found that while parents believed they praised their children far more than they criticised them, they used criticism three times more often than praise. Perhaps the artificial intelligence on our phones will one day give us handy data on the balance of praise and criticism we use with our children. I can imagine a dystopian parenting dashboard that rates us in horrifying detail across a range of indicators. Until that day, and in the absence of enrolment in an academic study, it's probably safe to assume that our balance is slightly off, and that we should err on the side of trying to amplify the positive things we say and to curtail the negative.[1]

It's important to think about what's driving children's behaviour. Children who feel angry, sad or frustrated are more likely to behave badly.[2] A child who is acting up is often trying to communicate that they need something – perhaps attention, rest or some degree of autonomy. Working out the need can help parents decide what to do about it. There's been a bit of experimentation in my family as we've tried to work out how to avoid one of my daughters having a blazing reaction to certain events or words. She needs calm surroundings, plenty of notice before we do anything and never to be asked to do more than one thing at a time. It's been a long process, and we don't always get it right, but she's been happier since we've been able to piece together some of the puzzle.

The knotty issue of cause and effect is worth considering when thinking about behaviour. Do warm, responsive parents cause their children to behave well, or do well-behaved children make it easier for their parents to treat them warmly and be responsive to their needs? The evidence is mixed on this point, but the answer is that it's probably both. Parents' actions don't exist in a vacuum. They often reflect and are reflected by a child's actions. The humble mirror is a handy object.

The discipline gold standards

Three key approaches to discipline are backed up by very high-quality research: praising or otherwise reinforcing good behaviour with words and actions, using natural or logical consequences in place of punishment, and using 'time out' where necessary.

Praising or otherwise reinforcing good behaviour with words and actions

In the words of one parenting intervention, 'Catch them being good.' Positive reinforcement includes praise, encouragement, a smile, a nod or touch. It can help children manage their own behaviour better – children don't naturally develop ways of controlling their behaviour without outside help, much as it would be wonderful if they did. One study of children between the ages of four and nine looked at the effect on children's behaviour of praise combined with eye contact. At the beginning of the study, children complied with their parents' instructions about a third of the time. After parents were trained to give specific instructions, using direct eye contact and praise when children followed instructions well, the success rate more than doubled.[3]

Praising actions is better than praising children's personal qualities. A focus on personal qualities – saying 'You're a good girl' – makes children feel ashamed when they fail, possibly because they link that failure to themselves as a person rather than the actions they've taken. This is especially true for children with low self-esteem. Praise linked to children's qualities can make their self-worth dependent on other people and can increase self-blame when they face setbacks. It also reduces how much they're able to persevere with something. Even a small amount of praise focused on a child's qualities or personality can knock persistence levels.[4]

Praise should be specific. Praising defined and straightforward behaviour such as dressing in time for school or eating tidily makes this behaviour happen more frequently.[5] It's important, too, to describe what you like in detail. Descriptive praise is about focusing on small things children are doing well or right, with a focus on effort rather than results: 'Thank you for helping me clear the table – I really appreciate it.' It could involve describing what you see when your child has drawn a picture and what you like about it: 'Oh, it's a picture of a bumblebee chasing a ladybird. I love the bright colours you've used and how well you've coloured in the ladybird's spots.' Of course, this can sometimes go terribly wrong: 'I really like how detailed it is and how you can see the light reflecting off the elephant's eyes.' 'It's not an elephant. It's a hummingbird.'

Advice for descriptive praise includes:[6]

▶ Praising things that are a bit of a stretch, not things your child can do without thinking.

▶ Making praise specific to your child, not comparing your child or what they've done with anybody else.

▶ Sticking with descriptive praise until whatever you're praising has become a habit.

▶ Saying your child should be proud of themselves. If you do this instead of saying you're proud of your child, as might be your instinct, it removes a level of pressure. Your child becomes less likely to need your approval when they do something – they can rely on their own approval in its place.

Shifting your attention from behaviour you don't like to behaviour you do is an important element of reinforcing good behaviour.[7] You might choose to ignore your child's slowness when trying to leave the house, but shower them with praise when they put on their shoes and coat quickly. Paying attention to certain kinds of unwanted behaviour can reinforce it in children who want or need attention, even if that attention's negative. Removing oxygen from negative behaviour patterns, and directing it instead towards positive behaviours, can help children make changes without turning things into a battle.

Individual children may need slightly different approaches. Some children find praise controlling, not supportive. It can make others, and especially anxious children, overly self-conscious. Praise can undermine children's motivation to complete easy tasks, because they're less likely to get praised for them than they are for more difficult ones. Praise that's exaggerated – when parents use words like 'extremely', 'hugely' and 'fantastic' – can erode children's self-esteem by setting standards that are impossible for them to meet.

(Returning to my perpetual frustration over the toothpaste lid, you can't praise something your child never does. I recently took to hiding my own separate tube in my washbag, thinking that at least I'd have a backup source of fresh, non-leaking toothpaste. My daughter found it and left it on the sink without its lid. I'm asking her to give me something to praise, but she's leaving me with less to work with than there is toothpaste left in its packaging.)

Using natural or logical consequences in place of punishment

In general, punishment is to be avoided. It won't always be possible – sometimes you'll lose your temper and change the Wi-Fi password, or you'll refuse to give your child a lift to a cherished event – and sometimes punishment may be the only thing you can think of. I have found myself in this latter position on more occasions than I would like to admit.

One of the reasons it's hard to avoid punishment, whatever your view of making children fearful of losing something (I file it in the Suboptimal Parenting drawer when I use it), is that it often works in the short term. It's less effective over a longer period, though. Fear makes children less able to understand reasons why an adult may or may not want them to behave in a certain way. If children don't internalise values at the time, they're less likely to be able to use them to guide their behaviour in future.[8] Anger may also get in the way of them being able to internalise their values. If my child's furious that I've told her she can't have screens due to her shooting an arrow into my bum (true story), she's less likely to take on board why shooting arrows at people, not targets, is unacceptable. One day, she'll read *We Need to Talk about Kevin*, hopefully not for tips.

Using natural or logical consequences for children's actions can reduce disruptive behaviour.[9] Natural consequences happen as a direct result of a child's actions. No adult involvement is needed if you want your child to feel the results of natural consequences, though it's probably fair to warn them what these will be. A child without a jumper in Scotland in November will get cold, a child who hasn't eaten much lunch will get hungry, and a child sporting two left shoes will get at least one sore foot. Logical consequences are, instead, imposed by an adult. They should be related to the behaviour in question, put in place in a respectful way and be reasonable in scope. You might explain to your child that you have removed their favourite Samurai sword as you can't have them using it to attempt fratricide. Logical consequences tend to work better when they're used in families who allow their children plenty of autonomy.

9. EXAMPLES OF LOGICAL CONSEQUENCES

A glass of milk is knocked over deliberately ➤	The child clears it up, or helps to clear it up, depending on age and ability.
A child hurts a sibling ➤	The child is removed from the room to make sure that everyone is safe.
Screen time limits have been broken ➤	The child is given a short break from screen time.
A road is crossed without looking (after an age where the child is allowed to cross independently) ➤	The child must hold an adult's hand for the next few crossings until they can demonstrate that they can cross the road safely.

Consequences, whether they are natural or logical, should be framed as the result of actions, not as a punishment. 'If your room is messy, you won't get TV' is a punishment. 'When you've tidied your room, you'll be free to watch TV' is a logical result of being able to do fun things once chores have been done. It also frames the situation more as a choice, meaning the child is more likely next time to remember what they've learned.

Children should ideally know in advance what the consequences are likely to be for certain actions. You might make it clear that you won't engage with your child if they are screaming at you, as you find it hard to respond well to them when they do – while saying you will always talk to them about something they find upsetting if they can communicate with you calmly. Similarly, you need to remain calm in any discussion of consequences or their aftermath. Consequences are much less effective if the parent comes across as angry.

You should also be willing to accept the child's decision if they decide they prefer to take the consequence. This means being prepared to see it through. Your child may be hungry until breakfast time if they've refused to eat their dinner, or they may be taken home early from a party if they're being unkind or disruptive. As with many other areas of parenting, consistency is key. If consequences are not applied in the same way each time, children are less likely to follow the rules.

Consequences should also be short. If a consequence lasts for days or weeks, children may not see the point in behaving well, because they can't see any immediate gains. I remember letting my younger daughter know she couldn't have TV until her room was tidy. She held out for over a week. Stubbornness runs in the family, but it appears to have crystallised itself particularly well in her – I gave in before she did. Her bedroom remained a tip.

Using time out

Time out is when a child has a short interlude without adult attention after misbehaving. You might, for example, get your child to sit in a chair in the middle of your living room for a few minutes if they've hit you. The idea is not to punish them – instead, you're removing the reinforcement of your attention on their behaviour. Despite some controversy about the use of time out, research evidence generally supports it as an effective tool that causes children no harm.[10]

This technique needs to be used carefully and appropriately to be effective. It should only be used where children have clear control over their behaviour and never for mistakes, a lack of understanding or ability, or where a child has acted out of fear. Parents should remain calm throughout the process and should be careful not to reject their child in any way.

When my children were much smaller, I remember how easy it was to snap at them. Saying angrily that a child is going on time out is very different to telling them calmly that time out is about to happen. I ended up not using time out for long – it didn't feel right, despite the research. I wonder if my temptation to use it in anger made me realise it wasn't a suitable discipline method for me or my children. It goes back to the point about selecting what works for your own family. Few approaches are right for everyone.

Giving a single warning has been shown to reduce the need to implement time out by three quarters. Children are more likely to comply with time out if you move quickly and confidently, keep a neutral tone and limit the amount of talking you do. It can also be effective to make the length of time out contingent on the child's adherence to it: 'You can sit quietly for two minutes, or we can do five minutes if you keep shouting at me – it's your choice.' When time out lasts between four and five minutes, it's more effective than when it's shorter and is less stressful (and no less effective) than when it's longer. There is no evidence to suggest that the length of time out should increase as children get older.[11]

Expert advice suggests that you should only end time out if your child has been quiet for five seconds immediately before you speak.[12] Using a phrase such as 'Now that you're quiet…' helps the child learn it's their quietness, not their expressions of rage, that will end a time out for them. Returning to personal fit, this piece of advice makes me feel slightly itchy in a manipulative and uncomfortable way. I haven't used it. Who am I, though, to argue with the evidence?

There's no consensus in the research as to what kind of location is best for time out, nor whether a parent should be present in the room, though it's worth avoiding children's bedrooms. One of the reasons time out works is boredom. There are often toys, books and games in a bedroom to distract children, so it may take longer to have the desired effect. An adult chair (which is harder to topple over if the child is upset) in a communal room – far enough away from walls so they can't be kicked – may be a better option.

The book *1-2-3 Magic* recommends a counting system ahead of time out.[13] With this approach, you count every five seconds while a child is behaving in a way that might (depending on the rules in your household) warrant a time out, moving your child to time out when you reach a count of three. According to the book's author, most children will stop on the count of one or two, once you've tried this a few times. He recommends going straight to three for certain behaviours, such as hitting. A friend of mine uses a reverse counting method, but without time out at the end of it – she counts down from five when her daughter acts up. Her insertion of fractions when she gets to the smaller numbers means she's never reached zero and has no idea what she'll do if she ever does. (I've heard my partner trying a similar reverse counting system with our dog, astonishingly without success.)

There are two keys to implementing the time-out counting system successfully. One is talking as little as possible, and the other is keeping feelings hidden. That means not appearing angry or hurt. It's up to you how you use this suggested system, although the author of *1-2-3 Magic* recommends using it for things that don't persuade me they're appropriate for time out, like a child arguing with a parent because they've been refused a snack. This kind of response from a child strikes me as a useful negotiating skill for later life and not something to be quashed, however irritating.

You may not see immediate results when time out is first introduced – children may escalate their behaviour in the beginning. And time out may not be appropriate for all children; very defiant children may not benefit from its use.[14] If parents need to use verbal or physical coercion to ensure time out happens, they're showing their children that compliance is achieved through force. This can make poor behaviour worse. It's not a great life lesson either, unless you're hoping to bring up a tyrant. Where positive parenting strategies have been successful, there's generally less need to use time out.

Despite many experts suggesting that time out might be damaging in the long run, large-scale studies don't support this. In one case, more than 1,500 children in the United States were tracked across three time points – between the ages of zero and three, just before they started kindergarten, and when they were in fifth grade (aged ten to eleven). To assess any side effects of using time out, researchers measured child discipline, children's mental health and the quality of relationships between parents and their children. There were no significant differences in children's mental health, nor in the quality of parent–child relationships, between families who reported using time out and those who didn't. The researchers concluded that the use of time out has no long-term negative outcomes for children.[15]

Other thoughts on effective discipline

Using rewards for good behaviour isn't as straightforward as it might appear. Physical rewards, like ice cream or a new toy, can effectively bribe children into behaving well. They remove children's responsibility for motivating themselves and regulating their own behaviour – so, even if they work in the short term, they may be storing up future behaviour problems.[16]

There are two ways of giving rewards so they don't undermine children's motivation to do things for themselves.[17] The first is when they're given unexpectedly. A one-off cinema trip to celebrate a good school report is an example of this, though parents should be careful not to offer them so often that they become expected by default.

The second is when you reward behaviour you've already seen in your child ('informational' rewards), instead of incentivising your child to change ('controlling' rewards). A controlling reward is clearly designed to change a child's behaviour in future: 'We'll make your bedtime later if you can show me you can go to bed without arguments for the next week.' Children feel pressurised by this kind of reward, and it can make them less likely to want to do things for themselves. An informational reward, on the other hand, is based on behaviour that's already happened: 'You've been great at getting ready for bed quickly this week, so I think we can start making your bedtime a bit later.' Informational rewards make children feel competent.

Some parents may be willing to risk children's internal motivation levels for a short-term fix, and there are plenty of parenting experts who recommend the use of control-based rewards. For those who do wish to use these, the consensus seems to be that tokens or star charts work best. They can be given for specific parcels of behaviour and saved up for something a child wants – having a film night with popcorn, or having a friend over to stay.

Control-based rewards are best used as a temporary intervention. They're most effective combined with copious amounts of praise, and when given immediately after your child has behaved in the way that you'd like: 'You did a good job tidying your bedroom. It's so clean. I'm adding a star to the chart now.' The short-term fix may be shorter-term than you'd like it to be, however, and your best intentions may backfire. Before I'd read the relevant research, I remember using a star chart to get my younger daughter to sleep in her own bed. She'd been sleeping in ours, positioning her elbows in my neck and her ankles in my partner's back with a frequency that had morphed us both into living zombies. Once she had ten stars, the idea was that she would get a Highly Desirable Teddy.* On the eleventh night, she padded into our bedroom at 12 a.m.: 'I want another Highly Desirable Teddy. I need to sleep with you so you can start the star chart again.'

Other sections of this book may boost your child's behaviour. Supporting their mental health (Chapter 9) is key. Children also tend to behave better when they get on well with their parents, siblings and friends, and when they aren't being bullied (Chapter 5). More physical activity, more sleep (Chapter 7), more opportunity for unstructured play and less screen time (Chapter 8) may all be helpful. Making mealtimes a positive experience for everyone, when possible, can also support behaviour. When your children are bickering about who gets to sit where and whose turn it is to get the water, this feels like an impossible pipe dream. I've noticed, though, that there's less bickering and more happy chattering when my partner and I are both in a good mood. If one of us is feeling stressed and snappy, it's infectious.

Children are more likely to comply with an instruction if parents have been positive with them, for example by hugging them or play-ing with them just before the command is given. The psychotherapist Philippa Perry has designed a five-step approach to working collab-oratively on behaviour:[18]

---

* Replace with appropriate brand name here.

10. THE FIVE-STEP COLLABORATIVE BEHAVIOUR APPROACH

Explain	➤	Explain what the problem is by saying what you would like to happen: 'I need your help sorting out dinner. I would like you to lay the table every night.'
Ask	➤	Ask your child what feelings are driving the behaviour, helping them if needed: 'Do you think it's unfair that you have to lay the table because you think it's a grown-up job?'
Validate	➤	Show your child that you understand their feelings, even if you don't agree with them: 'I can see that you think it's unfair.'
Support	➤	Ask your child what would help them to do the particular task or behave in the particular way you are seeking, reiterating what it is you would like them to do.
Enact	➤	Put any sensible ideas into practice, or repeat any steps if needed.

Another approach is to think about your child's need for connection and attention if they're acting up. Children often express a need to connect when they throw their yoghurt on the floor or tell you how much they hate you ('I didn't ask to be born!'™), however unlikely that may seem in the immediate inferno of their rage. Parents may find it easier to meet this need if they consider it when thinking about their children's behaviour. If my younger daughter comes downstairs after her bedtime and starts baiting my older daughter, who's sitting on the sofa beside me while we watch a TV programme together, it's likely because the younger one, at that point, feels less well connected to me than her sister does.

Giving children plenty of positive attention is a fundamental ingredient in discipline. A lack of input from parents can lead children to seek attention in any form, even if it involves their parents getting cross. Similarly, reacting strongly to negative behaviour by your child can backfire by reinforcing the behaviour; it shows your child they can have an impact, however unpleasant.

Children need guiding away from negative actions, but not negative feelings – they need to be able to show they feel angry or sad. If they're acting up, it may be that they simply need a bit of support around how to show these feelings appropriately. It's also important to focus on a child's actions, not who they are as a person, when trying to change their behaviour.[19] Labels like 'lazy' or 'rude' can make children more likely to behave in a particular way. If they're seen in that light already, why should they try to behave differently? Negative character labels can also knock their self-esteem.

Parents' language can shape the way children behave in other ways, too. Speaking to your child in the first person is more direct, and therefore more effective, than using the third person ('I'd like you to stop throwing Lego at me,' not 'Let Daddy have some air' or 'Please don't hit Mummy'). Language can be overused during behaviour flash-points. In periods of stress and misbehaviour, too many words can be confusing and can distract your child from what it is you want them to do. Spending lots of time explaining things can also invite your child to argue with you.

Positive family rules can be another way to use language in a way that supports children's behaviour. Having 'stick together' as a family rule makes it easier to respond positively if a child is running away from you when you're out together. 'We stick together' is more posi-tive than 'Stop!' or 'Don't do that.' It's a rule that offers reassurance to children who tend to misbehave, making them feel safe because they have the support and security of the rest of their family. This sticking together can apply even – or especially – when there are disagreements.

Language can determine how much children feel guilt or shame when they've acted up, both of which can get in the way of trust between children and their parents. Discipline works better when you and your child trust each other.[20] It's hard, though, in the moment, to ask your child politely to do something in a way that avoids guilting or shaming them. If I walk into the kitchen and find split milk all over the floor and Weetabix, which sets like concrete, slowly hardening on the table, it's more natural for me to ask them what qualifies them to think I'm the cleaning fairy than it is to state calmly that they need to clear up their breakfast.

Modelling is another tactic that may help. 'Effortful control' refers to the ability to use attention and focus to override impulses; examples include doing a couple of hours of work before having a coffee break or getting up when your alarm shrills instead of hitting snooze. While it may be deeply tedious on a cold, dark December morning to desert the pool of warmth created by your body, the children of parents who demonstrate effortful control are better able to regulate their own behaviour.[21]

An online parenting programme may also be useful if you and your child are struggling in this area. Triple P is one such course, and is often cited by research studies as being effective. And while the ideas in this section are presented separately from each other, they sometimes work better when used in tandem. You might, for example, combine being warm and affectionate with your child, using praise and clear guidance and being careful not to be coercive. These all work individually to support children's behaviour but are most effective when combined.

Promoting socially minded behaviour

There's a scene in *The Railway Children* where the three Waterburys collect birthday presents from people around the village as a surprise for Perks, the stationmaster. The labels fall off their pramload of offerings, leading Perks to assume they're charity. He's horrified, thinking people donated because he was poor, and the children are shamed. Later, when he realises they're gifts, he recognises what the children were trying to achieve in the first place – to make someone they care about happy. Socially minded behaviour, or 'prosocial behaviour' in the psychology literature, involves voluntary acts that are intended to help somebody else. It can show itself through helping, comforting and sharing.

Before digging into the research, my instinct might have been that if my child is happy and secure, she's probably more likely to show socially minded behaviours, and happiness and security may be more useful ambitions for her. It looks as if there's good reason to want children to show socially minded behaviour in its own right, though. The more children behave in a socially minded way, the less likely they become to develop mental health problems in adulthood. Children are also more likely to make friends if they act in a socially minded way.[22]

The question of whether there are downsides to socially minded behaviour is notably absent from the research literature. There must be drawbacks, though, if it moves to an extreme level: if people are so socially minded that they don't sufficiently consider their own needs. I've known and loved people who spend so much energy on other people that there's little left over, almost to the point that they can't recognise what they need for themselves. A likely solution as a parent is to model looking after your own needs at the same time as modelling socially minded behaviour, thereby showing your children it's important to do both. This might involve carving out time to do something you love or taking on other ideas from Chapter 1.

Socially minded behaviour isn't just a result of children (or indeed adults) wanting to do the right thing. They may want other people to think well of them, or they might want positive attention from an adult. But even very young children can show empathetic behaviour to someone who's been hurt, despite having little to gain by behaving in this way. In one study, a group of young toddlers was shown an adult removing something belonging to another adult or destroying it, while another group was shown a situation between two adults in which nobody was harmed. None of the adults in question showed any emotion – this was a test of how children imagined that the adults felt. Children showed more concern about the victim than they did about the other adults and, later, were more likely to behave in a socially minded way towards the victim.[23]

Between the ages of one and two, children tend to start displaying socially minded behaviour.[24] It gets more frequent and more mature as children grow older. Parents help their children develop socially minded behaviour when they set high expectations while helping them meet these expectations – like offering help with schoolwork when needed. When children are helped to meet their parents' expectations, they're more likely to develop traits that underpin behaviour intended to help others, such as empathy, conscience and moral reasoning. Be careful to set your expectations at a level your child can reach, though, so they don't constantly feel that they're failing.

Children's best way of knowing how to behave is through watching the adults around them. I grew up watching my parents helping other adults, arguing for fairness in politics and going to protests when they thought something wasn't right, all of which contributed to my own thinking – and later actions – in these areas. These things may not be your cup of tea, but the point is that demonstrating to your children how you want them to behave makes them more likely to take on that mantle for themselves.

There are links between socially minded behaviour and children's relationships with their friends and siblings, and when children have a secure relationship with their parents, they're more likely to behave in a socially minded way.[25] Ideas on how to support your child's relationships are available in Chapter 5. Taking part in sports can also help the development of these kinds of behaviours (see Chapter 7).

Eating together as a family may support children to be more socially minded, or at least to be more social. A survey of almost 25,000 children in the United States found that the more families eat together, the better children's social behaviour.[26] Discussing ideas together as a family and allowing children to take part in making family decisions helps ensure that decisions are fair and supports children to develop a sense of morality through being able to participate in a democratic process. I recommend not letting them have sole agency in this area, though, unless you want chocolate cake for breakfast, school boycotts and adult serfdom.

Encouraging children to do regular chores that benefit other people has been linked to the development of impromptu helpful behaviour in children.[27] A friend of mine takes her children litter-picking on the beach, which has the added benefit of getting them out into the fresh air. Making a desired behaviour part of a child's identity by using a noun (a helper, a finder, a cook) can motivate them more than asking them to help, if you are able to overlook the manipulative undertones of this.

Young children who play music with other people are more likely to show socially minded behaviour afterwards, possibly because music increases social bonding.[28] It doesn't need to be sophisticated: a tambourine would do. And having attended a concert performed by children who'd been learning the violin for a single term, I can confirm that the word 'music' may be a stretch in certain scenarios.

Children behave more in a socially minded way when the emphasis is positive: 'She'll be delighted to see you,' rather than 'She'll be really upset if you don't visit her.' Explaining to children why certain behaviour can make others feel upset can also be useful, though. They're also more likely to act in a socially minded way when discussions relate to a particular person or groups rather than more general situations.[29]

When discussing social and moral issues with children, moral development can be supported by asking them for their opinions, checking what they understand, checking why they believe what they do and paraphrasing what they've told you they think. 'So you believe children should be in charge of adults?' is an example of checking their beliefs, assuming you can quell the instinct to follow up with 'Whatever in your power-hungry nature leads you to that conclusion?'

It's important to avoid giving too much information to a child when talking about these kinds of issues, though – it can hamper children's moral development, possibly because they see it as lecturing. I've seen the eye-rolling when I try to explain why paying taxes is a good thing. On the other hand, it's important to give clear explanations during conflict with children. A study of toddlers found that these explanations can help the development of children's understanding of morals. Any explanations should be short. As the previous section explains, too many words during conflict can sow confusion and invite arguments.[30]

I have wondered occasionally about how I can encourage my children to behave in a socially minded way because it's the right thing to do, not because they want to get praise. This may not be a fair question, though. I'm not sure any of us, as adults, can say we always behave in a socially minded way because we *should*. There are complex social reasons why we behave the way we do. We might return a lost wallet because we know we'd feel terrible about it if we didn't. We might put a lot of thought into choosing a birthday present because we want the recipient to know how important they are to us. We might donate to charity because of the altruistic glow it gives us. I like to think I'm behaving in a certain way because it's correct and because I want to help, but I wonder how I'd behave if all social bonds and expectations were suddenly taken away. The same is likely true for most children. They live in a social world that contains multiple layers of expectation attached to their behaviour that will help them thrive in such an environment. It's perhaps less important to have an ingrained sense of the right way to behave than it is to have the flexibility to adapt their behaviour to live well and happily within a society.

Troubleshooting behaviours

Anger and aggression

It's useful to teach children that it's OK to feel anger. It's a real and valid emotion that needs to be expressed constructively. Constructive and safe ways of handling anger include rationally discussing feelings of anger with the person who's sparked them, fixing the part of the situation that has caused your child to be angry (for example, mending something broken by a friend) and looking at the situation again in case a different view of it can be taken. The friend may not have meant to damage the toy. Maybe both parties contributed to the situation getting out of hand. Perhaps the teacher who shouted was having a bad day. Role-playing different situations that might provoke anger can be a helpful tool in teaching your child how to express that anger appropriately.

Children who become angry easily are more likely to behave aggressively, and aggressive behaviour is intended to cause either physical or emotional harm to others. I notice my own children being more aggressive, usually with each other, when something stressful is happening at school or they're having friendship difficulties. Aggression in toddlers is common and not necessarily a cause for concern. Childhood aggression tends to happen in a curve in the shape of a double-humped camel, with peaks between the ages of two and four, and again between fifteen and twenty. This fact makes me wonder if I should move to another country once the late teenage years roll in. Some children, of course, are aggressive at all ages.[31]

Reactive aggression happens due to provocation – hitting a sibling who's broken a favourite toy – and anger tends to lie underneath it. Proactive aggression happens without provocation. They might, for instance, push over someone they dislike because they want to see that person hurt.

Boys are more likely than girls to be aggressive. Girls and boys often show aggression differently, with boys more likely to be physically aggressive and girls more likely to show aggression by harming relationships – leaving friends or other children out of games and activities, withdrawing or threatening to withdraw friendship, or spreading rumours. This difference is encouraged by the way children are taught to deal with anger. Boys are usually encouraged to express their anger, sometimes in the form of aggression, whereas girls are taught to suppress it. As a result, when girls' anger does spill out, it's often in indirect forms such as teasing.[32]

Negative parenting practices linked to children's aggressive, anti-social behaviour can lead some children to become insensitive to punishment. This in turn drives parents to behave more negatively.[33] These negative practices include inconsistent punishment and rewards, angry and aggressive behaviour by parents, and disruptive living conditions.

A separate study of studies describes 'coercive cycles', in which a parent gives an instruction, the child responds aggressively, the parent backs down and the child's aggressive behaviour is reinforced.[34] These coercive cycles can be broken, and children's behaviour improved, by using positive parenting techniques. These are outlined earlier in this chapter under 'Discipline and general behaviour' and also in Chapter 4;

examples include using praise and encouragement where appropriate, and applying logical consequences for poor behaviour.

Preventative measures include modelling the behaviour you want your child to show and openly discussing socially minded values (see the previous section for ideas here). If your child spends a lot of time playing video games, it may also be worth reducing this. In one study of studies, researchers compared children's aggression levels before they started playing violent video games with how aggressive they were once they'd been playing games for between three months and four years. They found a significant link between gaming and aggression.[35]

It may be helpful to have critical discussions about television, video games and the internet with your child. Lower levels of aggression are seen in children whose parents actively discuss media content with them and who try to develop their children's critical thinking around things like the choices characters make.[36] This background chatter drives my partner, who prefers silent contemplation when absorbing a TV programme, completely bananas.

If your child's school offers programmes targeting aggressive behaviours, and you're concerned about aggression in your child, it's worth enrolling them. These programmes tend to be very effective. Supporting your child to build their social skills, especially around how they interpret other people's actions, may also help them be less aggressive. Children who believe that other children are acting out of hostility towards them are more likely to act aggressively, especially in emotional situations. Those who have been rejected by other children can find it especially hard to interpret social cues and other people's intentions. This may be because they've not had the same opportunities as other children to learn these skills.

Being emotionally reactive

Children who respond with anger or sadness to the smallest thing are known as 'emotionally reactive'. One book aimed at therapists is particularly helpful in outlining strategies for reactive children.[37] I cover the main strategies here. Not sweating the small stuff is key – it's much better to choose three or four areas of behaviour you want to work on with your child and to ignore the rest for now. Praise should be the main approach to reinforcing good behaviour. You can also help your child feel good at something and, ideally, multiple somethings. You could do this by asking them to do household tasks that you know they can manage (such as stirring the soup or setting off the washing machine) or encouraging them to do hobbies they're good at.

Less is more with an emotionally reactive child. There's a particular need to reduce any activities that make children feel rushed. I've learned with my own emotionally reactive daughter that getting her out of bed with plenty of time to spare makes for happier mornings. If there's no pressure on her to eat breakfast or brush her teeth, she potters along cheerfully, whereas any sense of urgency sends her into a tailspin.

You can help your child calm down, then encourage them to do this for themselves. You might, for example, find you can help by sitting with them in a quiet place. They may be able to calm themselves further by doing some colouring. Gradually, your child may move straight to activities that help them to self-soothe when they get upset, without needing you to step in. You could create a calm-down space – perhaps a corner of a bedroom filled with cushions – and a calm-down box filled with soothing activities that your child enjoys doing. The box might contain a colouring book and pencils, a fidget toy, some putty and a Rubik's cube.

Asking your child for ideas can be useful. These can focus on what to do when they feel upset or find themselves in certain situations that are likely to set them off, including things you or other members of the family could do to help them. If bedtime causes regular meltdowns, your child might suggest you give plenty of warning before you want them to start getting ready for bed. You can promote self-reliance in your child by gradually encouraging them to play more by themselves, if they find this difficult, and by helping them recognise their emotions. Perhaps you could use a picture of some traffic lights or a mood meter to help your child identify when they start to feel upset and need to use calming strategies.

You can help your child tolerate frustration by acknowledging how they feel and offering them strategies to handle it, but without solving the problem for them. Strategies might involve your child taking a deep breath and thinking about what options they have, followed by visualising how they'll break through that frustration – perhaps seeing themselves running through a finish line.

Transitions can be made easier by giving your child plenty of warning when you're moving from one activity to the next, or leaving one place to go to another. This can be supported by giving your child something that makes them feel secure about your relationship – a favourite teddy or something that represents the next activity. Picture cards might work for younger children.

Emotionally reactive children may need more support than other children to develop the social skills they need to make and maintain friendships. Reactive children are more likely to interrupt conversations and find it hard to listen to others without disagreeing. Telling your child to breathe deeply while someone else is talking, at the same time as wearing a half smile, may help them wait to speak. They could also be encouraged to take themselves away from a conversation or a situation if they can feel their frustration building.

Sulking

Children tend to sulk when they think something is unfair or when their feelings are hurt. Hurt feelings can arise when a child believes that their parent (or another key person) has done something that wasn't deserved or appropriate, making the child believe the person in question doesn't value them enough. A sense of abandonment or sibling favouritism are two key causes of these feelings. It doesn't have to be real abandonment or favouritism – a parent might have answered a phone call mid-conversation with their child, or have asked one sibling to lay the table when the child believes it's the other one's turn.[38]

If people put huge emotion into something, such as family relationships, it brings vulnerability. Hurt feelings are an inevitable part of that. Even when children sulk because they don't get their own way, it can arguably be down to the child interpreting not getting what they want as a mark of disrespect from their parents.

Other reasons children may sulk include feeling overwhelmed, overtired or unheard, or that they lack control. Sulking may also signal that children haven't yet developed the ability to manage their emotions or communicate them effectively. Children sulk with the intention, conscious or otherwise, of getting either what they want or an apology. Those with very controlling parents sulk because they don't know how else to express what they want or need, and those with permissive parents do it because it tends to get them what they want or need.

There may be times where sulking is habitual or undermining family happiness, and where approaches may need to go beyond simply trying to support your child not to feel abandoned or jealous. Research-based advice is thin in this area, though, and the ideas here therefore come mainly from expert opinion rather than evidence.

If your child feels angry about something that's happened, it can help to ask them to tell you about it – what happened, how they felt about it and what they learned from it. Talking about experiences that make children angry can reduce the distress they feel and may make sulking less likely. Listening to your child's concerns and repeating back to them why they feel upset can validate their feelings and make them less likely to sulk. This is true even if you can't or won't do anything differently. 'You're feeling upset because I don't have time to read you a story right now.'

In conflicting advice, some experts advise ignoring any sulking behaviour.[39] If adults don't give it their attention, children are less likely to sulk. Giving a child what they want as a result of sulking can reinforce the behaviour. Instead, parents can make it clear that children need to communicate what they want using other means: 'I can't tell what you need from me if you're not speaking to me. I'm here to listen when you're ready to talk.'

As the evidence conflicts on this point, and as all of it is based on expert advice rather than high-quality research studies, you could try different tactics on different occasions and see how your child responds.

Non-compliance

It's normal and healthy for children to say no to things we ask of them. At the moment of asking, children might not want to go for a walk, do their homework, eat their vegetables or tidy away their toys. They can refuse to comply in several ways, as shown by the table below.

11. FORMS OF NON-COMPLIANCE IN CHILDREN

Defiance	➤ Explicitly going against directions.
Passive non-compliance	➤ Ignoring directions without reacting.
Self-assertion	➤ Telling the adult in a calm manner why they will not be complying.
Avoidance	➤ Physically distancing themselves from the grown-up who has asked them to do something.

Types of non-compliance change with age. Defiance and passive non-compliance tend to decrease as children get older and increasingly use negotiation. One of my daughters is still a master of passive non-compliance, though, even as she grows. She'll nod sweetly when I ask her to tidy her room, and the following day it's still strewn with clothes, books, artwork, teddies, pen lids, glass beads, elastic bands and most other random detritus you care to name.

Negative parenting responses to non-compliance, such as gentle reprimands, work best when combined with positive responses to the behaviour that parents want to see.[40] Fostering positive values in children, like concern about other people's well-being, may be a better option than trying to get them to be more compliant. If children are compliant because they're used to being told what to do, they lose an opportunity to practise making decisions for themselves, making them less likely to make responsible choices when they get older.

In contrast to the recommendations made earlier in the chapter, one large study of studies did not consistently find that compliance was improved by praise. Instead, the study found that praise works better for children who are already reasonably compliant.[41] The research authors suggested that the parents of non-compliant children may interact less positively with them, meaning that these children have less of a hook on which praise can hang to reinforce behaviour. Giving these children more positive attention, in addition to praise, is likely to be helpful.

If fostering positive values hasn't got you far, a first step may be to improve the way you're giving instructions to your child (you may, of course, be in the camp that says children should never be given instructions – in which case, good luck with all that cleaning and tidying up you'll be doing until they leave home aged twenty-seven and three quarters). Effective instruction-giving should include making eye contact, being within three feet of your child, speaking quietly and in a calm tone, giving your child several seconds to respond and praising them if they follow the instruction. One instruction at a time works best – 'I want you to brush your teeth,' not 'First, I want you to brush your teeth, then put on your pyjamas.' Instructions should be framed according to what you want your child to do, not what you want them not to do: 'I'd like you to talk to me in a normal voice,' not 'Don't shout at me.'[42]

You could also try asking your child to do a few things they're likely to want to do, and praising them as they do so, then immediately asking them to do something they'd usually avoid. This is known in the research literature as a 'high-probability command sequence'.[43] For a young child and using games or play, it might be 'Touch your toes, wriggle your nose, touch the floor, high five! Put on your shoes.'

'Errorless compliance training' is similar to high-probability command sequences, but it takes place over a longer period of time, moving gradually from easy requests to more difficult ones.[44] Over a few days, parents give their children lots of easy requests that they're likely to put into action. Examples might include getting a screen from the living room so they can play some games, getting a biscuit from the cupboard, getting a cup so they can have some juice or getting out a board game you can play together. Lots of praise is given each time the child completes these requests. Gradually, slightly more difficult requests are introduced, again with lots of praise attached when these are completed successfully. This positive reinforcement, coupled with an absence of negative reinforcement, generally leads children to be able to comply more with difficult requests by the end of the process.

Parents may sometimes unwittingly reinforce their children's lack of compliance. If a child has a tantrum when asked to put away their shoes, and a parent responds by putting away the shoes instead, the child is more likely to have a tantrum next time they're asked to do the same thing. Non-compliance can also be reinforced by a parent soothing and comforting a child who has responded badly to a direction or a request. Praising a child when they do what they've been asked, after initially putting up a fight, can reinforce the original non-compliance. A simple 'thank you' or 'OK' is better than copious praise – and you can praise them vigorously the next time they do something you ask straight away.

Reprimanding children for non-compliance can reduce its occurrence, so long as parents are careful not to be harsh and to avoid doing it in a way that gives the child lots of attention. Attention, even when it's negative, can make children more likely to misbehave in future. Using discouraging gestures, such as shaking your head or crossing your arms, is another effective way of getting children to comply. Note again that these gestures should not be harsh or punishing.[45] It's also worth being wary of not slipping into areas of psychological control (see Chapter 3) by withdrawing affection or attention.

Compliance is less likely when parents attempt to control their children's behaviour instead of guiding them towards a particular goal. If I ask my child to clear up her clothes after a bath, or if I explain that the bathroom needs to be clear so her sister can have a shower, she is more likely to listen to me than if I threaten punishment.

An element of pragmatism is needed here. Toddlers, in particular, should be offered alternatives when they refuse to comply. If your child refuses to put on the blue T-shirt you've got out for them, you might ask if they'd prefer to wear the orange T-shirt or the black T-shirt. It's also worth checking you're being reasonable in terms of what you're asking of your child. Adults who place fewer demands on children give them less opportunity not to comply. Trying to focus on what children do right a lot more than what they do wrong makes them more likely to cooperate with parents, while also helping them feel good about themselves.

Being a bully

Bullying is behaviour intended to hurt. It's done over a sustained period by a child who has more physical or social power than another child. Bullying may be physical (child A regularly thumps child B), verbal (child A spends weeks taunting child B that he smells and is disgusting) or relational (child A encourages the rest of the class to exclude child B from conversation and games). Often bullying is physical and verbal at the same time, though this overlap gets smaller as children get older. Note that teasing is different in nature from bullying. The intention of teasing is to make the person being teased laugh, and it stops if anyone gets upset.

When children don't have a good way of getting something they want or need – for instance, a way to boost low self-esteem – they may bully other children to achieve this. Children who bully others are more likely to suffer from depression and anxiety, to have other behavioural problems and to be disliked by other children. They tend to think badly of other people and themselves, they find school hard and they struggle to work through conflict with other people. Children who lack a secure relationship with their parents are more likely to bully other children, as are those who have witnessed domestic violence. Bullies are more likely to be the children of authoritarian parents. Boys are more likely to bully than girls.[46]

Children who are bullied at the same time as bullying others may be the most at risk of all groups. So-called 'bully/victims' are both bullied more and do more bullying than stand-alone bullies or victims. Bully/victims are more likely than other bullies or other victims to be depressed, perform badly at school and behave badly.[47]

If you discover that your child has been bullying other children, a first step is to work with your child's school or nursery. You should meet your child's teachers to work out how best to address the bullying. Bullies learn to behave this way in social situations and institutions such as school, making these good places to unlearn this behaviour.

You should give your child a clear message that bullying won't be tolerated, ideally in tandem with a similar message from your child's school or childcare setting. It's important to try to keep lines of communication open, discussing the bullying with your child and working out what may have caused it. It's important, too, to keep calm in any discussions and not to grill your child. At the same time, getting into a debate should be avoided, in case it helps your child feel justified in their behaviour.

One option is to teach your child that there are other ways of exercising power. This might be through helping other people. Community service projects are one good example. Supporting children to develop other interests and hobbies may also be helpful. If positive behaviour gains a child respect and recognition, they have less need to engage in negative behaviours.

If possible, consequences should be applied that are relevant to the bullying behaviour, for instance returning or repaying anything that's been taken. Consequences should be unpredictable, to reduce the risk that the child will decide on other occasions that the costs of bullying are worth the rewards. After an incident, parents can teach their children to manage their own behaviour by monitoring it themselves and reporting back regularly.

It is key to offer your child time and support. Parents of children who bully others while being the victims of bullying themselves tend to spend less time doing activities with their children. Depending on the child's age, activities might include board games, puzzles, art and craft projects, football or cooking. Children who are bullies also believe they get less support from their parents than other children.[48]

You can reduce the chances of your child becoming a bully by sup- porting them to develop their social skills, if this is an area with which they struggle. Bullies tend to lack the ability to solve social problems.[49] You could help your child understand other people's perspectives and learn how to take turns better in conversation. Supporting your child to develop a more positive view of other people may also help – bullies view other people more negatively than their peers do. Developing and agreeing some family rules can be another useful tactic. If possible, these should be written down and displayed prominently, perhaps on the fridge.

Depending on your child and how they respond to these ideas, professional counselling may be necessary.

CHAPTER CHECKLIST

High-quality research

► **Use some of the gold-standard behaviour techniques.** Reinforce good behaviour with words and actions. Use praise, a smile, a nod or touch. Be careful about using material rewards, which can undermine children's motivation to do things simply because they're the right things to do. Use natural or logical consequences in place of punishment. Try using time out, if necessary. Make it effective by avoiding giving more than one warning when you're about to implement it, making the length of time out contingent on your child's adherence to it, and limiting it to five minutes at most.

► **Give effective instructions.**[50] Make eye contact, be within three feet of your child, speak quietly and calmly, frame instructions according to what you want your child to do (not what you don't want them to do), give one instruction at a time, give your child time to respond, and praise them if they follow the instruction.

► **Support your child in other areas that may help their behaviour.** Help them with their relationships (Chapter 5), their physical health (Chapter 7) and their happiness and well-being (Chapter 9). Also check their screen use and get them to move more, including playing sport (Chapter 8). Try to make family mealtimes a positive experience for everyone. Try a parenting programme if you're struggling with your child's behaviour.

Moderate-quality research

► **Refocus and reframe.** Move your focus from poor behaviour to your child's good behaviour. Don't ask your child to help; ask them to be a helper.

► **Educate, but carefully.** Try explaining to your child why certain behaviour can make others feel upset. During conflict, give clear explanations to toddlers that help their understanding of morals, but be careful about giving too much information when discussing social and moral issues as children grow; they may see it as lecturing, which can get in the way of moral development. Instead, try asking them what they think and why.

▶ **Do other things that may support your child's behaviour.** Eat together as a family. Encourage your child to play music with other people. Model how to control your impulses. Give your child plenty of opportunity to play in an unstructured way.

Anecdotal research/expert advice

▶ **Praise smartly.** Be specific in what you're praising. Praise things that are a bit of a stretch, not things your child can do without thinking. Make praise specific to your child, rather than comparing your child or what they've done with anybody else. Tell your child they should be proud of themselves (not that you are proud of them). Stick with descriptive praise until the behaviour becomes a habit.

▶ **Add some nuance to your use of natural and logical consequences.** Make sure you frame consequences as being the result of certain actions, not a punishment. Inform your child of any likely consequences in advance, where possible, and accept your child's decision if they are willing to experience a consequence. Calmly discuss consequences. Keep any logical consequences time-limited. Be consistent.

▶ **Communicate effectively.** Speak about yourself in the first person. Choose the right moment to give instructions.

▶ **Try a five-step collaborative approach to behaviour** as designed by the psychotherapist Philippa Perry. Explain what the problem is by saying what you'd like to happen; ask your child what feelings are driving the behaviour; show your child you understand what they feel; ask your child what would help them do the task or behaviour you'd like; put sensible ideas into practice; and repeat as needed.

▶ **Give your child the right messages.** Be careful to guide children away from negative actions, not feelings. Avoid shaming your child or making them feel guilty. Don't spend too much time trying to explain why your child should act in a certain way. Emphasise the positive effects of certain behaviour.

- ▶ **Involve your child.** Discuss ideas together as a family, and allow children to take part in making family decisions. Consider having 'stick together' as a family rule.
- ▶ **Check your own behaviour and thought processes.** Model the behaviour you're seeking. Try not to react too much to negative behaviour, otherwise you might reinforce it. If your child is acting up, think about their need for connection and attention.

Troubleshooting: aggression

Don't walk away when a child becomes aggressive. Don't give in to the aggression. Reward positive behaviour. Minimise the amount of time your child spends playing violent video games. Have critical discussions with your child about television, video games and the internet. Support your child to build their social skills, especially around how they interpret other people's actions. If your child finds it hard to make friends, help them build relationships with other children. Avoid unhealthy cycles of punishment. If your child's school runs a school-based programme for aggression, enrol your child in it.

Troubleshooting: sulking

If your child feels angry about a particular event, ask them to tell you about it: what happened, how they felt about it and what they learned from it. Listen carefully to your child – or, in conflicting advice, ignore the behaviour. Don't give in.

Troubleshooting: non-compliance

Make sure you're giving instructions effectively (see above, under high-quality research). Immediately after asking your child to do a few things they're likely to want to do, ask them to do something they'd usually avoid. Gradually move from easy requests to more difficult ones. Gently reprimand your child when they don't do as you've asked. Use discouraging gestures such as shaking your head or crossing your arms. Use guidance, not control. Offer toddlers alternatives. Don't give in to a child who dials up their negative behaviour in response to a request.

Check you're being reasonable in what you're asking of your child. Focus on what your child does right a lot more than what they do wrong.

Troubleshooting: if your child is bullying another child

Work with your child's school or nursery. Be clear to your child that bullying won't be tolerated. Apply clear consequences. Discuss the bullying with your child and work out what may have caused it. Keep an eye on things going forward. Get outside help, if needed. Support your child to develop their social skills and a more positive view of other people. Spend more time with your child and do activities together. Make sure your child feels supported by you. Teach your child there are other ways of exercising power. Agree some family rules. Reward your child for socially minded behaviour.

CHAPTER 7

PHYSICAL HEALTH

Periods of ill health make you realise, retrospectively, how easy it is to take good health for granted. When I moved from London to Brighton, my elder daughter – at the time, there was no sister – was two and in nursery. She spent the next year consisting of 90% human matter and 10% snot. My partner was similar, to the extent that he eventually booked a doctor's appointment. After running through the relentless stream of bugs he'd had, the doctor stopped him. 'I don't suppose you moved to the city around the time you started getting ill?' she asked. 'Yes,' he replied. 'And do you have a child in school or nursery?' 'Yes again,' he replied, slightly perturbed at the doctor's all-seeing eye. 'There's your answer. Your child has access to a whole new suite of bacteria and viruses, and so, by extension, do you. Give it a few months and you'll start to feel better.' My partner was sceptical until, like magic, the veil of illness lifted and he went down from ten colds per year to a more normal three. My daughter wasn't far behind him.

At other moments, a child might become more seriously ill. When my younger daughter was five, she got a vomiting condition that meant she was ill several times a night on a periodic basis. I was lucky to have a paediatrician friend who told me the right questions to ask at the hospital and how to advocate for her, but it was a tough time, made harder by the fact that we couldn't get a clear diagnosis. Our daughter's immune system eventually got so run down that she contracted shingles. After more than a year, the stonewalling consultant at the hospital was proved correct, and her vomiting episodes cleared up on their own. We were fortunate. If you have a child with chronic health issues, you have my sympathy (and may I please, with the benefit of hindsight, refer you back to the section in Chapter 1 about looking after yourself?).

This chapter isn't so much about ill health, though, as it is about supporting good health. There are plenty of aspects of physical health that parents can't reasonably expect to influence. You have no control, now your child's other parent has made their genetic contribution, over your child's DNA (and no, eating asparagus after conception can't change a child's sex, as a friend once confidently informed me[1]). By now, you probably don't have a huge amount of scope to increase how much you earn nor to move to a bucolic, pollution-free zone.

The good news is that your child's physical health is influenced by plenty of things over which you have at least some control – their diet, their sleep routines and how you travel to school or nursery. This chapter looks at the aspects of physical health you can reasonably hope to influence. It covers general health and sleep. It also looks at how you can develop and sustain attitudes that will set up your child to look after their own physical health in future, namely good exercise habits, a healthy attitude to food and a healthy body image.

General health

I can see three states of health in my own children. There's the obvious patina of illness: flushed faces or ghostlike wanness, floppiness and heat. There's robust good health, when there's a bounce in their step and a glow to their cheeks that's not fever-induced, and they chat happily and smile easily. And then there's an in-between condition, usually seen towards the end of a school term when exhaustion rolls in. They're caught in a state of nothingness – not ill but lacking energy, not miserable but hard to make laugh, not avoiding friends but a little reticent. Good health, though, is not just an absence of illness. The World Health Organization (WHO) describes it as being physical, mental and social, so there's some crossover with Chapter 5 on relationships and Chapter 9 on happiness and well-being. The WHO also suggests that children's healthy development means being able to live 'harmoniously' while everything around them changes.[2]

This section on general health is, for good reason, broad. Medical advice should come from doctors. This maxim can be demonstrated by evidence on children's weight – parents are likely to believe their overweight children are a healthy weight, while those who believe their underweight children are at risk of obesity may end up underfeeding them as a result.[3] In light of this, I've avoided discussing issues relating to children's weight. This section looks instead at how you can support your child to be healthier. More specific advice on areas that span beyond general health, such as sleep and exercise, is given later in the chapter.

Being moderate in your approach is key. It's all too easy to create health anxiety, perhaps in the form of children who think obsessively about one area of health, in this post-pandemic world. Weaving healthy behaviours into family life without making too much fuss about them is optimal in terms of how children engage with the issue. A moderate and wide-ranging approach is also better than any kind of extreme for children's health. One study, made up of around six thousand children from twelve countries, divided children into separate groups according to those who were very physically active, those who were very physically inactive, those who had lots of screen time and ate unhealthily, and 'all-rounders', who did moderate levels of physical activity, ate healthily and didn't have much screen time. The all-rounders were the healthiest group.[4]

Movement, as you might expect, is key to positive health outcomes. The research on sitting still is more contradictory. One study of studies suggests that the amount of time children spend sitting down isn't a particular concern as long as they're active. Another says the opposite: time spent sitting down is bad for children's health. I'm putting my money behind the study that doesn't object too much to time spent sitting when children are active at other times – it's a better-quality study, as it crunches numbers as well as synthesising conclusions from a range of research. It's also more recent.[5]

Getting children moving moderately or vigorously is therefore more likely to be important than preventing them from spending periods of time sitting still, as long as they're not sitting for long stretches at a time. Aerobic exercise is particularly good for health, and team sports are likely to be better for your child than individual sports, due to their social nature. Muscle strength is also linked to a number of positive outcomes in children, including bone health.[6] Ideas for getting your child's muscles to be stronger – these are more of the 'bunny hops' than the 'pumping iron' variety – are available in the exercise section later in the chapter.

Outdoor play is good for health, as are active video games. Screen-based games that get children moving around have similar health benefits to doing more mainstream types of physical exercise. A friend's son has a virtual reality headset that removes him visually from the physical space of the room. We've learned to keep a safe distance while he's slaying orcs.

Children who walk or cycle to school tend to be fitter, with a healthier balance of muscle and fat, than those who don't. Of course, if you live a long way from your child's school, this may not be an option for you. My own primary school was across a stretch of water or mud, depending on the time of day, then a mile-long dirt track, then a busy two-mile main road with no pavements. Boat, car and bus were the only logical options, although this didn't stop my mum occasionally shoehorning me onto the back half of a tandem.

If you're choosing a childcare provider for your child, it's worth looking for settings in which carers let children get on with things without becoming overly involved in what they're doing. Young children tend to have higher levels of stress hormones when they attend childcare that's intrusive and controlling.[7]

A varied, balanced diet such as the Mediterranean diet is likely to support your child to be healthy. Eating as if you're on the sunny terrace of a taverna beside the Med allows you to incorporate a wide range of fruit and vegetables, whole grains, beans and nuts, fish and olive oil. Moderate dairy consumption is also part of this way of eating. Children who eat this kind of diet have healthier arteries and are less likely to wheeze. There hasn't been a great deal of research in this area for kids, though adult studies have found wide-ranging positive health outcomes. Having a rich and varied diet is likely to have effects beyond health, too – early-stage research points to a link between composition of the gut microbiome (which is likely to be affected by diet, although this study didn't demonstrate a clear link) and children's behaviour.[8]

It can be hard to map what you eat as a family onto a regime like this, so some scientists have tried to simplify the advice. One expert, Professor Tim Spector, recommends eating thirty different plants across the course of a week. It sounds a lot, but herbs and spices can up the numbers quickly. Frozen fruit and vegetables, and tins of pulses (baked beans count, according to Spector), can be a cheap and relatively easy way of increasing the number of plants you and your child eat.[9]

There's little evidence to support the common recommendation that young children eat low-fat versions of dairy products. There's also little support for the idea that sugar causes kids to have a 'sugar high' and behave manically. I struggle with this finding, having seen what happens to my own kids when birthday cake gets layered on ice cream. It's possible some children have an idiosyncratic response to sugar, but a more likely explanation is that I notice behaviour that confirms my preconceptions, and I don't pick up on evidence that contradicts them.[10]

Eating meals as a family is linked to better nutritional health in children.[11] The downside is that you get to eat less interesting food, at least until you've trained your children's taste buds to tolerate chilli by casually leaving out occasional bowls of Bombay mix or hot pepper tortilla chips as pre-dinner snacks. This works.

Indoor air pollution can affect children's respiratory health.[12] Sources of air pollution include wood-burning fires, certain carpets and paints, clothes that have been dry-cleaned, air fresheners, incense and mould. Our open fireplace is a bone of contention between me and my partner – he thinks the risks are minimal. I don't. I still long to sit in front of a crackling log fire on a cold winter's day, though, or even a mild spring one.

There are some links between physical health and the topics covered in other chapters of this book. Stress (Chapter 9) has been linked to later negative health outcomes. If your child gets more than their fair share of headaches and stomach aches, you might want to probe gently whether they are being bullied (Chapter 5). Friendships (Chapter 5) are linked to children's health in later life. And it's worth keeping your child's screen time below two hours per day (Chapter 8), or less if they are very young. Children who have more than two hours of screens a day are more likely to be unfit two years later.[13] This link may not be causal, of course – parents who allow their children to spend a lot of time on screens may be less likely to encourage them to get outside and exercise.

I promised that this was a general section, but I'm going to be specific about one area – those abominable creatures that challenge cockroaches in their indestructibility: head lice. Around one in twenty schoolchildren in Europe is estimated to have head lice at any one time.[14] We had them on a loop between the start of nursery and the end of primary school, passed around between children and horrified adults like canapés at a Downing Street party. It took four months of a pandemic and no physical contact with other children for our household to become permanently free of repeated, repulsive infestations.

So what does the research say? Treatments that kill head lice and nits by coating them with jelly or oils are as effective as those that are toxic to lice, and may even work better. If you prefer a more natural approach, there are several options. Herbal head lice treatments can be effective when combined with combing. Treatments containing kunzea oil look promising. Tea tree oil kills adult lice. Nerolidol, which can be found in fragrant plants such as jasmine, lemongrass and (again) tea tree, acts on the louse eggs or nits. Using tea tree oil in combination with nerolidol can be particularly effective on lice and eggs in a lab, although this hasn't been studied directly on the heads of children. And this is an issue with a lot of the treatments. What works in a lab doesn't necessarily translate onto your child's head. You can destroy almost every louse that has set up its comfortable encampment there, as well as its eggs, but miss a couple and you're screwed. It's a particular issue when you have a child with thick hair.[15]

Yet again, general research findings may not work for all children. We found conventional treatments to be next to useless – we always missed a patch on our daughters' voluminous mops (or perhaps we're spectacularly useless with the application). Instead, we've found the only effective thing to be weeks upon weeks of plastering hair with conditioner, then combing it through with a contraption called a Nitty Gritty. This is done once every two days to catch the lice before they get big enough to lay eggs. I feel itchy just writing this.

You may also have an issue with reinfestation. One enduring cycle of lice in my daughter's class was only broken with an irritated plea from a parent on the class WhatsApp group for everyone to treat their kids over half-term. Your best solution may simply be to get stroppy.

Sleep

If you're reading this book, you'll probably have a child who's at least two. If this is the case, you will presumably have emerged from the thick mental fog of confusion and despair that results from prolonged, baby-induced sleep deprivation. If your child has a sibling who is younger than two, you might want to put down this book and have a nap or a cup of coffee. I remember a time when I'd have given away my pay cheque (or possibly my daughter) for one uninterrupted night's sleep.

When you're through the tyranny of sleep deprivation wrought by an infant, sleep problems in an older child can worry the calmest of parents. You might feel you're going to descend back into the never-ending wakeful fug of the early months. Just as you learn how to sleep again, it gets whipped away from you.

It may help to know what's normal in terms of children's sleep, but researchers don't yet have good enough data to be able to say how much sleep children should get according to their age, even at a broad average level, and individual children can need different amounts. Rather than looking at how long your child sleeps, there are other measures you can use to work out how well your child is sleeping.

One study of studies defines good-quality sleep for a school-aged child as taking less than thirty minutes to get to sleep and waking only once, or not at all, during the night. Other factors included in this definition of good-quality sleep include sleep efficiency (the ratio of time spent asleep to time spent in bed) of more than 85% and spending less than twenty minutes awake between going to sleep and getting up the next day, but these factors are not something parents can easily measure. Sleep is defined as poor quality when children wake up four times or more during the night.[16]

Sleep problems are common. At least one in five young children suffers from some kind of sleep disorder, such as difficulty getting to sleep, night terrors and sleepwalking. Sleep is also crucial for children in several areas, not just the basic fact of staying alive. Poor sleepers are more likely to suffer from poor health and to be overweight. Children who sleep badly as babies are more likely to have sleep problems a couple of years later. And in what might fairly be described as a 'no shit, Sherlock' study, researchers have confirmed that sleep problems in children can affect their parents' sleep, and that getting less sleep can make parents tired. If your child is a poor sleeper, don't panic reading this – there's lots you can do to help them.[17]

Gut instincts may well override research findings when it comes to sleep, as it is incredibly personal. Children's sleep is a controversial area in the expert literature, and one where conflicting advice abounds. It's also something over which parents themselves can feel strongly. In particular, the evidence on sleep training set out a little later may not sit well with you if you're someone who takes a child-led approach to being a parent. In one view, sleep training can result in instant relief and better long-term well-being for the whole family, and in another be horrifically damaging. I've tried to keep this section clinical in terms of highlighting research findings according to the strongest evidence.

One of the most important things for children's sleep is to create consistent bedtime habits. Calming activities you can weave into your child's routine, in addition to getting into pyjamas and brushing teeth, include:

▶ Telling stories, reading or gentle singing, or some kind of combination. Families of faith might include praying here. Singing and speaking help children sleep for longer at night when they're combined with evening routines. They may also support brain development.[18]

- ▶ Having a warm bath.
- ▶ Practising deep breathing or massage.
- ▶ Quiet play.
- ▶ Listening to music.
- ▶ Making sure teddies are present and correct.
- ▶ Dimming lights half an hour before sleep.
- ▶ Lying down with and/or cuddling your child. Ideally this shouldn't be done while your child is falling asleep, as kids tend to sleep better without an adult in the room.

The most common elements of a bedtime routine are reading a story, having a bath or shower, and putting on pyjamas. Routines are important for all children, not just the younger ones, even if showers and a quick game of cards have replaced a nightly bath and nursery rhymes. School-aged children with consistent night-time routines sleep for almost an hour longer than those without. Children also sleep better when social maturity is encouraged through self-care routines (cleaning their bedrooms and making their beds) alongside relevant family rules (having set homework times and bedtimes). While it's important to be consistent, a degree of flexibility is also needed. Being too strict can make bedtime stressful, which itself gets in the way of good sleep.[19]

Ideally, children's bedrooms should be dark and quiet. If your child needs to sleep with the light on, a dim bulb is less likely to disrupt their sleep rhythms than a bright one. Bedrooms should also be a temperature that's neither very hot nor very cold. One thing that finally persuaded my younger daughter that her own bed was preferable to my own was the temperature of the bedroom (I like to sleep with the radiators off and the window open all year, though I have to compromise on this predilection with my warm-blooded partner). My daughter has duly declared our bedroom to be 'like the Antarctic' and is happier in her more temperate environment.

Active play near bedtime is something to avoid, as it's stimulating. Nobody's going to be ready for sleep if you've all just sprinted round the park playing tag. And bedtime matters. Children who go to bed after 9 p.m. sleep less than those who go to bed earlier. This is true even of older children. School-aged children who go to bed after 9 p.m. take longer to go to sleep and average one hour less sleep than those who go to bed earlier.[20] Daytime schedules are also important. Having too much to do, like after-school clubs and homework, can get in the way of bedtimes. The same might be said for adult pressures. It's usually when my partner and I both have to finish a piece of time-critical work that mealtimes and bedtimes slip.

While spending longer with your child at bedtime is linked with better sleep in young children whose parents are sensitive to their needs, it's worth trying to keep out of your child's room when they're falling asleep. If parents are in the room with children when they go to sleep, school-aged children are almost three times more likely to wake up at night, and babies average an enormous hour and forty-two minutes less of sleep.[21] This is a strong argument against sleep-training methods that involve parents sitting in the same room as a child while they go to sleep.

Pets should also be kept out of bedrooms. Cats, dogs, hamsters and other fluffy things, while irresistible to many children, can disrupt their sleep. It's been a hard no on keeping our greyhound out of bedrooms, much to our children's annoyance. This has been possible principally because he hasn't yet worked out how to climb the stairs indoors, even though he skips up and down staircases outside. Like Pooh Bear, the dog is a creature of very little brain. If he ever does ever work it out, though, I suspect there may not be much we can do to prevent his thirty-five-kilo heft from doing so.

Screens can interfere with sleep. Children who have screen time close to bedtime tend to sleep badly and to be sleepy during the day. Having a screen in the bedroom overnight, even if it's not used, can lead to worse sleep. School-aged children with TVs in their rooms sleep around twenty minutes less a night than other children.[22]

It's worth minimising your own use of screens at bedtime, as well as that of any siblings, or at least ensuring that screen use by other family members isn't going to disturb a child trying to sleep. When asked directly what gets in the way of them falling asleep, children mention other people's media use.[23] My younger daughter went through a stage of playing the soundtrack to *Hamilton* loudly and obsessively. Her bedtime is earlier than her sister's, so while they share a bedroom wall, it may not have contributed directly to her sister sleeping less. It certainly contributed to tempestuous sibling arguments, though, which themselves are linked to poor sleep.

Children who regularly consume caffeine sleep less than those who don't, and some kids may be especially sensitive to caffeine.[24] As someone who can't drink coffee after midday, I suspected my children might be the same. This case was closed when one of my daughters went to McDonald's with family friends and drank a pint of Coke. That night, she couldn't get to sleep. In her view, though, it wasn't the Coke that stopped her sleeping. It was just an extraordinary coincidence.

When children eat plenty of fruit and vegetables, and generally avoid fast food or other energy-dense, low-nutrient food, they tend to sleep better. The link between diet and sleep could be nutritional, or perhaps children who have slept badly find it harder to make healthy food choices. If your child needs a snack near bedtime, you could try offering food that promotes sleep, such as a cracker with a glass of milk. Snacks full of carbohydrate and calcium are better for sleep than food high in protein.[25]

Ways of supporting your child to sleep covered in other chapters include improving your relationship with each other and addressing sibling tension (Chapter 5), supporting your child's well-being (Chapter 9), ensuring they have a chance to play outdoors regularly (Chapter 8), and avoiding alcohol if you drink it problematically (Chapter 1). If your child is sleeping badly, you might also want to check if they're being bullied (Chapter 5). Insomnia, nightmares and other sleep problems can result from bullying.

What should you do if your child is sleeping especially badly? One thing you might consider is cognitive behavioural therapy (CBT), which you can access through your doctor or online. Having four or more CBT sessions has been shown to help children sleep better. Teaching yourself about sleep can also help, possibly because children absorb messages about sleep from their parents.[26]

If your child regularly wants to sleep in your bed, it could be that they feel worried about being away from you. It may be that you don't mind them being there, or perhaps having a small child lying diagonally across your bed is getting to you; it's a known fact that children take up at least 120% of any space available to them. If your child might be sleeping in your bed because they're feeling anxious, you can try some of the ideas suggested in Chapter 9.

It might be that your child isn't sleeping for long enough. If this is the case, something as simple as an earlier bedtime might be worth a try; one study of studies found that it gives children a solid forty-seven minutes of extra sleep a night, on average. If your child is having difficulties falling asleep, on the other hand, temporarily delaying bedtime may work. However, this contradicts the research on consistent bedtimes, which is informed by stronger evidence – so while temporary delays may work for some children, it's worth being cautious and moving back to a consistent bedtime as soon as possible. You might also try removing your child from bed for twenty minutes or so if they're not sleeping. Getting out of bed reduces the chance that children form an association between lying in bed and not being able to sleep. Once your child is out of bed, any activity during this period should be low-key and dull. This removes a possible incentive for not going to sleep – having fun activities to do out of bed makes getting up more appealing.[27]

Finally, on to the controversial bit: sleep training. Sleep-training programmes improve the quality and length of children's sleep, but many experts worry they may create other problems for children, such as a belief that they won't be comforted when needed, or an insecure relationship with their parents. But the research, on balance, doesn't support this view. One study followed more than three hundred families, half of which used sleep-training programmes when their children were babies, and assessed five years later whether there were any problems, including whether sleep-trained children felt more stress. The study found that children experienced no long-term harm (or, indeed, long-term benefit) as a result of sleep training. A separate longitudinal study has found that not intervening when children sleep badly risks them being less well able to regulate their emotions as they get older, causing (among other issues) further sleep problems.[28]

Researchers and experts who are sceptical of sleep-training programmes use a combination of theory and study critiques to argue against these findings and those of similar studies. The theoretical critiques don't stand up for me; why would we take a model explanation, however clever and thoughtful, over hard evidence? The critiques of individual studies showing no adverse effects of sleep-training programmes – such as that they are not big enough – hold more weight. But there is minimal evidence suggesting that sleep-training programmes are harmful, and your own stress levels may affect your child's stress levels more than the approach you use to help them sleep.

Until we have bigger, more powerful studies, we can be reasonably confident in saying there's no real evidence to show that sleep-training programmes cause harm, and there's quite a bit of evidence showing they are beneficial. That said, a recent study of studies found that sleep interventions with children aged five and below leads to them sleeping nine minutes longer each night, on average.[29] Only you can decide whether the extra fifty-five hours a year are worth it.

There are several ways to approach sleep training, and more than I've covered here. Given that there are entire books written about children's sleep, I've selected a few key ones:

▶ **Extinction, or 'cry it out'.** This sleep-training approach involves leaving children to cry themselves to sleep. It can be emotionally distressing for children and parents alike, and requires parents to stick to it fully. It's successful in improving sleep.[30] It's also incredibly controversial.

▶ **Graduated extinction, or 'controlled crying'.** This involves leaving a child for gradually increasing periods of time up to a specified maximum, perhaps ten or fifteen minutes. When parents go in to check on their child, they offer some brief comfort while minimising interaction, with the theory that chatting and smiling gives the child an incentive to stay awake. Graduated extinction helps children with sleep problems and is less upsetting for parents than extinction. Graduated extinction has been linked to reduced anxiety in children, better behaviour and increased family well-being within two weeks of starting an intervention.

▶ **Bedtime pass.** The child in question is given a pass which they can exchange for a single trip out of their room or a visit from a parent. The pass is given to the parent after it has been used and is given back the following night. Once the pass has been used, the parents leave children to settle themselves to sleep. It's been shown to work well in a trial of three- to six-year-olds, but may work for other ages.[31]

▶ **Extinction with parental presence.** With this approach, the parent sits in the room with the child, giving reassurance that the child has company but (as with other forms of extinction) ignoring unwanted behaviour. This method can be particularly helpful for children with separation anxiety. But while some experts recommend this approach, and there is support for it in studies of babies, there's also very high-quality evidence to suggest that having a parent in the room at bedtime is linked to children waking more frequently at night.[32]

I've seen parents tear themselves apart over whether to use sleep-training programmes. It's an area where your instinct is probably as valuable as the research. Sleep training worked well for one of my children, and seemed less appropriate for the other. It took around seven years for her to be keener to sleep in her own bed than mine, though, so make of that what you will.

Exercise

My childhood exercise exploits were a mixed bag. I was rubbish at team sports and hated being dragged out for family walks, but I had specific, limited skills in table tennis, tree climbing and diving. I loved swimming, and swam in the sea most days from March. These days, the chilly English water is just about warm enough for me in August. I could also cycle pretty much forever, as my parents and I spent two weeks most summers carting our camping gear across northern Europe by bike. In general, though, it took me a good eighteen years to learn how to enjoy exercise and find things I could do well.

I try to remember this when my children resist my attempts to get them moving. These endeavours have included a mini indoor trampoline in the hope that they'd bounce while watching TV (they didn't, and we ended up with lots of stubbed toes), a dog (which causes arguments about whose turn it isn't to walk him) and moving further away from school ('Muuuuuuuum, why can't we just driiiiiiiive?'). The low point was persuading my elder daughter to come on a run with me and howling with frustration when she needed to walk a few minutes after we set off. Strangely, she hasn't run with me since.

Children's activity levels have fallen steeply. Between the early 1940s and the early 1990s, the calories that children burn during physical activity are thought to have fallen by around six hundred a day.[33] I haven't been able to find more recent estimates based on large-scale studies but, given the increasing access to screens and declines in children walking and cycling to school, it seems unlikely that physical activity levels are on an upward curve again.

Ideally, children should be physically active for no less than an hour a day, and get at least a little out of breath while doing so. Activity should be mostly aerobic, with some muscle and bone strengthening thrown in about three times a week. Weight-bearing exercise helps children to build bone mineral. Anything that includes jumping is great. Younger children can develop muscular fitness through exercises such as bunny hops and frog jumps. PE lessons and sports clubs might be necessary to help older children build muscular fitness and skill in a way that's age-appropriate and challenging.[34]

Parents' encouragement, and their willingness and ability to take children to places they can exercise, also influences how much exercise their children do. Playing catch or football together, or going for walks as a family, shows your child you think exercise is important. Children are more likely to choose to be active at other times if you provide lots of opportunities for them to be active. The more time children spend outdoors, the more likely they are to be physically active and fit.[35]

Sometimes it's a question of finding an activity your child loves. If children enjoy exercise, they do more of it (respect to the persuasion skills of the researchers who got a study commissioned to show this).[36] There may be other barriers here, though. One of my daughters loves trampolining, but we have no trampolining club in our city and other activities are never as appealing to her. Friends may also be useful in making movement part of weekly routines. You could find a regular activity for your child to do with a close friend that allows them to see each other out of school or nursery and potentially allows you to share drop-offs or pickups with another family.

When parents take regular exercise, children tend to be more physically active.[37] Through your attitudes to physical activity, and by doing it yourself, you can affect how much your child chooses to exercise. Modelling isn't always successful, though. Anecdotally, showing too much enthusiasm for something can even put older children off it altogether. I've run three marathons, but my girls won't even lace up a pair of running shoes. Helping your child feel physically competent can be another subtle way to induce more activity. Children are more likely to take part in vigorous exercise if they feel they're good at something. Perhaps they're strong, they have a particular skill, they're flexible or they don't give up easily.

Children who have good relationships with their parents and whose parents are responsive to their needs are more likely to exercise than other children. Kids who eat well are more likely to exercise, as are those who spend less than two hours per day on screens.[38]

My children move more when they choose the activities. They'll often ask if we can go swimming, even if they'd rather eat courgettes than go for a walk. War games appeal when other children visit or we stay with other families. And while I suspect there are negative consequences of tying rewards into movement, it's a foolproof strategy. 'Does anyone fancy a walk?' is greeted by tumbleweed. 'Does anyone fancy walking up to the hilltop cafe to get ice cream?' is met with more enthusiasm.

You could also find something that appeals to your child's personality and current interests. A friend of mine lives in central London. Her location has meant she's struggled to find ways of getting her daughter to be physically active. She's had to get creative. A bit of trial and error has led to the discovery that a pair of *Frozen*-themed, light-up trainers and a superhero cape gets her daughter running performative laps of the park most days.

If your child is reluctant to exercise, it may be that they face particular obstacles to doing so. Overweight girls often have less support from teachers or other adults to exercise.[39] Children who are overweight may also find that other kids tease them or that their own bodies present barriers to exercise – if they're not as fast as other children, for example. Your child might feel uncomfortable about their body or have a low level of baseline fitness that prevents exercise being fun. They might have poor skills in a particular sport or activity, perhaps because they haven't done much of it before or because they lack hand-eye coordination. You could play catch with them in the park if a lack of throwing or catching skills is undermining how motivated they feel to exercise, or take them to the pool if they don't feel they're as strong at swimming as other children.

Children who are bullied or otherwise left out by other children are less likely to exercise, possibly because they're put off doing so by their experience, or because it's hard for lonely children to take part in social activities. You may be familiar with the hot feeling of shame if you stand awkwardly, as an adult, on the outside of a group who get on with each other and are familiar enough to have in-references you don't understand. The special horror of networking events is a case in point. Apply this feeling to lonely children, and it may become clear why they're less likely to want to do group sport. At the same time, evidence suggests that children who exercise more are less lonely. There's an amazing camaraderie that comes from team sport. It may therefore be a combination of loneliness making children less likely to exercise, and exercise (or group activity) driving away feelings of loneliness in those who do more physical activity.[40]

In other cases, the barriers may be ones you face as a family – for example, if it's hard to find spare cash for clubs and equipment. If you live in a city, it's worth looking at your local children's or community centres. Many of those offer free activities. My local centre ran free toddler movement classes when my daughter was at the right age for them, with lots of dancing and a ground-anchored parachute. At the risk of morphing into Captain Obvious, charity shops can be a good source of balls, Frisbees and skittles, and local parks and playgrounds often have play equipment or space for games. Your child's school, if they're old enough to have one, may have free or subsidised after-school activities.

Families in low-income neighbourhoods generally have less access to areas that are safe and suitable for play and exercise, though, such as parks and community centres.[41] There's a real need for support from local and national governments to create more spaces where children can be physically active. This requires improvements to urban design, increasing the safety of streets and reducing traffic where possible, as well as the provision of low-cost sports programmes in areas that need them.

A healthy attitude to food and a healthy body image

A good relationship with food sets up children to be healthy as they get older. It's something that should be simple, yet it can seem overwhelming. Food can be used as succour and comfort, as a tool of control and as a battleground when, at its best, it's simply sustenance, pleasure and shared ritual. When drawing together the research for this section, I wanted to think not only about how we ward off the spectres of future eating disorders and their milder forms, but also about something much more fundamental – how can children develop a straightforward relationship with food that enables them to make mainly healthy choices without having to think about them, and enables them to take pleasure in food without feeling guilt?

One thing that's entirely normal, and nothing to worry about unless it becomes extreme, is fussiness around food. Fear of new foods, particularly for toddlers, is normal and a natural defence mechanism that protects children from their increasing ability to decide what they put in their mouths. If they're in a wood and see a toadstool, they're more likely to make it to adulthood if they choose not to eat it. One study followed children between the ages of two and eleven to assess how common it is to be fussy. It found that between one in eight and one in five children are picky eaters at any given age, and this pickiness lasts for more than two years for 40% of picky eaters.[42]

Offering a decent variety of ingredients and flavours is a common recommendation. This is easier said than done when your child just wants to eat pasta with tomato sauce. I felt hubristic pleasure when

I'd managed to wean my daughters onto curries, thinking it would develop their palates for later culinary adventures. Their willing acceptance of spice lasted all of four months until the bland kid food preference took over.

Food variety is also challenging when your child has extremely fussy friends to visit. One daughter had a primary school friend who would only eat beige food. After one disastrous dinner where she kept saying, loudly, 'Excuse me! I don't like this!' (and I heroically resisted responding 'Well, don't bloody eat it then'), I asked her what she'd like for dinner next time. She said plain pasta. I duly made this the next time she came over. She refused to eat it because I'd made the fatal error of tossing it with olive oil. I can't pretend I was devastated when she and my daughter drifted apart.

As most public discourse and research on body image focuses on teenagers, particularly teenage girls, it might feel a bit early to be thinking about body image. However, body image concerns can start a lot earlier than puberty. Depending which study you read, between 20% and 70% of young children are dissatisfied with their bodies.[43] I remember hating my body when I was as young as eight, although being called 'thunder thighs' by other children probably didn't help. (Being strong of thigh has helped me as an adult to lift weights that would unquestionably defeat their puny limbs and to run far and fast, so I win.)

Girls are more likely to want to be thin, though it's also common for boys to have a poor body image. One issue for girls may be how hard it is to see accurate representation of themselves and their bodies in media, or even any representation at all. A lot of published data in this area is old, so I analysed the current output of the children's TV channel CBeebies. I found that of programmes with either male or female lead characters, 68% had a male lead and just 32% had a female lead.[44]

There's also a real issue with media messaging around body ideals, even for young children. And where progress has been made, it's limited. Barbie dolls have diversified recently, with a new range depicting a greater range of body shapes than their forerunners. The original doll is famously a shape that, transferred to a living human, would prevent said human's body from being able to support its head. Even having a wider range of dolls, though, isn't enough to cut through the toxic messages that filter into our children's heads – recent research has found that girls, on average, prefer the original dolls and still value thinness.[45]

A healthy attitude to food

Children often eat more healthily when they have a good relationship with their parents (Chapter 5), and they're more likely to eat unhealthily if their mental health is poor (Chapter 9). As with many other areas in this book, parents can only do so much to help their children develop a healthy relationship with food and with their bodies. Children are influenced in what they eat by the world around them. Junk food adverts make a significant difference to children's food choices. Short of never switching on the TV or going with them to the shops, there's not much you can do about this. Like much else, it's a matter for policy.

The food children eat is linked most strongly to two things. The first is the food available to them. They can't eat what they're not given. The second is the extent to which their parents act as healthy role models.[46] This means showing children what it means to eat healthily and that you like eating different types of food – eating the way you want your child to eat, in other words. Even if children are fussy right now, they're more likely to end up eating a variety of food if they've seen their parents enjoying it. The adult who eats lots of Maltesers and cheesy Wotsits, and the one who enjoys stir-fries packed with vegetables, probably have parents who ate similarly when they were growing up.

Modelling eating a range of fruit and vegetables is particularly useful in getting your child to do the same. Parents skipping meals can make children more likely to miss meals themselves once they reach adolescence.[47] Offering your child lots of different types of food is a good idea, including, occasionally, things you don't like yourself. Young children's food preferences are affected by what their parents don't offer them, and parents don't tend to offer food they don't like.

I'm highly unlikely to cook a plate of Brussels sprouts without some evidence-based encouragement (or even with the evidence base right in front of me. They taste like drains).

Being exposed to lots of different flavours early on is linked to healthy diets as children get older.[48] And if children always get the same pizza or fish and chips off the children's menu if you go out to eat, they'll start to think other food is not for them. My hard-earned nuggets of truth wrung from years of trying to increase variety include these: children can detect a finely chopped mushroom (so fine that it's basically dust) from ten paces; if you have more than one child, there will be precisely one meal they both like enough not to complain about; and putting purple carrots in your egg fried rice will turn the rice blue, and your kids will refuse to eat it.

Children naturally gravitate towards sweet food. Tasting something sweet releases dopamine, which is the neurotransmitter responsible for pleasure, in the brain. Children aren't equally responsive to sugary food, though – some children can be twenty times more sensitive to sweet tastes than others.[49] Others lose this preference as they grow. My dad's aversion to sweet foods came, he said, from saving up his post-war sugar ration to gorge himself at the local sweet shop. In later years, he could be persuaded by a good Jamaican ginger cake or blackberry and apple crumble, but otherwise he avoided sweet things in the way my children sidestep mushrooms.

As a rule, when family members eat together frequently, children eat more healthily.[50] They're also less likely to skip breakfast when they reach adolescence. This has been more possible for us in the evenings since pandemic and post-pandemic working practices have changed, as there's been less commuting and getting home late. Breakfasts, though, are still a chaotic free-for-all. Making mealtimes reasonably consistent is worth considering too. If children don't know when to expect food, they're more likely to eat as much as they can when they're offered it, rather than responding to their natural feelings of hunger.

It's best to plan mealtimes to be away from the TV or other distractions, as it's hard for children to pay attention to the hunger they feel and the food they're eating if they're concentrating on something else. If children graze on snacks throughout the day, they can become less able to recognise when they feel hungry. A good relationship with food comes from feeling hungry – healthily hungry, not excessively hungry – before a meal, and full afterwards. My children seem to think they'll die if they get mildly hungry. I've been trying to convince them that avoidance of snacks an hour before dinner does not lead to immediate demise, but evidence has not yet persuaded them otherwise. Drinking lots of milk tends to affect young children's appetites, so this may be something to look at if your child doesn't get that hungry at mealtimes.

At the same time, children shouldn't be pressured to eat more than they'd choose naturally, though you can still praise young children when they make healthy choices. At mealtimes, more than four in five parents try to get their children to eat more than they would do other-wise.[51] This can lead to children ignoring their natural hunger cues. This suggestion has been incredibly hard to put into practice for me. I have to override decades of conditioning to disregard the instinct to encourage my children to eat a little more, particularly when it comes to vegetables. It is tough for me to trust that their bodies know what they need better than I do, especially when I know how much ice cream they're able to consume.

The research literature contains conflicting findings on rules and restrictions relating to food and mealtimes. It's not entirely clear from the research done to date why they can be helpful in some situations and unhelpful in others. It may be that setting rules around food doesn't work when those rules are associated with shame. One study found that parents being restrictive with food can lead to girls feeling sad, guilty or shameful about what they eat. Another study looked at the eating habits of girls across several years. Girls whose parents were very restrictive with their eating at age five were more likely, at times they weren't hungry and when adults weren't around to supervise them, to overeat when they were older.[52]

Restrictiveness was measured by parents:

▶ Making sure their child doesn't eat too many sweets, too many high-fat foods or too much of their favourite foods.
▶ Keeping some foods deliberately out of reach of their child.

► Offering sweet food or other favourite foods as a reward for good behaviour.

► Believing that, without guidance or regulation, their child would eat too much junk food or too much of their favourite foods.

Restricting access to food they like increases children's focus on that food and can make them more likely to eat it once any restrictions are no longer there. One way to allow children choice within a framework of healthy options and minimal restrictions is to choose what to give your child to eat, as well as when and where to give it, but to allow your child to choose whether to eat it and how much to eat. You might choose to offer some cheese and fruit at 3 p.m. for an afternoon snack. Your child decides whether to eat this snack and how much of it to eat. If they choose not to eat, they wait until the next meal before being offered anything else.

This approach can be helpful in several ways. It removes the counter-intuitive anxiety that children may feel if they have unfettered choice. It gives them a sense of control over whether and how much they eat. It also supports them being able to regulate themselves according to how hungry they feel, and it reduces the chances of mealtimes becoming a battleground. As child-feeding specialist and therapist Jo Cormack says, 'If the adult is not invested in the child's eating decisions, the child can't use them as a way of taking power or striving for autonomy.'[53]

A community or school gardening project might be worth joining, if you live near one – or, if you have your own outside space, you could grow some vegetables with your child. Children who get involved with gardening tend to eat more vegetables, either because gardening means vegetables are more available to them or because it makes them more likely to try new foods. This reminds me of a highly accurate graph developed by a Twitter humorist that depicted an inverse relationship between children's ability to help you in the garden, which increases with their age, and their interest in doing so, which falls off a cliff.[54]

If your child already has difficulties around food and mealtimes, a group parenting course focused on this area may be helpful. Courses such as Hassle Free Mealtimes Triple P can help families and children improve both behaviour and confidence. Finally, if your child is overweight, you're better off not criticising their weight or encouraging them to slim down. A focus on weight can lead to children having a dysfunctional relationship with food and affect their well-being.[55] Instead, you can encourage healthy eating and physical activity without referring to how much your child weighs or what size they are.

A healthy body image

A healthy body image can be supported by making mealtimes as relaxed and happy as possible, showing you accept different body shapes and sizes, and being open with your child about how the media can promote an appearance that's unrealistic for most people. These are all strategies that were used in the Confident Body, Confident Child programme, which demonstrably helped parents support their children to have a healthy body image.[56]

Other recommendations made by the programme included praising your child about things unrelated to how they look – like how much hard work they've put into a painting – and modelling healthy eating. It's also important to avoid discussing foods as being good or bad, and to avoid using food to reward or punish your child. You might want to avoid proffering a doughnut as a reward for doing well in a test, or threatening to withdraw dessert from a child who is throwing peas.

Another recommendation of the Confident Body, Confident Child programme was to avoid criticising how you or others look in front of your child. It's also not a good idea to diet or to encourage your child to diet. A separate study has found that when mothers criticise their own weight, shape and what they eat, it causes their daughters to be more dissatisfied with their bodies.[57] If you're concerned about your own body, it's worth making sure your child doesn't know about it.

Wariness around media is the order of the day when it comes to body image. If you have magazines aimed at adult women in your home, it's a good idea not to leave them where your daughter (if you have one) can find them. Girls who look at these kinds of magazines are unhappier with their bodies. They're effectively being told, 'Here's what society finds beautiful, and you're not it.' Media containing sexualised messages – for instance, children's television programmes that show boys valuing girls for their physical appearance – can lead girls to internalise those messages, damaging their body image. *iCarly* has been highlighted by one study as the kind of programme that does this. And it's worth minimising the amount of time older children spend on social networking sites, which have been linked to increases in body dissatisfaction. I can confirm that implementation of this suggestion will probably be met with mutiny by said older children.[58]

Children tend to have a better body image when they have a good relationship with their parents (Chapter 5), when they have plenty of opportunities to exercise (this chapter), when they're not being bullied (Chapter 5), and when they have good levels of self-esteem (Chapter 9) and are self-compassionate.

If you focus on what your child's body can do, not what it looks like, you'll be setting them up well for a healthy body image.[59] Your child needs to know you don't attach importance to how they look, and nor do other significant adults. Recognising your child for being strong is more likely to give them a healthy body image than recognising them for being pretty. Someone close to me has a daughter who looked particularly doll-like when she was a toddler. She used to find that people would breathe 'She's so pretty!' in front of her daughter. Prettiness is of such fundamental value to many people that my friend struggled to persuade people that their words might be better focused on other attributes.

CHAPTER CHECKLIST

High-quality research

▸ **Look at what you can personally do to support your child's health.** Be physically active – you can act as a role model. Eat the way you want your child to eat. Rely on your doctor, not your own judgement, to highlight any concerns about your child's weight. See if there are any ways of improving your relationship with your child (Chapter 5 has some ideas). Minimise air pollution inside your home.

▸ **Give the right messages.** Show you accept different body shapes and sizes, and be open with your child about how the media can promote an appearance that isn't realistic for most people. Don't discuss foods as being good or bad. Don't criticise how you or others look in front of your child. If your child is overweight, don't highlight their weight or encourage them to slim down.

▸ **Do things together.** Spend time outdoors with your child. Try to find a community or school gardening project, or, if you have your own outside space, grow some vegetables with your child.

▸ **Prioritise movement.** Make sure your child is getting plenty of exercise, including movement that will support their muscular fitness. Your child should be doing at least an hour of physical activity a day, ideally something that gets them at least a little out of breath. If your child's reluctant to exercise, though, be mindful of any barriers they may face. Consider letting your child play active video games. Avoid driving your child to school, if possible.

▸ **Prioritise sleep.** Make sure your child's room is cool and dark. Create consistent bedtime routines, and make sure your child goes to bed at the same time each evening. Keep screens out of bedrooms, especially at night. If possible, avoid being in the same room as your child when they're falling asleep. If your child is sleeping badly, check whether they might be being bullied. Use a sleep-training programme for children who have significant sleep problems, or consider enrolling them for CBT through your doctor or online.

- ▶ **Be careful with messages about food.** Rules and restrictions in your child's diet may have unintended consequences. Praise young children when they make healthy choices, but don't use food to reward or punish your child. Steer your child away from caffeine. If your child has difficulties around food and mealtimes, consider finding a group parenting course focused on this area. Be mindful of any junk food advertising your child may watch. Eat meals together as a family when you can, and make mealtimes as happy and relaxed as possible.
- ▶ **Identify other areas that may affect your child's physical health.** See if there's anything you can do to improve your child's mental well-being and lower their stress levels (see Chapter 9). Encourage your child's friendships (see Chapter 5). Keep your child's screen time below two hours a day (less, if they're very young), and make sure they avoid screens in the hours before bed (see Chapter 8).

Moderate-quality research

- ▶ **Be balanced in your approach.** A moderate and wide-ranging approach to children's physical health is better than any kind of extreme. If you have magazines aimed at adult women in your house, don't leave them where your daughter (if you have one) can find them.
- ▶ **Make necessary changes yourself.** Minimise your own use of screens at bedtime, as well as that of any siblings, or at least ensure they're not going to disturb a child trying to sleep. Teach yourself about sleep. Avoid alcohol if you drink it problematically. Keep pets out of bedrooms.
- ▶ **Strengthen your child's body image.** Help your child feel physically competent. Be careful not to let your child watch TV programmes that contain sexualised messages, which can affect children's body image.
- ▶ **Think about the quality of your child's diet while maintaining a light touch.** Aim for a varied, balanced diet for your child, such as the Mediterranean diet. Offer your child lots of different types of food, including, occasionally, things you don't like yourself. Avoid letting your child drink too much milk if they tend not to be hungry at mealtimes. At the same time, don't pressure your child to eat more than they'd choose naturally.

▸ **Look at what else you can do to support your child's health.** Spend more time with your child at bedtime, if you are able to. If you want to help your child learn to cycle, a balance bike can help. Try to avoid overfilling your child's schedule. If you're choosing a childcare provider for your child, look for settings in which carers let children get on with things without being intrusive. If your child has a sibling and they're fighting a lot, see if you can calm things down between them. Promote maturity in your child by encouraging self-care routines.

Anecdotal research/expert advice

▸ **Try other dietary advice.** Choose what to give your child to eat, as well as when and where to give it, but allow your child to choose whether to eat it and how much to eat. Limit snacks. Make mealtimes reasonably consistent, where possible, and avoid eating with the TV on or with other distractions.
▸ **Troubleshoot sleep issues.** Avoid active play near bedtime. If your child needs a snack near bedtime, try offering food that promotes sleep. If your child needs to sleep with the light on, try using a dim night light or a bulb that gives out very little light. If your child is having problems falling asleep, try temporarily delaying bedtime.

CHAPTER 8

LEARNING AND PLAY

Play is the area in which I've struggled most as a parent. When my elder child was still small enough to snooze on my shoulder, I anticipated future problems with sleep or behaviour, but not play. Who finds it difficult to play with their own child? I do. I desperately want to be able to do it and to enjoy it, but there's a yawning chasm where my imaginative play instinct should be. 'Mum, let's pretend…' used to send spikes of dread through my nervous system, unless it involved something easy, like chasing my children and tickling them until they squealed. I remember sitting in my half-sister's kitchen in Whitstable, watching her join in with children's games while mixing them some home-made slime, making pizza dough and chatting to the other grown-ups. I felt a mixture of deep love for her and hot shame that I lacked this skill set, as well as respect for how little slime–pizza cross-contamination she'd achieved.

I've always found it easier to facilitate independent play. Some friends with similar-aged kids once commented, slightly wistfully, on my children's independence. These friends were sceptical at my response, which was something about independence being a natural consequence of a parent whose brain recoiled from messy, free-form play. But it was true, and one more thing to add to my parental shame list (incidents on this list include placing my potty-training toddler on the supermarket packing shelf while I paid for my shopping, with the inevitable denouement).

Ideally, children's learning and play should be a source of delight for parents. This chapter covers free play and outdoor play, the thorny matter of screen time and how to cultivate a love of learning in the most resistant of children. It has been difficult to find high-quality evidence on learning and play for this chapter, because evidence tends to focus on educational settings rather than home ones. There's plenty of research on academic achievement, but research on fostering curiosity and a love of learning is rarer. Little of the reams written on play is of practical use in guiding parents how best to play with their children. (For any research funders reading this, commissioning academics to fill some of these gaps would be a worthy enterprise.)

Outdoor and free play

I make mental notes each time I visit a certain set of friends. They've perfected outdoor play. On any given weekend, there might be a game of stuck-in-the-mud in a field near their house. This is a riff on a game of tag. Anyone who gets tagged must stand still with their legs apart and arms out at the sides. They can be untagged by someone else crawling between their legs. The game is over once everyone is, effectively, stuck in the mud. My children (and I) have spent many happy hours like this. These friends might find a large piece of plastic and a hill, and place a hose on full blast at the top so the kids can bomb down at full speed. They even made it onto a radio show at the height of the pandemic. This followed their voices as they hunted their children across a nearby heath, as part of an elaborate cat-and-mouse game they'd invented.

Children who spend time in parks or countryside are less likely to be depressed when they're older, probably because their familiarity with nature leads them to seek it out as adults. People who spend time in nature as children are more likely to be committed to the environment or to feel close to nature in other ways when they grow up. There may be physical impacts too. I'm quietly proud of the scars on my feet that I got as a ten-year-old on holiday while swimming over hidden rocks. In retrospect, perhaps I could have been more careful in a part of the river known as Suicide Rapids.[1]

Long-term effects may also be seen in what children miss by time spent playing outdoors. I spent a lot of time outside as a child, with no supervision. I made dens in the woods, skimmed stones on the beach and made occasional forays into terrifying military bunkers on the ends of the island. This time I spent outdoors was inversely proportional to my knowledge of popular culture. Such is the extent of my 1980s cultural abyss, friends have a theory that I'm a foreign agent who landed in England in the early 1990s. If they make a reference to Michael Jackson's 'Thriller' or Ferris Bueller and I respond blankly, it's taken as further evidence. I'm trying to catch up now by watching the 1980s back catalogue. I brook no arguments, though, with the opinion that these films have failed to stand the test of time. (My partner loves them. Perhaps you had to be there.)

When children play outdoors, they often try to make themselves scared. A four-year-old might try something new, overcome a fear or feel slightly out of control, perhaps by scaling the top of a climbing frame or spinning on a roundabout. They experience joy and fear at the same time. This kind of play is fun, teaches children to assess risk, increases their ability and confidence, and challenges them to think creatively. It helps their physical and cognitive development. Being in nature also supports children's ability to learn from their environment. When young children are able to engage in unstructured, free play, they're more likely to develop the later ability to regulate their feelings and behaviours.[2]

Living circumstances dictate how easy it is to let children play outdoors freely and with minimal supervision. Wild nature has a bigger impact on well-being than city parks. But while children living in inner cities have limited access to nature, they have more access than suburban children to spaces in which they can play outdoors. Options in towns and cities might be parks, playgrounds, allotments and your street; and in more rural areas, they might involve surrounding countryside, woods, beaches, rivers or nature reserves.

Other possibilities for your child include the gardens of friends or family (if you don't have an outside space yourself), or children's clubs that organise outdoor activities, such as the Scout Association or Girlguiding if you're in the UK. Taking part in school gardening projects has been linked to more scientific learning and healthier eating habits.[3] Outdoor activities can include playground games like hopscotch, kite-flying, jumping in puddles, building dens or throwing snowballs. (Kite-flying should come with a hazard warning, though. I've bought my children three kites in their lifetimes. Each has had precisely one outing before becoming so diabolically tangled that unpicking them would require a minimum of 167.5 hours and the patience of a better human than me.)

Reading your child adventure stories set outside can make playing outdoors more attractive, and children also spend more time outside when their parents encourage them to do so.[4] As with all things, it's best to be balanced in your approach, though. My mum, as a child, was turfed outside after breakfast and told not to come home until dinner time. If you can avoid going to this kind of extreme, it's worth letting children take appropriate risks when playing – being able to get lost, if old enough, or going to the top of a climbing frame. You can teach outdoor safety skills, such as road safety, from an early age, so that children are better able to take risks safely.

A degree of risk is crucial for healthy development. Children need to be able to take risks when playing outdoors, and risk may be what deters parents from letting their children do this. But the risks posed by strangers are small, and commonly believed to be higher than they are. Children are more at risk from someone they know than they are from a stranger. The Royal Canadian Mounted Police, for example, assessed previous cases of child abductions that were logged as having been perpetrated by strangers, and found these so-called strangers were most often acquaintances or family members. None of us wants our child to be the incredibly rare victim – but the chance of this is heavily outweighed, says the research on outdoor play, by the benefits children experience from greater freedom, more movement and working out how they themselves can manage risk. The health risks of being injured while playing are outweighed by the benefits too, according to the research. That tumble out of the tree is worth it.[5]

Age is likely to be important to your risk assessment here. Playing somewhere a child can get lost clearly works better for a ten-year-old than it does a two-year-old. You can encourage your child's independence, if you can't leave them alone safely, by staying discreetly nearby while they play alone or with other children. If you're indoors, you could wait until they are concentrating fully before you gently withdraw from the activity.

Your child or the area in which you live may influence how much you let them play outdoors. A sensible child can probably have a little more freedom than one who sees a shiny balloon and chases it wherever it blows. And children are more likely to play outdoors every day if their parents trust their neighbours to look out for them.[6]

You may also need to modify your rules as the situation changes. Our old house was in the city centre, on a small, scrubby cul-de-sac behind a busy shopping street. There was a gloriously flat piece of asphalt behind our row of houses that was perfect for roller-skating. We decided it was safe to let our girls play there from the age of about seven, on two conditions: first, that they were with a friend, and second, the friend's parents had given permission. Unfortunately, the nature of our road – central, with no through traffic – made it perfect for drug dealing. We had to adapt our street training swiftly the day our older daughter ran into the house saying she'd just seen a deal (it says something about where we lived that she knew what one was) and that she'd filmed it on her phone. I get cold sweats thinking about it.

Boundaries are key when teaching your child to be safe when playing outdoors. You don't want your child to be the other side of a busy road they might struggle to cross safely or somewhere they don't feel safe themselves. In terms of teaching, you can help your child with road skills, drum into them never to go anywhere or accept anything from strangers, and make sure they know their way home. On average, boys are allowed to play outside more, to be out more without an adult around and to go further from home than girls.[7] You may therefore wish, if you have a girl, to give her more freedom than your instinct might allow.

I've found camping trips with posses of other children to be good moments to encourage safe outdoor play. My children were given walkie-talkies a few years ago, meaning they could go out of sight while staying in touch. For a few years, better-intentioned parents than me organised annual class camping trips. The enforced socialising under canvas made me want to escape to the familiar, polluted spaces of the city, but my children loved it. They roamed in packs with torches and marshmallows. I undid all that good, though, by booking a trip with friends – easier company for me, though less exciting for my children – on a June weekend when it was forecast to rain. And rain it did, continuously. The tent started floating. My daughters never want to go camping again.

Whether you are playing outdoors or inside, making your child's days a little less structured leaves more time for free play. It's worth being led by your child when you're playing together. Adult-led activities can squeeze out the time available for free play or limit what your child does. Being child-led can, in some limited circumstances, also be helpful for you. You might want to limit being child-led when it comes to cooking, unless you want to eat tomato spaghetti with cupcakes for every meal.

Finally, it's good to let your child get bored occasionally, as boredom encourages creativity.[8] If your child says they're bored, you could try telling them you have confidence in their ability to find something they'll enjoy doing. This phrase has the added benefit of getting my children to exercise their eye-rolling muscles.

Screens

For many of us, screens come bound up with both utility and guilt. *Octonauts* or Roblox have their benefits when you're trying to write a paper, work out or cook dinner. Cleaning is virtually impossible without screens. My children are mini hurricanes – as soon as one corner of a room is tidy and scrubbed, a book and a pile of crumbs magically appear there. Dirty socks multiply like rabbits under recently wiped-down tables. The other side of the coin is unease that screen time may be damaging to them, at least in the volumes that allow these jobs to be done.

Discussion of children's screen time is often binary. There's either an assumption that more screen time is bad and less is good, or that screens are fine and we should leave children to it. The research paints a slightly more nuanced picture. In general, an extreme amount of screen time doesn't seem to be good for children, but up to two hours a day – an amount that would leave my pre-parent self appalled and my current self intensely relieved – doesn't seem to be too bad.[9] Even this two-hour barrier is frequently vaulted, especially when my kids are on holiday but I am not.

Age is also important, with negative links such as worse fine motor skills and less ability to construct images in the mind's eye seen mainly in younger, preschool children.[10] Children ideally shouldn't be offered screen time below the age of two. While they're still babies, screens don't substitute for real-life chat and play in terms of learning and development. The later the age at which children begin watching screens, the better their language skills tend to be. They might call you out on it, though, if you try to delay screens until adulthood.

A recent study of studies found the increased use of smartphones and tablets by young children to be weakly linked with worse developmental outcomes.[11] It is worth bearing in mind, though, that the studies on which the findings were based tended to be of low quality, and causality wasn't clear. If my child has worse outcomes from lots of screen time, is it because she's not spending the same time reading a book or playing football, or is it because I don't have much time to spend with her, and screens are a side effect of my need for her distraction?

Quality may matter more than time. Discussion of children and screens often focuses on how much time they're spending in front of screens, but the quality of the content they're consuming can be more important. Use of computers in middle childhood has been linked to better achievement at school, and programmes with an educational focus are linked to better language skills. Video games are related to the development of visual–spatial skills and problem-solving skills in children. Children's abilities in this area also have the diminishing effect of making all adults within sight line feel they're turning into their own parents when it comes to technology. When I was younger, my dad could work complex video-editing software but couldn't set a basic timer or – here's a throwback task for you – tune the television without help. I suspect a lack of will rather than ability on his part. But then my kids probably think the same about me when I fail to understand why they'd watch a YouTube video of people playing computer games.[12]

Screens can be negative when the quality of the content is poor, more malevolent dimensions such as junk food advertising or online bullies impinge upon the children using them, or when they get in the way of children's personal space and rest. The real question seems to be not whether children should have access to screens, but instead how children can engage with them in a way that's healthy, fun and supportive of their development.

Children whose parents monitor their screen use and set rules, especially when they're still young, spend less time on screens, are less aggressive and are less likely to view harmful content. Children with smartphones whose parents set related rules and limits are less likely to get harassed online. Monitoring and rule-setting become less appropriate as children approach adolescence, with the greater independence that implies.[13]

Rules for younger children might include:

▶ Limiting your child to two hours' screen time a day, or one hour under the age of five.
▶ Not offering snacks or meals to your child while they're on screens, or at least not regularly.
▶ Keeping your child away from violent or age-inappropriate content, and steering them away if they accidentally come across it.
▶ Not having screens near bedtime.
▶ Keeping screens out of bedrooms, especially at night (as discussed above, having screens in a bedroom, even if they're not used, is linked to poor sleep).

When children watch age-appropriate sitcoms, it can foster their altruism, tolerance and cooperation. Programmes like *Dora the Explorer*, that spark conversation by asking questions of children who are watching, can support learning. Finding programmes containing characters with whom your child can identify is also useful, as young children are more likely to learn from TV programmes when they've developed a relationship with the main character. A 'parasocial' relationship is a one-sided relationship with someone on-screen, with the child feeling they know the character and trust them. These relationships engage children and make them more likely to learn. There's a yellow, Lisa Simpson-shaped reason my daughter decided to learn the saxophone.[14]

I remember an obsession with the 1980s TV programme *ThunderCats* when I was seven, in particular with the character Tygra. (*ThunderCats* is proof that I'm not a foreign agent who bypassed the 1980s after all, although my friends argue I must have taken some cultural studies courses before I landed.) When my children were a similar age, I found some old episodes on YouTube to show them so they could experience the magic for themselves. Unfortunately, like cheese and pineapple hedgehogs, as well as so much else from the 1980s, the Cats didn't stand the test of time. My children have had to develop their own parasocial relationships – ones I'm destined never to understand.

While screens allow parents to get things done and have a break, it can be good to spend some time watching TV with your child or playing video games together, too. Viewing screens together is linked to better language development in children and higher levels of family connection. It also allows your child to laugh at you if you sob at *Coco*, or indeed any programme or film in which somebody dies or cries. Children also spend less time on screens when parents spend more time watching TV with them. This may of course be because parents would rather keep the TV remote hidden than experience the nails-on-blackboard effect of yet another *PAW Patrol* episode.[15]

During quiet times, we have a weekly family film night. Every so often we top up the 'film jar' with a few pieces of folded paper per person, each of which has the name of a film printed on it. One piece of paper is pulled out of the jar each time we watch a film. If everyone contributes ideas, it minimises the risk that you have to watch *Frozen* or *Hamilton* forever. Family weekend rituals spent away from screens – game nights, perhaps, or car boot sales – can reduce the amount of time children spend in front of them. And it's amazing what the opportunity to buy some cactus seeds and a broken watch can do to a child's mood.

If you're worried about your child's screen use or the broader impact of screens on the family, you might want to look at how you engage with screens yourself. Mobile phones, in particular, give away no clues about what the user is doing. Children learn by imitation, but there's little to imitate with a smartphone, other than holding it and looking at it.[16] When parents spend time with their children, they're less able to derive meaning from this time and feel more distracted if they are simultaneously on their phones. Guilt is another factor. I get pangs of conscience when I've lost myself down an online rabbit hole containing critical information on election forecasts, how to reduce my 5K time or reasons my chilli seeds haven't germinated.

There's also a strong link between the amount of time parents and their children spend on screens.[17] If your partner is the one spending hours of their leisure time on screens, though, it leaves you a bit more stuck. 'But Dad's always on screens' is a common refrain in my household.

Scheduling screen-free time for everyone in the family can be useful, if you can manage it with work or other commitments, for instance when you're eating together or talking to each other. This is generally accepted by parents and children alike. My half-sister had a rule with her stepchildren that if a message arrived during a meal and got looked at, the recipient had to read it out to everyone at the table. (If you're waiting on any sensitive messages from friends, it's an amazing incentive to leave your phone alone while you eat. 'Val says her date was joyful and she's feeling extremely well shagged' is going to take some explaining.)

It may not always be better to restrict screens, though. Parents may not have the time or capacity to find alternative activities for their children. Reducing screen time may also cause conflict between parents and children ('But Mum! It's not fair! I didn't realise you were going to ask me to come off screens, and I've only just started watching something'), as well as increasing sibling bickering. I've sometimes found myself on the threshold of asking my kids to come off their screens, considered the likely ensuing battles and stepped smartly away.

Learning

My elder daughter made a bid, aged eight, for an early entry into the Darwin Awards when she ran an experiment to see whether she could get two magnets to stick through her cheek, one on the inside of her mouth and one outside. She came sheepishly downstairs at bedtime to admit that she'd swallowed a magnet. We sent her back to bed, reassuring her it would re-emerge the other end in the form of some literally attractive poo. As soon as she left the room, we both went straight online to check that it was as safe as we'd told her. It wasn't. Five minutes later, I was bundling her into the car to take her to A & E. She was fine – the real damage would have been caused by swallowing two magnets, apparently. These might have tried to find each other as they tracked their way through her intestines. As science experiments go, we awarded her 10 for curiosity and learning, and 0 for sense.

It's worth being generous with your child's errors when they're less potentially lethal. Mispronouncing words shows that the person doing the word-mangling probably learned that word through reading rather than teaching or conversation. This was something my friend Sara kindly pointed out between sniggers when I pronounced albeit as *al-bite* at the grand age of twenty-four, thinking it probably had Germanic roots rather than being a contraction of the more prosaic 'all be it'.

This section covers how to facilitate a love of learning in your child, and what you can do to support them to develop the skills and attitudes to help them learn. I won't pretend that it's going to be possible to foster a love of learning in your child in all areas. I'm never going to persuade my child that she loves learning maths, no matter how hard I try to persuade her of the beauty of a well-designed and functional spreadsheet. Encouraging a more general curiosity about the world seems more realistic, particularly when combined with encouragement of the skills and attitudes needed to answer that curiosity.

Getting your child to learn things can sometimes backfire, like when I realised I couldn't help my children with their long multiplication homework. The method I used when I was at school, and which raised baffled objections from my daughters when I tried to explain it, is gathering dust back in my childhood. My children also graffiti 'learn to write!' on any notes I leave for myself written in what they and many others believe to be illegible scribblings and I insist to myself is precise lettering. Perhaps teaching them old-fashioned respect should have been further up my list.

You probably already know about the value of reading to your child, as well as helping them with numbers. Data from Canada, the United Kingdom and the United States show that parents are less likely to spend time reading to their children or doing number-based activities if they have boys. This finding helps to explain a good proportion of the difference between boys and girls in their reading and maths ability (boys score worse, on average) before they start school. While reading to your child is good at any age, it's particularly effective in fostering a love of learning in children between the ages of three and five.[18]

Parents often reduce their focus on reading once children can read fluently, meaning children read less than they would have done otherwise.[19] Reading aloud to your child, whatever their age, has multiple benefits, as does them reading aloud to you. If you don't have enough time to sit down with your child and concentrate fully, it's best to wait until you do, or they can be put off reading. It's also better not to correct every small error when your child reads to you, tempting as it is to tell your child that *The Guffalo* would be a smellier story. It's more important for the experience to be enjoyable than it is for it to be correct.

Research has shown that children appreciate parents' efforts in reading aloud to them, even if this reading isn't fluent.[20] A lot of the value lies in closeness and a shared experience, and the reading itself doesn't need to be perfect, or even good. This is reassuring for me as an intermittent insomniac. At times of low sleep, I yawn my way through bedtime stories, miss key words and forget where I am on the page. My daughter, who reads along next to me, jubilantly highlights my errors.

It's good to read books yourself, too. Seeing parents read encourages children to read themselves, and children notice when parents don't do as they say. It's a delightful excuse to curl up next to your child on a rainy Saturday. You can also model other things you want your child to pick up from you – you can show your child what it means to be curious, to have diverse interests and to interrogate opinions or theories the media might be presenting as fact.

Your child may be more likely to learn if they see intelligence and ability as things that can be changed with effort, otherwise known as a 'growth mindset'. If your child tells you they can't read a tricky word or they don't understand number lines (me neither), you could tell them they can't do it *yet* – it simply needs some time, work or support from an adult. But although positive links between learning and a growth mindset have been found in previous studies of studies, a recent one suggests there is no causal link once study quality and bias have been taken into account.[21]

'Scaffolding' your child's learning can be helpful. This means supporting them to do tasks that are just beyond their ability to do independently; you provide the scaffold that helps your child to learn. If your child can write letters but not words yet, you could help them learn how to write short and simple words like 'cat' and 'hat', making sure you avoid those beyond their ability. Taking over from a child when they're trying to do something tricky can make them less persistent in future. Symbolic play, in which you and your child use objects or toys to symbolise something else (the banana becomes a phone), can help scaffold learning in younger children.[22]

I had imagined, before a long-term relationship and children, that I was good at giving information and instructions. There is no lack of clarity in the feedback from my partner and children, though, that I'm wrong. Apparently there are layers of implications hidden in my words that are obvious to me and yet may as well be rendered in the Enigma code as far as my family is concerned.

If you are better able than me to be clear, though, it's worth trying to do so when giving your child instructions, and not just to make them more likely to clear the congealing porridge out of their bowl before dumping it the wrong way up in the dishwasher. Knowing what it means to receive clear instructions makes children more likely to seek clarity from their teachers at school when they're unsure about something.[23] If children are used to receiving fuzzy instructions, they're more likely to put up with a lack of clarity in other situations (sorry, kids).

While being clear is a good idea, oversimplifying your language is not. Hearing rich language can be good for development. Expectations are another area to consider, as having high expectations of children is linked to them doing better in school. This should be balanced with not putting too much pressure on them. Your expectations can also affect your child's attitudes and beliefs about their own learning.[24]

If you don't know the answer to something your child asks you, it's best to front up (or perhaps you could employ Google together). Children's learning is predicted by how well their parents answer their questions, independently of parents' education levels or intelligence.[25] Answering a question well means showing your child how to manage when you don't know something, or how to think about broader ideas if you don't know the details. If your child asks you why bees pollinate flowers, you don't need an A level in biology to be able to think about how pollinators support nature to thrive, or how they help us to have food to eat.

Touchscreen devices, such as smartphones and tablets, can support children's learning, with the effect being stronger the older the child. Books, puzzles, blocks and shapes are good things to have around to support learning, too – charity shops can be a good source of these. Having resources like these available at home can help young children who struggle with maths to be better at it a year later. Number games and easy sums are also linked to later maths ability and understanding in young children.[26]

Children do better at school when they have a good relationship with their parents and friends, and when they're not constantly fighting with siblings or experiencing bullying (Chapter 5). Aggressive behaviour is linked to children doing worse at school (Chapter 6), and children tend to do better when their mental health is good (Chapter 9).

Learning a musical instrument, if that's something available to your family, is one of the few things that has been shown to boost IQ, as well as making children more conscientious, more ambitious, and more open to new ideas and experiences. Music training can support the development of mental processes and skills, and can support children to be able to recognise and distinguish between different sounds. I can also tell you that saxophones are louder than you think and (drawing on the experience of friends) to be grateful if your child doesn't want to learn the drums. If you're in the UK and on a low income, many councils run heavily subsidised schemes to help children learn an instrument.[27]

I'm going to look at two areas more specifically – teaching children how to be good with money, and teaching them how to do chores. Considering your past (or perhaps current) relationships may demonstrate why these are undervalued as life skills. People are more likely to have healthy financial attitudes and behaviours as adults if their parents have supported their financial learning as kids.[28] Teaching children how to budget and encouraging them to save help them to be better at managing their money.

If you can afford to do so, it's worth giving your child pocket money. Children who have been given pocket money throughout their childhood are more likely to manage money well by the time they reach adulthood.[29] It's also a good test of whether you can avoid stepping in when your child wants to spend all their money on something you find utterly useless. There's a drawer in our house full of scented pencils and erasers standing as testament to me resisting the temptation to intervene.

On chores, the first point is to make sure you're being fair in your allocation. Girls do more household chores than boys do.[30] As someone with two daughters, I can't test whether my chore allocation would be equal if I had sons. I'd like to think it would be, but these decisions may be biased by culture. Bringing these potential distortions into full sunlight is a first step in uprooting them.

Once you've decided (either solo or as part of a family meeting) what your child will be doing, you are more likely to shift them out of mutinous dissent if you present any jobs you give them as helping, not chores. Children are motivated to assist others. Chores, on the other hand, don't feel particularly inspiring. Tying chores to pocket money is unlikely to work in the long term.[31] If children help out because it's the right thing to do, they're more likely to take responsibility for things when they get older, instead of waiting to get paid first. In the short term, kids may also be more likely to say no to certain jobs if they're getting paid to do them. If my child fancies stacking the dishwasher less than she fancies getting her pocket money, she may well walk away. If it's an unpaid expectation that she'll stack the dishwasher, it's harder for her to do this.

I've noticed with my own children that predictability and fairness are key. If there's prior notice of a chore and it happens reliably every day or every week, serious resistance is temporary. Eye-rolling and muttering may be a permanent consequence, of course, no matter how predictable you've been. And if one child believes the other child is getting off more lightly when it comes to chores, the gates of hell are opened.

CHAPTER CHECKLIST

High-quality research

▶ **Don't be afraid of risky outdoor play.** Let children take appropriate risks when playing – allow them to get lost safely or go to the top of a climbing frame. If your child's school has a gardening project, encourage them to enrol. Make sure girls have as much opportunity as boys to play outside; you're more likely to give your child freedom to play outdoors if you have a boy.

▶ **Frame your thinking and language.** Have high expectations of your child. Encourage your child to see intelligence and ability as things that can be changed with effort (despite research controversies, it's unlikely to hurt). Don't oversimplify your language when talking to your child.

▶ **Spend time on basic skills.** Read with your child and help them with numbers. Make sure you give boys as much opportunity as girls; parents are less likely to do this with sons.

▶ **And facilitate trickier ones.** Encourage your child to learn a musical instrument, if that's something available to your family.

▶ **Have some rules around screens.** If your child is still very young, try to delay the point at which they start to have regular screen time. Monitor your child's screen use and set rules, especially with younger children. Spend some time watching TV with your child or otherwise interacting with them while they're on screens. Let your child use touchscreen devices to support their learning. Don't let your child have screens near bedtime. Limit your child to two hours' screen time a day, at most. Keep phones, televisions and other screens out of your child's bedroom, especially at night. Try not to offer snacks or meals to your child while they're having screens, or at least not regularly.

▶ **Support your child in other areas.** Consider whether there's anything you can do to support your child's relationships (see Chapter 5), behaviour (Chapter 6) and well-being (see Chapter 9). These all link to learning and play.

Moderate-quality research

▶ **Be curious together.** Try to answer your child's questions correctly and, if you don't know the answer, it's best to say so – or perhaps you could search online together. If you need to give your child instructions, make sure you're clear. If you can avoid it, don't take over from your child when they're trying to do a tricky task. Try to get toys and activities that support your child's learning, such as books, puzzles, blocks and shapes. Help 'scaffold' your child's learning, supporting them to do tasks that are just beyond their ability to do independently.

▶ **Know your weak spots.** If you're not interested in science yourself, make an extra effort to do science-related activities with your child – for instance planting seeds under different conditions to see how they fare.

▶ **Think about your needs and how routine/surroundings can support your child's learning and play.** Look after your own well-being (see Chapter 1). Try to do some regular activities as a family at the weekends. Declutter.

▶ **Be realistic about screens.** They aren't always bad, and sometimes it's better for the family not to restrict them. Make sure your child isn't accessing content that's inappropriate for their age, and avoid violent content. Set clear rules about gaming, but don't be controlling. If your older child has a mobile phone, make sure you're keeping an eye on their mobile phone use. If you're worried about the amount of time your child is spending on screens, look at your own screen use.

▶ **Go outside.** Encourage your child to play outdoors. If you live in a city, try to access the countryside with your child when you can.

Anecdotal research/expert advice

▶ **Challenge your expectations and teach necessary skills.** Be aware that your own expectations can affect your child's attitudes and beliefs about their own learning. Teach outdoor safety skills, such as road safety, from an early age.

▶ **Consider the content of the screens your child watches.** If your child is young, try to encourage them towards programmes like *Dora the*

Explorer that stimulate conversation by asking questions of children who are watching. Sitcoms aimed at children also tend to be positive.

- **Aim for variety in what you do together, and prepare.** Try a range of activities with your child and dress for the weather. Try reading your child adventure stories set outside.
- **Be led by your child sometimes.** Encourage your child's independence. Be led by your child when playing together, rather than trying to suggest or lead activities yourself. Try to make your child's days a little less structured.
- **Think about balance.** Consider how screen time balances with the time your child spends doing other things, such as time with other people, exercise and time outdoors.

CHAPTER 9

HAPPINESS AND WELL-BEING

My happiest childhood summer was my tenth. My dad was working on a television programme in Canada called *The Turkey* that, aptly, never got off the ground. My mum and I joined him there for the length of my summer holidays. We stayed in his producer's wooden cabin on the pine-shaded shores of Stony Lake. A girl my age was staying in the cabin next door, and our friendship was forged under the blazing Ontario sun. We dived and swam. We paddled up creeks in canoes. We salted fleshy leeches off our tender skin. We ate fruit with bowls of vanilla ice cream. We read Archie comics by torchlight, and we laughed. There was so much warmth, literal and metaphorical, in that holiday. Thinking now about what made that summer such a joyful one, it had some key ingredients for happiness and well-being: connection, exercise, nature, deep sleep and – the research won't tell you about this last one, but it's true – the gluttonous consumption of wild blueberries.

This chapter covers well-being, resilience and self-esteem. There's a troubleshooting section at the end for parents of children who are feeling worried or sad. Supporting children's happiness and well-being is probably one of the most important parts of this book. It's a particular concern given the isolation that most children experienced during the coronavirus pandemic. Covid-19 won't be too much of an issue for children who were born after national lockdowns, but anyone whose child had to miss nursery, school, family or mixing with other children will recognise its impact. Even outside the context of the pandemic, children's happiness and well-being have been falling for a long time in lots of countries. Many causes of this are outside parents' control, making the areas we can influence even more important.

As with behavioural conditions, this book doesn't cover diagnosable mental health conditions. If you think your child is suffering from clinical anxiety or depression, you should seek medical advice or psychological support.

Well-being and mental health

Like all children, my own have had periods where everything is right with the world and others in which they're laid low by sadness or worry. They may be open about the reasons for this, but sometimes it's a guessing game or a process of elimination. At other times, I only realise afterwards that they've been dealing with difficult feelings. Well-being is complex and highly nuanced, and at any one moment your child may need something different from you than they have done previously.

There are two main components to supporting children's well-being and mental health. The Agatha Christie part involves working out when children are unhappy or worried, and helping them to feel better. The Mary Poppins part involves being proactive about well-being and working out what we can do to support our children to be mostly well and happy. No child can or should be happy all the time – developing resilience to life's knocks is also important. Resilience is covered later in this chapter.

While parenting can play a role in your child's mental health and well-being, your influence has limits. What happens at school affects well-being, as children of school age spend so much of their week there. Within schools, factors such as bullying and friendships have a bigger effect on well-being than the type of school your child attends. Girls have worse mental health, on average, than boys.[1]

Those who grow up in cities are also more likely to have poor mental health than children who grow up rurally. There may be a few reasons for this. Green space, which is hard to come by in cities, is critical for children's well-being. Traffic noise and air pollution both negatively affect mental health. Parents may be less likely to let their children go outside in built-up areas, particularly if those parents are working long hours. And children are more likely to live in areas with social problems, such as high crime levels, if they live in a city. Within cities, children living in more spacious, suburban areas with lots of out-of-school activities on offer have, on average, better mental health.[2]

So much of children's well-being also depends on national and local policy, which affects whether children have access to green space, playgrounds or safe bike paths. In my previous home, I had five playgrounds within walking distance, but they were all a little over a mile away in different directions. This is fine on a weekend when you have the time and the means to propel a child who is too small to walk there and back; a scooter with a pull cord fashioned out of a scarf is underrated as a mode of transport. It's less useful during a working week. If you pick up your child at 5.30 p.m and want them to stretch their legs before dinner, a two-and-a-half-mile round trip is a hefty obstacle.

Crime rates were also high. The first time we began to think seriously about moving was when my daughter was woken by the sound of screaming after a drug deal had gone wrong outside. She was terrified. A few nights later, we were woken by armed police stopping a car outside our front door. We were lucky to have the option to move – many people don't. We're now on the edges of the city, with easy access to nature, and my children desperately miss being in the centre of everything. The lesson I take from this is that wherever you live, there will be upsides as well as downsides. The key is going to be making the most of what you have available to you.

Your child isn't necessarily the best judge of what's going to make them happy. My own children believe their lives would be perfect if they had limitless access to sugar and screens, never had to do any chores and were given a hamster, two ferrets and a pet pig. If nothing else, this is teaching them valuable campaigning skills and a life lesson that not all campaigns are successful. As with other parts of this book, the ideas given here may be more or less suitable for different children. You will know what's most likely to work for your child. Alternatively, you will soon find out, as I did when my attempts to steer one of my children towards mindfulness and strenuous exercise were vigorously rejected.

Physical activity is linked with good mental health (see Chapter 7), while sedentary behaviour is linked with the opposite. Lots of time spent watching television or playing video games is connected to worse well-being in children, but this link may be more about time being inactive than about screens themselves. I know that my chances of encouraging my children out of an armchair when they're engrossed in a TV programme or even a book, without having an alternative activity to offer them, are like my chances of winning a 1980s music round at a pub quiz: minimal. Going to the park to meet one of their friends is a more successful strategy.

Activity in natural environments can have positive effects on both mood and self-esteem. Being near water – a river, a lake or the sea – can be particularly helpful for mental health. Getting into nature can be hard if you live in a city, though you may have canals, parks or city farms you can access. It can be good to give children greater independence to play outdoors and explore, away from their house or flat. Children have less freedom to ride bikes or go to the park without adults than they had in the past. This limits their sense of place and negatively affects their well-being.[3]

Other sections of this book likely to help in supporting your child's well-being and mental health are on sleep (Chapter 7) and relationships (Chapter 5). Having good friends can help to compensate for any parenting shortcomings when it comes to your children's mental health. This knowledge has been consoling when my partner or I are going through a patch of suboptimal parenting.

Helping your child manage their emotions (Chapter 4), for instance by encouraging them to express feelings of anger constructively, is worth particular attention. Children who suppress their angry feelings tend to have poorer mental health. Trying to work out what's going on in your child's head, beyond the obvious, may be worth your time – it can make you a more competent parent, which in turn supports your child's well-being. Parents can help children digest news and world events in an emotionally healthy way by talking about what is happening, including what's good and what's bad about it, being clear about potential bias in news sources and guiding children to feel OK about what has happened.[4]

Self-compassion is something to cultivate in your child. There's some evidence to show that mindfulness-based interventions may help children develop greater self-compassion, but this evidence isn't that strong, despite being highlighted in a study of studies. You can also help your child develop active coping mechanisms by talking about problems, working out potential solutions, taking part in relaxing activities such as listening to music, or doing exercise to help deal with stress. Children who use these kinds of strategies to deal with problems tend to have higher levels of well-being than other children.[5]

As discussed in Chapter 7, children's mental health is better when they're eating a healthy diet with not too much in the way of highly processed food. This is hard when kids tend to favour food like pizza, chips and fish fingers. The Nigellas reading this may make these from scratch, avoiding the factory processing, but who among us has the two hours needed to prove pizza dough more than occasionally? It's probably more realistic to accept that kids are sometimes going to eat processed food, but to get in the fresh food where you can.

Your child is likely to have better mental health if you're looking after your own well-being (Chapter 1). There may be areas of your well-being you can't control, of course. I've certainly had periods in which work stress and high levels of underlying anxiety have corroded the veneer of competence that cloaks my parenting. There will still be things you can do, though, to help your child; for example, if you suffer from depression, you can make sure your child knows it's not their fault. Children with a depressed parent, and who blame themselves for how their parent feels, are more likely to suffer from poor mental health.[6] As an adult you may know they are blameless, and assume they realise this too, but children's minds have an uncanny ability to fabricate stories to plug an information gap.

Be aware that your beliefs may also contribute to your child's well-being. Children, and especially boys, experience better mental health – and, in particular, less social anxiety – when their parents believe intelligence can be changed through effort. Your child's well-being may also be affected by specific issues. Children who witness racism against other people of their own race are more at risk of poor mental health than other children, for example.[7]

In families who don't live together, children tend to do better when they have a good relationship with the parent who isn't living with them, and when there are lots of different types of involvement.[8] You might go on walks, have movie nights and visit grandparents together. It's also important to place children at the centre of any activities. The actual amount of contact children have with their non-resident parent doesn't seem to affect their well-being. Don't stress too much if you don't have much time with your child – it's the quality of the time you spend together that's important.

Parents may worry about the effects of childcare on their children's well-being. This is an emotive issue, and one that has often been weaponised for clickbait headlines. A recent study of studies shows a short-term negative impact on children's well-being, as measured by levels of the stress hormone cortisol by the afternoon of a day in care. The impact on well-being in home-based childcare settings is less when they are of high quality, with sensitive, attuned staff. Parents may also want to consider some of the beneficial effects of high-quality childcare when thinking about these findings, which include social competence and learning. And it goes without saying that childcare is often essential. The needs of parents and the wider family have to be taken into account, too.[9]

The quality of a childcare setting is clearly important to children's outcomes. A high-quality centre should have plenty of staff for the number of children, several small rooms with a few children in each – rather than one big room containing a cacophony of children – and staff who are sensitive and responsive to the children's needs. When I first put my younger daughter in nursery, she was miserable. I should have heeded the staff's lack of engagement and the complete absence of any kind of system. After a week of being told that my daughter had refused to eat anything that day, I pulled her out of nursery and into the warm, capable hands of a childminder. She immediately started eating again and seemed back to her usual self. When she was a bit older, she started at a different nursery. This nursery was in a tiny, rough-around-the-edges building where the ceilings were so low they felt they were closing in and the 'garden' was five square metres of sand, but everyone there knew my daughter's name, each room had a maximum of five kids, and warmth and care were paramount. If there's a negative impact on your child of putting them into one day-care setting, you'll probably notice, and if you live somewhere big enough, you'll have the option to move them elsewhere.

If you're very concerned about your child's mental health, you may want to seek professional support, but children's mental health services can be hard to access. In the UK, up to 75% of referrals are turned down – and, for those who are accepted, children can wait for two hundred days for treatment. If you're in the UK, you can get a referral to Child and Adolescent Mental Health Services (CAMHS) through your GP or your child's teacher. You can also make a direct referral yourself by contacting your local CAMHS service. If you haven't been able to access real-life support and are concerned about your child's welfare, online or similar resources can be effective. A range of resources is available on the CAMHS website.[10]

Resilience

Resilient children respond to challenges by being proactive. They're realistic about what they can influence versus what's out of their control. They find it easier than other children to adapt to new and challenging situations. Children with resilience tend to feel appreciated, are able to set realistic goals and solve problems, and recognise their strengths while seeing weaknesses not as fixed character traits but as areas that can be worked on. They are able to interact well and comfortably with friends and adults.

Children can be resilient in different ways. I was physically resilient as a child, as holidays spent cycling thirty miles a day across windswept, rain-drenched flatlands can attest. My parents cultivated this resilience by tying it to my competitive nature – they assigned points to the first person who could spot a windmill emerging into view on the endless horizon. This is harder than it sounds when you're hunched over a set of handlebars trying to blink the raindrops out of your lashes. They also smartly dropped their usual rules on sweet food by pretending they hadn't seen the sugar lumps I swallowed when we stopped for coffee.

I was also resilient when it came to knotty maths problems or exam revision. When it came to personal criticism, though, my resilience matched the underbelly of a soft-shelled crab in my assumption that what other people thought of me must be true. One child can show resilience in how brilliantly they can adapt to life in a new country but may lack resilience in being able to finish a task. Another may win cross-country races but worry frantically about problems they can't control. Resilience can also vary according to how well resourced children feel at a given time. Even today, I know my resilience levels can falter if I'm under-slept or I've had a row with someone I love.

Resilient children are better able to deal with stress. What children define as being stressful depends on the child and on the cultural expectations of those around them.[11] And because a child copes in some ways, it doesn't mean they're able to cope in others. It's important to be mindful of the type and extent of stress in your child's life, and to support them in areas they may not be managing well by themselves. One child may find it stressful to be asked to do something new with little warning. Another might feel stressed by travel or school. There are some stresses – including illness, poverty and losing someone they love – that will land a blow to the resilience of the most assured child.

Children can cope in various ways when stressful things happen to them. They can cope actively by problem-solving or thinking positively. They can cope in an avoidant way by repressing feelings or by wishful thinking ('If only I had nicer friends'). They can seek support from somebody who can help them manage their feelings or develop a plan of action. Finally, they can distract themselves by focusing on something else or taking part in an activity, such as sport, that can help them release their feelings. Children who use active coping mechanisms are less likely to misbehave than other children, and they're more socially competent. Active coping mechanisms are only appropriate for situations your child can control, though – perhaps they keep handing in homework late or worrying about things that aren't likely to happen. Using active coping strategies in other situations can cause difficulties.[12]

There's a lack of good-quality evidence on resilience, as it hasn't been clearly defined by researchers in a way that allows it to be compared across studies. Resilience is also complex. There are lots of different influences on its development in children, and these influences work together in ways not yet entirely understood. Simple ideas and recommendations are therefore hard to draw out.

A lack of resilience can show itself in the form of anxiety or depression, so there's some overlap between this section and the contents of the rest of this chapter. There are also sections elsewhere in the book that support resilience – self-esteem (in the next section) and relationships (Chapter 5). Support from extended family and friends can help children to develop this skill. This is what children missed so much over the worst months of the pandemic. Resilience is higher, too, says the research, in children who spend time in nature (Chapter 8).[13] Personal experience says this is temporarily untrue if your daughter falls into a muddy stream from a rope swing in January and you're a forty-minute walk from a change of clothes. It remains untrue if your other daughter does the same thing a year later.

Children need to experience stress that's appropriate for their age and level of development, and that you know they are able to manage. Being able to cope with stressful experiences is a skill. Protecting children from these experiences altogether makes them less resilient to stress when you're not there to shield them from it. Children are naturally exposed to healthy levels of stress through experiences such as starting school, meeting new people or being told they can't do something they want. These experiences aren't usually too difficult for them, in part because they're over quickly. Having cursory, limited exposure to stress can help children learn and develop in a positive way. It's particularly helpful if parents can encourage the use of active coping strategies and help children feel they've got the hang of a new or tricky situation.

Imagine that my child needs an injection. In Scenario A, I'm so stressed myself by the idea of her being hurt that I have to leave the room. She's left to cope alone, knowing that I'm terrified and leaving her with a lifelong fear of needles. (Scenario A happened to a friend of mine as a child. She eventually got hypnotherapy so she could inject herself with the needles that allowed her to do IVF and become pregnant with her own child. The echoes of her original experience sounded long into her future.) In Scenario B, I do everything I can to minimise the stress for my child. I bring her a tablet and headphones so she's oblivious to what's happening. Scenario B does nothing for her. She's not exposed to any healthy stress, as I've protected her from it entirely. When she later has medical procedures and I'm not there, she won't know how to cope with it. In Scenario C, she knows she's being injected, but I'm there chatting to her about other things – perhaps her favourite television show or what we're going to do at the weekend. Importantly, I'm not showing her any of my own anxiety. It's this time-limited exposure to healthy stress, supported by an adult, that helps children develop resilience.

Part of developing resilience is making clear to your child that you believe they're capable of coping with stress. This message can be underlined by accepting their feelings and encouraging them in their efforts. I remember the start of secondary school being hard both because it was intense – I learned more in my first term there than I had in the whole time at my breathtakingly crap primary school – and because I was travelling for three hours a day. My parents made it clear they thought I could cope, so I did.

Helping children frame stressful situations as challenges, not catastrophes, can make them appear more manageable. A stressful scenario can also be presented as something from which they may gain in the longer term. If your child has a test coming up at school and feels worried about it, you could talk about how practice doing tests can help them to feel less stressful in future. Children may also need your help to work out when they're likely to face challenges. Stress is easier to cope with when it's predictable than when it lands with no warning bell.

Children need to understand when they can do something about a situation (for instance, practising more if they're finding something tricky) and when to accept it (such as when schools close due to a global pandemic). In some stressful situations, children have control. In others, they don't. When situations are out of children's control, any negative impact can be reduced by discussing the situation to help them make sense of it and put things into perspective. It's also important to help your child understand when a source of stress can be ignored and when they should get help. A lost eraser is less of an issue than a lost pair of glasses. A one-off incident of teasing by somebody they're unlikely to see again is less of a potential issue than persistent bullying.

You can foster resilience in your child by demonstrating healthy ways of coping when you encounter something stressful yourself. Your child needs to be shown positive examples of how to cope, and will look to you to provide these. As becoming a mass of reverberating stress isn't quite the model I'm after for my children – if I were an object, I'd be a tuning fork vibrating to the note of A – this is something I'm working on.

If you struggle in this area too, it's worth trying to understand your coping style, as well as your child's. In the absence of professional support, you could look at the types of coping described earlier in the chapter (active, avoidant, support-seeking and distraction). You could also consider how you might be able to cope more actively and access support from other people. For my part, I know I'm good at problem-solving and finding physical outlets for stress, like running or cycling. I also know I tend to catastrophise and ruminate about problems I can't solve. My job is to work out how to bring myself back to the present so I can help my children do the same.

Children's resilience can be supported by positive experiences in Scout groups, sports clubs and the like.[14] My friends' son plays rugby every Saturday. Afterwards, he goes to their local swimming pool, which has trapezes and rope swings set up over the water. These friends credit their son's experience of playing sport and being active with his uncomplicated, robust approach to life and an ability to deal cheerfully with whatever is thrown at him (not just rugby balls).

You can cultivate resilience by showing your child empathy or working to see a given situation through their eyes. It can also help to highlight your child's strengths. Believing they have skills that other people value helps make children more resilient. Having realistic expectations of your child is important, too. Expecting too much can make children feel they're constantly failing. Expecting too little of children, on the other hand, can mean they never push themselves far enough to make mistakes. In the words of Elizabeth Day on her brilliant podcast *How to Fail*, 'Learning how to fail in life actually means learning how to succeed better.' If children don't make mistakes, they can't learn from them. Having low expectations also risks children believing that you don't think they're good at things. Realistic expectations foster resilience.[15]

If you're concerned about your child's ability to be resilient, you could try enrolling them on a mindfulness-based cognitive therapy programme, if that's available to you. While a sensitive child may be more vulnerable to stress, they're likely to benefit from supportive experiences more than another child might. Authoritative parenting (being warm and accepting of your child, while having clear rules that are consistently enforced; see the Introduction) can be particularly helpful for highly sensitive children. It may also be helpful to see your child as being sensitive, not oversensitive. The 'over' implies a judgement that it's a bad thing, but it may be a marker that your child will be an empathetic adult who sparks some good in the world. From your child's perspective, personality traits are better accepted than scored as too much or too little. Instead, it may be more helpful to work out how you can help your child with the rough edges of these.

Something as simple as a weekly family meeting can be an alternative. Each member of the family can bring their child-appropriate problems to this meeting. Working together to solve problems can help strengthen children's abilities in this area. Telling them what to do, or even giving them gentle advice, can rob children of the opportunity to practise problem-solving, undermining their potential to be resilient.

Self-esteem

Self-esteem represents how someone feels about their worth as a person. It's based on two main things in kids: feeling they're good at things they value, whether that's schoolwork, sport, music or another hobby; and feeling supported by parents, friends and other important individuals. This is where this book gets tricky for me. Self-esteem is my bête noire when I'm writing about things to do with childhood and parenting. My professional self-esteem has always been high, a level that was first set by an entertaining, complex waitressing job as a teenager and a brilliant boss who made me feel clever and capable. My personal self-esteem, though, is a shameful, creeping creature, like Gollum in *Lord of the Rings* after the ring has started to corrupt him. My experience of being bullied and dismissed as boring is my own Isildur's Bane. For whatever reason, this label – let me refer you back to my total lack of knowledge of the 1980s – stuck. And no matter how much evidence I gather to the contrary, being boring to others is a deep-seated fear that underpins every conversation I have.

As my examples can attest, self-esteem can vary according to what's being measured. One child may have high self-esteem relating to character, responsibility and academic achievement while at the same time feeling insecure about their athletic ability and appearance. For another, these levels may be flipped. Boys tend to rate themselves better in athletic ability and girls in personal character. One study found that girls and boys had similar self-esteem relating to body image in the early stages of school, but girls' body image was worse than boys' by the age of ten.[16]

Researchers have divided self-esteem into two types. The first type is explicit self-esteem, measured by how people describe themselves. If you're Donald Trump, you might characterise yourself as a top human who did a VERY GOOD JOB. The second type is implicit self-esteem, which is more unconscious. One way of measuring implicit self-esteem is to look at how much people prefer the letters of their own name when compared with other letters from the alphabet. It's possible for children to have high levels of explicit self-esteem while having low levels of implicit self-esteem. It's these children who are most likely to show narcissism. They have high levels of self-belief on the surface, while being deeply insecure.[17]

Supporting children's self-esteem and bolstering it where necessary are crucial jobs for parents. You may, like me, prioritise these even more if your own self-esteem is shaky. Occasionally, when my younger daughter tells me confidently how great and prodigiously talented she is, I worry that I may have taken this pursuit too far.

As with other areas of mental health, both sleep and exercise (Chapter 7) play an important role in children's self-esteem. Exercise may require a little more than simple encouragement, though, as low self-esteem can be a barrier to children being more physically active. Enabling your child to play in nature (Chapter 8) and supporting their relationships (Chapter 5) are likely to help, too. Bullying is worth watching for – low self-esteem puts children at greater risk of being bullied, and being bullied in turn undermines their self-esteem.

Unconditional acceptance is a key ingredient in children's self-esteem. This mean showing you love them, whatever their behaviour, and not imposing your own standards on them. It's even better if your child doesn't need to call you out on this last point, as mine has done: 'Mum. I'm ten. I can't possibly be expected to clear up after myself to your standards.' Unconditional acceptance means recognising and validating your child's feelings, including ones you might find difficult. (It doesn't necessarily mean accepting how they show this anger or other feelings. You don't need to condone things being thrown across the room.) It also means showing your child how important you think they are. One parenting and family expert suggests telling your child things like 'I enjoy being with you,' 'You're important,' 'I'm glad I'm with you,' and 'I'm lucky to know you.'[18] The response of my youngest to this last statement, returning to the fact I may have tipped the self-esteem scales a little too far in the opposite direction, would be 'Yes. You are.' Unconditional acceptance is easier when you're well slept and your child is treating you like a human rather than just a supplier of food, clean laundry and lifts.

Using praise or feedback appropriately is important in the development of self-esteem. As mentioned in Chapter 6, parents should praise children for what they do, not who they are, and make sure feedback is realistic. When your child shows you a drawing, it's good to say what you like about it while being careful not to overpraise it. Overpraise can risk the development of narcissistic traits in children with high self-esteem.[19]

Parents tend to give children with low self-esteem lots of praise for their personal qualities in an attempt to bolster their confidence, but this can backfire and further damage fragile self-esteem. It can lead children to believe that if they don't manage to do something, it's a result of who they are as a person, rather than the result of an action they have (or haven't) taken.[20] Praise given to children with low self-esteem should therefore be realistic and focused more on what they do than on who they are. Examples might include 'I'm proud of the way you did that,' 'Nice job,' or 'Thank you for being so patient.'

You can also bolster self-esteem by continually reinforcing the message that your child is capable. This could be in response to something small, like being able to pick up a cup without spilling the drink inside it, or something big, like constructing a detailed model for a school project. Supporting your child to focus on their own growth, avoiding comparisons to other people, can also help. Achievements are best measured by what your child can do compared with what they could do last week or last year, not what they can do compared with their siblings or their friends. 'You've really learned how to paint shadows – they've come on so much in the last few weeks,' not 'You've really learned how to paint shadows. I bet your friends can't paint them as well yet.'

In general, it's better to talk about what to do than what not to do. But if you do find you need to give a negative message to your child, one that requires you to say what you don't want them to do, telling them why not and giving them an alternative can help them feel capable and build self-esteem. You might say 'Please don't bang your cup on the table. It might spill if you do that. Put it down carefully, like this, instead.' As with praise, any negative messages should be focused on your child's actions, not who they are.

If your child's interested in lots of different things, it's good to support them to pursue more than one interest, if practically and financially feasible. This means that if children feel they're failing in one area, they have other things to support their sense of self-worth. My daughter got turned down by the local surf life-saving club as her front crawl wasn't strong enough. After an evening of mild wobbles, she was able to stop caring so much. I suspect her music and aerial circus class gave her a stable base from which to handle this rejection with reasonable equanimity.

On the question of how to raise children with high levels of self-esteem while avoiding narcissism, achieving a balance means giving children realistic feedback while not over-praising them; helping them to focus on their own growth, not on beating or outperforming other people; accepting children for who they are, including when they fail; and not showing disappointment when children don't meet parents' standards.

My partner is a product of an upbringing that finely planed such an approach. My mother-in-law was a health visitor who'd read every book on child development she could find. She developed her own theory on raising children that centred around the idea that if parents' needs were met, their children would likely be fine, too. My partner was loved and accepted no matter what his behaviour. This was impressive, given that incidents included the fire brigade being called out after he'd blown the roof off his garden shed. Don't play with matches around petrol canisters, kids. It seems that Darwin Awards eligibility is another thing to run in the family. This acceptance by his parents was often demonstrated after an initial blow-up between them. They still have fiery rows. As someone brought up in a household in which conflict went unspoken, these rows make me want a turtle shell so that I can disappear until they're done – but they blaze quickly. Once they're over, the closeness and acceptance are palpable again.

Nobody else's approval is needed for my partner to feel OK. Approximately 97% of the time, he's confident without being arrogant. If someone around him is in a terrible mood, he doesn't assume it's his fault. His own self-belief makes him good at understanding people's flaws, and even valuing them. I'm not sure his family entirely followed the blueprint of this book when he was growing up – there was too much fighting for that, even though its resolution was a beautiful thing. His story shows, though, that there are different ways of moulding a healthy, balanced, independent human.

Troubleshooting mental health concerns

Anxiety and sadness are included in this section in a non-clinical sense. The advice here is for children who are worried or sad. If your child is clinically anxious or depressed, professional support is advised.

Anxiety and stress

At the start of the pandemic lockdowns and school closures, one of my daughters seemed fine. She was spending quite a bit of time in her room, but she was getting to an age where this seemed normal. I wasn't too concerned. I also wanted to respect the boundaries she had set. Later, her worry, sadness and loneliness came pouring out. In that moment, I realised I'd got it wrong. My daughter would have felt less alone with her worries if we'd wrapped our family web around her more, and if we'd spun it so that she could intersperse her sorely needed space with more of our company. We started to course-correct.

Fears are normal in children, and don't necessarily mean your child is unusually anxious. The table overleaf shows common fears at different ages.

It may be unwise to assume that fear is irrational. My dad used to tell a story about a time before I was born, when my half-sister Catherine was staying. She crept into the kitchen and told him there was something moving under her bed. 'Don't be silly, Catherine. No there isn't. Go back to sleep,' he told her. This happened two or three more times before he went through with a torch to prove to her that there was absolutely nothing to fear. He found a corpse of a bird that a cat had brought in. It was heaving with maggots. My sister was vindicated.

12. NORMAL FEARS[21]

	AGE 2	AGE 2–3	AGE 5	AGE 6	AGE 7–8	AGE 9–10
Loud noises	◆					
Large objects	◆					
Changes in the house	◆					
Animals	◆	◆	◆			
Separation	◆	◆	◆	◆		
Dark	◆	◆	◆	◆	◆	
Masks		◆				
Noises at night		◆				
Bad people			◆			
Bodily harm/injury			◆	◆	◆	◆
Sleeping alone				◆		
Staying alone				◆	◆	
Supernatural beings				◆	◆	
Thunder and lightning				◆	◆	◆
Tests/school performance						◆
Physical appearance						◆
Death						◆

Anxiety in children is most often the crystallisation of several factors; it is rare for it to be caused by a single thing. While parenting can contribute to children's anxiety, this impact is very small. Many things that influence children's stress and anxiety, such as how violent their neighbourhoods are or whether their parents are getting divorced, are not particularly controllable. Stress is also an inevitable part of life. If your child's anxious or feeling stressed, you may be better off supporting them with those feelings than removing the cause.[22]

Sometimes it's not obvious that your child is feeling anxious, and you may need to look out for other physical or behaviour signals. Children who are irritable may, in fact, be anxious.[23] Anxiety, through having to focus on a particular threat and how to avoid it, can be tiring for children. It can leave them feeling grouchy and unable to concentrate on other things. Children who are both anxious and irritable tend to suffer worse with anxiety than children who are merely anxious. Other signs that your child may be anxious include physical symptoms such as headaches, tiredness and trouble sleeping; behavioural symptoms such as fidgeting, crying and clinging; and signs of avoidance, such as wanting to stay off school or – for those who find social situations stressful – avoiding eye contact.

13. SIGNS OF ANXIETY

PHYSICAL SIGNS	BEHAVIOURAL SIGNS
Trouble sleeping	Irritable
Headaches	Has safety rituals
Feels sick, stomach aches, etc.	Fidgets
Feels sweaty	Paces
Rapid heartbeat	Cries
Difficulty concentrating	Clings
	Shakes
	Freezes
	Direct avoidance (e.g. dark rooms)
	Subtle avoidance (e.g. eye contact)

When asked to describe what they think and feel when something stressful happens, the most common feelings children describe are anger, worry, sadness, nervousness and fear. The top physical symptoms are headaches, stomach aches, feeling sweaty, having a fast heartbeat and feeling sick. Shy children are more likely to be anxious than other children. Those with learning disabilities are also more likely to be anxious, as they tend to experience more stress. When children are presented with something threatening, anxious children are more likely to identify information that confirms their fears.[24]

Just as there isn't a single reason for a child to be anxious, it's worth trying a range of strategies to help them feel less worried. Any solution to anxiety, though, is unlikely to be a quick fix.

Improvements in anxiety symptoms are seen in children who are more physically active, and children who take more than 12,000 steps a day are less likely to be anxious than those who take fewer than 9,200.[25] (Researchers are nothing if not precise.) For ideas on how to help your child to exercise more, please see Chapter 7. There's a link between anxiety and being bullied, particularly in girls (see Chapter 5). Anxious children often have problems sleeping. They have frequent insomnia and nightmares, and sometimes they don't want to sleep alone (see Chapter 7).

Parents who have certain beliefs about their children's anxiety are more likely to have children with high levels of separation anxiety.[26] These beliefs include the world being full of danger for your child, your child not being able to deal with things independently, and you (not your child or your partner) being the only person who can fix things.

When parents show their own anxiety, their children also tend to be more anxious.[27] It helps to hide from your child that you worry about them doing dangerous things or making a mistake, and to avoid showing fear when your child does something on their own. On the other hand, reinforcing your child's courageous behaviour – by offering them lots of praise when they've been brave, for instance – may help them to feel less anxious. I'm sure most of us have been the parent who calls out 'Don't climb too high!' when their fearless monkey scales the dizzying heights of the climbing frame for under-fives, but doing so is unlikely to make your child safer, and it's more likely to make them fearful in other scenarios.

Similarly, when discussing anxiety-provoking situations with your child, such as a test at school, being positive and helping your child feel they can cope works better than showing your own anxiety or negativity. Often, listening to your child can be more useful to them than giving advice. It's also important to accept your child's mistakes and praise efforts, not successes. Anxious children can have perfectionist tendencies. It's easy for these to be reinforced if parents set their standards too high or if they make it clear that children's achievements are very important to them.

Unwitting reinforcement of children's anxious behaviour sometimes arises from letting them avoid anxiety-provoking situations. That's not to say you should lock your arachnophobic toddler in a room full of spiders, but it can reinforce an older child's fear if you let them take sick days when they're worried about something at school, and social anxiety can get better when children are exposed to social situations. Even providing lots of comfort when your child's behaving anxiously, as counter-intuitive and unnatural as it sounds, can make them more anxious in future. On the other hand, reinforcing your child's courageous behaviour – by offering them lots of praise when they've been brave, for instance – may help them feel less anxious.[28]

Patience is key. Anxious thoughts and behaviour are difficult to control, and impatience is likely to make the problem worse. You can set your child a good example by showing them how to relax. I'm terrible at doing this; my children are much better than I am at relaxing. In our case, they're providing me with an inverse role model. You could also encourage your child to read, listen to music, take naps, play quiet games, stretch or do anything else that helps them soothe themselves. Art is another good activity to deal with stress. It's important to communicate the message that play and fun are related to health.

Breathing exercises with your child can be done set to music – Bach's 'Air on a G String' is recommended by one handbook for therapists.[29] Your child should be comfortable, sitting in a chair or lying on a cushion, and asked to pay attention to their breath as they slowly breathe in and out, noticing their body as it relaxes. Another technique involves sitting with your child in a quiet room for around five minutes, breathing in while tensing a group of muscles, and relaxing those muscles while breathing out. It could involve muscles in the feet, legs, hands, arms, stomach, chest, neck and shoulders, and face.

Laughter is brilliant for children who are feeling stressed. You could make use of funny films and TV programmes, books and jokes, and maybe have a place such as the fridge where family members can put up things they find funny. 'Cheese-touch' and 'six fish' have both been successful in my family. You might know cheese-touch from *Diary of a Wimpy Kid*. It's like 'it', in that you have to tap someone on their body and say 'cheese-touch!' They then have the cheese-touch until they can cheese-touch somebody else or cheese-touch you back. (Cheese-touch became 'coronavirus' for a period of early 2020 in my kids' school playground.)

With six fish, if somebody farts, you yell 'six fish!' and start tickling them. You carry on until they name six different fish. My older daughter learned six fish that she can recite at speed – dogfishcatfishsalmonanchovyhaddockhake – to minimise thinking time while being tickled. You can ward off the tickles by farting and swiftly saying 'safety'. This means that over dinner or a family film, my children sit there quietly interjecting with 'Safety,' 'Safety,' 'Safety.' I think we eat too many beans.

If your child spends a lot of time worrying, you could help them to set aside a particular time of day to focus on the concerns. If worries come up at other times, they can be set aside until this worry time. It's important to make sure that this time isn't scheduled just before bed. Worry dolls might also be worth a try. These are tiny dolls, originating from Guatemala, which can take on a worry for your child so they don't need to think about it. The child gives each doll a worry before going to sleep each night, leaving the dolls under their pillow. A friend bought these for my daughter when she was finding things tricky. I think even the idea of someone outside the immediate family looking out for her helped my daughter feel better. Another technique for slightly older children is to write down worries on different pieces of paper and to store them somewhere safe, encouraging them only to think about that particular worry when they open the piece of paper.

There are other things you can look at if you've tried these approaches and your child remains anxious. If they are involved in lots of extracurricular activities, you could think about discussing whether they might want to drop any and, if so, which ones. Children increasingly identify taking part in lots of activities as being a source of stress. (My younger daughter, reading this section over my shoulder as I was editing it, said, 'WHY would you want to get parents to cut their children off from getting into a good university, and all the other opportunities they'd get from doing loads of extracurricular stuff?' Perhaps my pressure-free parenting antidote to my own achievement-driven psyche hasn't been as successful as I thought.)

Another option is to use a book specifically targeted at children with anxiety, incorporating activities and passages for both parents and children to read. One study found that families using such a book were less likely to have children with clinical levels of anxiety three months later than families who were part of the control group.[30] If your child's severely anxious, you could consider a group therapy programme. This works better than using a book alone.

If your child's anxiety is accompanied by perfectionism or by them being otherwise hard on themselves, it's worth – and I'm sorry to be blunt – looking at your own perfectionist tendencies.[31] This is where I would like to challenge my own interpretation of the research findings. If it were that bloody easy for people with perfectionist tendencies to stop trying to reach standards that dangle enticingly just out of our collective grasp, we'd have done so already. Perhaps a more appropriate aim is to avoid making a big deal of our perfectionist tendencies in front of our children.

Another recommendation, especially if you're female and have a daughter, is to avoid criticising yourself. There's a link between self-criticism in mothers and their daughters' own self-criticism. This may be a case of modelling – if a child hears their parent talking about how portly or incapable they are, it's a gateway into doing this themselves. Children's perfectionism also tends to be higher in families where parents put more pressure on them.[32]

One way to get off the perfectionist treadmill may be to help your child to focus on excellence, not on perfection, and on the development of a 'growth mindset' (as mentioned in Chapter 8, alongside the research controversies surrounding it).[33] This is a mindset in which children and adults are always learning and where intelligence isn't fixed. It sees mistakes and failures as opportunities to learn something, not a blemish on the individual's character. You can also remind your child to make enjoyment an important goal in what they do. Enjoying the process of doing things means they're not simply ticking things off a list.

Sensitivity to criticism by others may be an aspect of your child's anxiety, especially if they feel isolated by others. Children excluded from friendships and play between the ages of six and twelve are more likely to be sensitive to being excluded when they're teenagers – a sensitivity strong enough to show up in the neural patterns made by their brains.[34]

A strategy to help with this sensitivity is to be clear with your child that most people aren't judging them. If they're worried about what others are thinking, it's most likely to be their own worries and judgements, rather than those of other people, that are making them fret about being judged. Another is to try not saying no automatically when your child asks you for something. Children may interpret this as rejection, and rejection by parents can make children more sensitive to being rejected more generally.

It's also worth passing on the message to your child that it's not possible to please everybody all the time, and nor is it desirable to do so. Self-assertiveness can be supported by teaching your child to show empathy, while also stating their feelings or needs in the first person: 'I don't want to do that,' or 'That makes me feel scared.'

Sadness

Sadness can hide worlds of meaning and experience beneath its sodden surfaces. There's sorrow in the child who leaves her favourite teddy on the steps of the British Museum; in the child whose parents quietly criticise the way she eats and the volume at which she plays; in the child who sits alone on a playground bench, endlessly hoping that someone will ask him to play; and in the child whose grandparent is ebbing away to cancer. There's sadness in arguments with friends or family, in lost pets, and in sentimental books and films. The first film I ever saw in the cinema was *Bambi*. I cried for days. My children have been set off by friendships, by world events and by the losses that stem from moving home.

Sometimes your child will tell you if they feel sad. Other times, you'll need to work it out. The diagram below shows signs that could mean your child's feeling sad. Due to an absence of research literature on symptoms of sadness, this diagram covers the main signs of depression.

14. SIGNS OF SADNESS/DEPRESSION

PHYSICAL SIGNS	BEHAVIOURAL SIGNS	OTHER SIGNS
Trouble sleeping	Grouchy	Unable to feel pleasure in 'fun' activities
Obese	Withdrawn	Poor school attendance
Little energy	Disobedient	Doing badly at school
Feels unwell	Distracted	Unpopular
		Scared of leaving home

If your child's feeling sad, some other sections of this book may help – in particular, the ones on exercise (Chapter 7), friendship and bullying (Chapter 5), and sleep (Chapter 7). Feelings of sadness can come from disintegrating at the edges with tiredness. If you've ever mentioned mildly suboptimal news at a time when your child has heavy lids and the slight mania that comes from exhaustion, you'll know this already. Resilient children are less likely to become sad, so some of the ideas earlier in this chapter may also be useful.

Where your child is young and their sadness is about something trivial – perhaps they won a disappointing prize or their favourite socks are in the wash – you might want to try distraction. When my children were this age, I used to scrabble around for something suitable to use as distraction, while I watched other parents effortlessly saying things like 'Oh, look at the pretty butterfly! I'm going to the shops in a moment, what flavour ice cream should I get?' Distraction works less well for older children, and if your child is sad because of something important, such as a friendship, they should be able to talk about it.

You could also try working with your child to turn a negative into a positive. If a planned afternoon with a friend is rearranged because of illness, the new date can become something to look forward to. Your child needs to be fully involved in the process of reframing something negative into something positive; it's doing this together that helps the child be less sad and/or angry. It's important to be supportive when your child expresses sadness. Instead of discouraging children from expressing their sadness or ignoring them when they do so, you could say something like 'I hear you're feeling sad. I'll sit here with you until it passes.'

Grief is a reaction to a significant loss, such as that of a grandparent or a pet, and it's not just death that can cause your child to feel grief. It might be caused by leaving behind an old home or an old school, falling out with a friend or losing an important toy.

Children deal with grief in very different ways. When my beloved dad died from cancer, my girls were three and six. The six-year-old was distraught for months, and grief caught her at unexpected moments for years afterwards. The three-year-old wasn't hugely affected when he died, but sadness came crashing around her in waves when she was seven or eight. It was a delayed reaction to a momentous loss that she didn't understand at the time. My friend's daughter, two at the time, had a more matter-of-fact reaction to her own huge loss: 'My granny bumped her head and went into hospital. And guess what?! Dead!'

Depending on how old they are, children need different things to support them with their grief. Children aged two to four need lots of repetition and reassurance, consistency, and short, honest responses to their questions. They deal with grief through their play. Children under the age of five don't generally understand that death is final – this understanding develops gradually between the ages of five and ten. Those aged four to seven need a physical outlet for their grief. The use of drawing and stories is important, as is talking about their sadness. And children aged seven and over need your comfort but also time alone. It's good to be available to listen to them and talk about death, if that's the reason for their grief, as much as they need. As with slightly younger children, drawing and stories can help them process what's happened.[35]

Children need something concrete to help them with their grief. This might be in the form of photographs, visits to a grave, or rituals such as lighting a candle on important days for the person who has died. I light a candle for my dad on the anniversary of his death, his birthday and on days where we might have spent time together as a family in the past. My natural suspicion of custom has been capsized. It's a way of keeping his past in my present, and it's offered my children a solid connection.

If your child goes to school, the teacher should know what has happened. Children will often let out their grief more at school than at home, particularly if you're less available to them because you're grieving yourself. When you're talking about someone who has died, using positive words can be helpful. Children are better able to cope with their grief when parents use words like 'love' and 'happy'. 'He loved us so much,' 'She'd be happy to know you,' 'I'm glad we had the chance to know him and spend time with him.'

An age-appropriate book, such as *Michael Rosen's Sad Book*, may help children deal with grief. If your child shows signs of trauma or their grief is overwhelming, you will need outside help. Complex grief and trauma – which your child might show if they've seen somebody die in person – require professional support.[36]

Professional support

Lack of access to professional support is an issue facing a growing number of parents who seek it out. Many families are on waiting lists and having to find their own sticking plasters to cover the breach. This doesn't solve the problem, but you're not alone.

For those of you who are in the UK and needing urgent advice, the parent helpline number for YoungMinds is 0808 802 5544. It's open Monday to Friday between 9.30 a.m. and 4 p.m. They also have a live webchat option. There are several websites with useful resources, including e-wellbeing (https://e-wellbeing.co.uk) and Mind (https://www.mind.org.uk/information-support/for-children-and-young-people/information-for-parents/). You might be able to access specialist services or support groups through your local area; your council should be able to guide you in the right direction. Finally, online parenting forums can be a good way of linking to other people who have experienced similar disquiet with their children.

The advice on anxiety and sadness above may be helpful to you while you wait for specialist support. You'll also need to look after yourself in order to care for your child; the ideas in Chapter 1 are worth a bookmark.

CHAPTER CHECKLIST

High-quality research

▶ **Take the elements from the rest of this book that are likely to support your child's happiness and well-being.** Consider whether there's anything you can do to strengthen your child's relationships (Chapter 5). Get your child to be more physically active and to spend less time sitting down. Get out into nature together. Avoid giving your child too much processed food, and support your child to get a better night's sleep if they struggle with it (Chapter 7). Reduce your child's screen time if they have a lot of it (Chapter 8).

▶ **Take account of your own circumstances.** Look after your own well-being. If you don't live with your child, try to build your relationship and do lots of different child-centred activities with them. If your child finds it difficult to be self-compassionate, consider whether a mindfulness course might be useful for them.

Moderate-quality research

▶ **Support your child to develop healthy habits.** Encourage them to express feelings of anger constructively. Help them to develop 'active coping' strategies. Such strategies might include talking about problems, working out potential solutions, taking part in relaxing activities such as listening to music, or doing exercise to help deal with stress.

▶ **Adopt behaviour-related tools to support your child's well-being.** Use praise or feedback appropriately (Chapter 6).

▶ **Spend some time with your thoughts.** Think about what's going on in your child's head, beyond the obvious. This can make you a more competent parent, which in turn supports your child's well-being.

▶ **Tailor your actions to your circumstances.** If you suffer from depression, make sure your child knows it's not their fault. If you live in a Black, ethnic minority or mixed household, encourage conversations about race and ethnicity.

Anecdotal research or expert advice

▶ **Bolster your child.** Highlight their strengths. Keep reinforcing the message that they are capable. Support your child to focus on their own growth, avoiding any comparisons to other people. Accept your child unconditionally.

▶ **Help your child learn to handle stress.** Make it clear to your child that you believe they're capable of coping with stress. Allow your child to experience stress that's appropriate for their age and level of development, and that you know they can manage. Help them to work out when they're likely to face challenges. Help your child to frame stressful situations as challenges, not catastrophes. Teach your child when they can do something about a situation – for example, practising more if they're finding something tricky – and when to accept it. Demonstrate healthy ways of coping with stressful situations.

▶ **Reframe your thinking and communicate with care.** Try to see your child's point of view, even (or especially) when it's hard to do so. Have realistic expectations of your child. If you need to give negative messages, tell your child what not to do, why not, and give them an alternative.

▶ **Support your child's interests.** Encourage extracurricular activities your child enjoys. If your child's interested in lots of different things, support them to pursue more than one interest, if practically and financially possible. Consider giving your child greater independence to play outdoors and explore away from their house or flat, when it's safe to do so.

▶ **Find a balance between family cocooning and external input.** Have meals together as a family. Consider a weekly family meeting so problems can be solved together. Make sure your child has relationships outside your household. If your child is in regular childcare, try to select a high-quality centre with plenty of staff for the number of children.

The troubleshooting sections below should be read in tandem with the less targeted advice given above.

Troubleshooting: anxiety

Use a book specifically targeted at children with anxiety, incorporating activities and passages for both parents and children to read. If your child is severely anxious, consider a group therapy programme. Find out, if you can, whether your child's being bullied. Interrogate your own beliefs if you feel very anxious for your child, and don't show your child your own anxiety about them doing dangerous things. If your child is involved in lots of extracurricular activities, think about dropping some. When discussing anxiety-provoking situations, try to focus on being positive and helping your child feel they can cope. Be patient with your child. Accept your child's mistakes and praise efforts, not successes. If your child spends a lot of time worrying, think about helping them to set aside a particular time of day to focus on the worries. Encourage your child to read, listen to music, take naps, play quiet games, stretch, and do anything else that helps them relax. Show your child how to relax by doing it yourself. Try breathing exercises together. Get your child to laugh.

Troubleshooting: perfectionism and self-criticism

Try not to criticise yourself, particularly if you have daughters. Look at your own perfectionist tendencies. Try to be less harsh with your child. Move your child's focus from producing the best schoolwork to learning from the process of doing it. Remind your child to make enjoyment an important goal of what they do. Help your child to focus on excellence, not perfection.

Troubleshooting: sensitivity to others' criticism and rejection

Try not to say no automatically when your child asks you for something. Be clear with your child that most people aren't judging them. Teach your child to listen carefully when they think they're being criticised; they may be at the receiving end of feedback, not criticism. Pass on the message to your child that it's not possible to please everybody all the time, and nor is it desirable to do so.

Troubleshooting: sadness and grief

Be supportive when your child expresses sadness or anger. Try to find out whether your child is having friendship problems or being bullied. Try distraction if your child is young and their sadness is about something trivial. Try working with your child to turn a negative into a positive. Support your child according to what they need for their age (see the main part of this chapter for details). Recognise that it's loss, not just death, that can cause your child to feel grief. Use positive words when talking about a person who has died. Use images and physical objects with your children to support them in their grief. Find your child an age-appropriate book. If your child goes to school, let the teacher know your child is grieving. Get help if your child shows signs of trauma or if their grief is overwhelming.

EPILOGUE

Your own approach

CHAPTER 10

A SIMPLE ROAD MAP

The basic plan of action is simple. Be warm with your child. Be specific with your praise, making it about what your child's done and not who they are. Help your child feel competent. Pick your battles. If your child does something wrong, and it's big enough to be worth mentioning, describe simply what behaviour you want to see from them, and don't use words that judge. Don't criticise or shame your child. Give them easy choices as often as you can ('an apple or a banana in your lunchbox?') and avoid asking them to make choices that are likely to overwhelm them. Have routines, especially at bedtime. Be predictable. Make sure your child knows it's OK to show they're scared or angry. Be sensible with screens but don't be afraid of them, and know how useful they can be when you want to get something done or have some time to yourself. Help your child be active and eat well. Eat together when you can. Don't forget to look after yourself.

Interpret parenting ideas loosely. The suggestions in this book only work in the context of your own child and how you fit together as a family. Even the ideas with the strongest evidence base might only work for 80% of families 70% of the time. Treat them instead as an experimental toolbox. Some will be more successful than others for your child, and even the successful tools might need adapting or replacing as your child inevitably grows and changes.

When things go wrong – and they will – you're not necessarily responsible. Perhaps your child has a chemical imbalance in their brain.

Perhaps they've fallen out with a friend. Perhaps you don't have the help you need for your family. Perhaps a pandemic hits.

Sometimes, too, you might stop using techniques that have worked in the past because your child is happy, and problems eventually re-emerge. Or perhaps your child hits a developmental milestone and a new concern arises. Remember to come back to the research.

Keep in mind that everything's linked. Children behave better when they're happy and well-rested. They're happier when they have lots of opportunities to charge around in the fresh air and when they get on well with their family and friends. They have better relationships when they feel good about themselves and eat well. Everything's linked, too, when it comes to what you do as a parent. Tinkering around the edges may not have a dramatic effect on your child, but knitting together different elements – being warm, creating and sticking to sensible rules, carving out routines and being consistent – create security and a springboard for your child in a way that individual elements alone cannot.

There are also links between what your child does and what you do. If your child's calm, it's easier for you to be warm and responsive, calming your child further. If your child is lying down screaming in the middle of a cafe, it's hard to respond well, making it less likely they get what they need to settle themselves. Sometimes it's a question of building on positive cycles or interrupting the negative ones. It can even be useful just to be aware when you and your child are feeding well off each other and when you're not. Since I've started to watch out for it, it's made me feel better equipped to interrupt the cycle of 'You are grumpy, so I am grumpy, so you are grumpy.' I'm not always able to do this, though, which brings me on to my final point…

Don't aim for perfect. 'Good enough' is fine. It's actually better. Holding ourselves up to impossible standards as parents means we can only fail. It's a useful lesson for our children to see us mess up, own the mess and say we've got it wrong. Having parents who present themselves as infallible means that when something goes wrong, children are more likely to blame themselves. Having human parents – ones who make mistakes and model how to apologise for them – gives children something healthy and attainable to which to aspire. It's lucky for all of us that our children need something less than perfection.

APPENDIX 1

LIMITATIONS AND APPROACH NOTES

There will always be a degree of bias when reviewing and selecting evidence relating to parenting. The body of literature is vast, and the studies reviewed relate to the search terms used as well as the sources selected. There are also limitations in categorising studies according to their quality, no matter which approach is taken. A poorly designed randomised control trial, with few participants and a biased sample, may well represent worse evidence than a well-designed study that doesn't use a control group.

Where multiple studies exist showing the same research findings, the reference I've used is either the best-quality study or, in cases of multiple studies of similar quality, the first one to be reviewed. Sometimes the findings of good-quality studies contradict each other. Where this has occurred, I've tended to select a reference study that represents the balance of evidence across the studies reviewed; there is, inevitably, a degree of bias in this process. Many studies involve specific subsets of children and families, for example Canadian pre-schoolers. Where this is central to the findings, I've said so, but in other cases findings have been generalised to make the book easier to read.

There are a few other things that should be borne in mind when reading this book or thinking about its implications:

► The research literature that could potentially inform this book is probably impossible to read in a lifetime. I can't pretend to have captured all the relevant research not only on parenting but on all the areas that inform parenting.

► In some places, I've simplified research terminology. This may shift the definition by a minuscule amount, but not enough to change the key meaning for parents.

► I've included published books but excluded dissertations. The majority of the books I've read haven't included primary research, so they're assigned to the anecdotal or expert evidence category. Dissertations often include primary research, meaning they could, theoretically, be given a higher-quality assignment, but they've not been quality-assessed through peer review or a publishing and editing process.

► In most cases, the original research doesn't explicitly recommend an action in the form stated in this book – instead, I've drawn out actions based on links between research findings. In some cases, I've made assumptions about causality when deciding which studies to include in the 'Ideas' section. I've excluded health as a possible predictor of a good parent–child relationship, for example, as it seems more likely the causal link runs the other way round.

► There are some areas in which more research would be useful. These include involving more fathers in research, increasing the range of systematic reviews to cover studies whose focus makes them unsuitable for testing through randomised control trials, and doing more work to understand how inputs and outcomes vary for different groups of children and families.

While it's never possible to be entirely free from bias, taking a research-based perspective to the distillation of parenting advice can, I hope, provide other parents with useful tools and strategies to support their children into adulthood.

Endnotes and references

There isn't enough space to include all the studies I've used. The full list can be found online at www.matildagosling.com/parenting.

APPENDIX 2

LINKS BETWEEN PARTS ONE AND TWO

The chart overleaf summarises the links between the areas explored in Part One (listed on the left) and the outcomes examined in Part Two (listed at the top). Links are not necessarily causal.[1]

	RELATIONSHIPS	BEHAVIOUR	PHYSICAL HEALTH	LEARNING AND PLAY	HAPPINESS AND WELL-BEING
Positive ★ / Negative ○					
Parents' well-being	★	★	★	★	★
Parents' healthy management of emotions	★	★	★		★
Parents reflecting on childhood experiences	★		★		
Parents having home/work boundaries	★	★	See note		★
Parenting confidence	★	★	★	★	★
Unhealthy family conflict	○	○	○	○	○
Parents' relationship quality	★	★	★	★	★
Household chaos	○	○	○	○	○
Physical punishment	○	○	○	○	○
Being critical	○	○	○		○
Shouting/being hostile	○	○	○	○	○
Psychological control	○	○	○	○	○
Permissiveness	○	○	○	○	○
Helicopter parenting	○	○	Mixed	Mixed	○
Warmth/responsiveness	★	★	★	★	★
Consistency	★	★	★	★	★
Helping children with emotions	★	★	★	★	Mixed
Giving guidance and having boundaries	★	★	★	★	★
Giving children autonomy	★	★	★	★	★

ACKNOWLEDGEMENTS

My agent, Rufus Purdy, took a punt on a non-fiction pitch, for which I am deeply grateful. Thank you to Mark Richards and Diana Broccardo at Swift Press for wanting the book, and for the absolute ease and pleasure they bring to a working relationship.

There are too many people who have talked through book-related ideas with me, shared anecdotes and given their support to thank here, and I hope they will forgive omissions. Particular thanks, though, go to Camille Gatin, Dora Napolitano, Gemma Dunn, Gregor MacLennan, Janet Graham, Jo Blackman, Kate McSweeney, Lucy Lambton, Maryna Tkachenko, Natalie Orringe, Rowan Diamond, Sarah Maber, Simon Fanshawe, Simon Gallacher and Suvra Datta.

I don't have words to express what Sara Fakhro has done for me and what she means to me, but I hope I have failed to communicate this enough times that she knows what lies underneath the mangled language.

I'd like to thank clinical psychologist and parenting expert Dr Natalie Cheatle for reviewing an early draft; Sarah Terry for her skilful copy-editing; Rachel Nobilo for press and publicity; and the proficient production team at Tetragon. Thanks, too, to Jules Mercy and Chris Hollis for giving me a deeper insight into human relationships and behaviour, without which I could not have written this book.

Thank you, of course, to my family – my mum, Imogen Gosling; my half-sisters (whom I love like whole-sisters), Amanda Gosling and Catherine Gosling Fuller; their partners, Andy Wroe and Ben Gosling Fuller; and my parents-in-law, Mary and John Daly. If my dad, Andrew Gosling, were still here, I would be thanking him over a glass of wine while we watched the sun go down over a river estuary.

Thank you to my daughters for their complicated, strong-willed, interesting and deeply wonderful selves. My attempts to Research Everything are driven by the fact that I adore them.

Finally, thank you to Pete Daly for so many things – but mainly for his warmth, wit, companionship and unending support, and for allowing me to tell the asparagus story.

ENDNOTES

Introduction

1 This grid was adapted from a framework originally conceptualised by Diana Baumrind in 1967, and built on by Eleanor Maccoby and John Martin in 1983. See e.g. Kuppens, S. and Ceulemans, E. (2019). Parenting styles: a closer look at a well-known concept. *Journal of Child and Family Studies* 28: 168–81. doi: 10.1007/s10826-018-1242-x.

2 Mental health: Pinquart, M. (2017a). Associations of parenting dimensions and styles with internalizing symptoms in children and adolescents: a meta-analysis. *Marriage & Family Review* 53(7), 613–40. doi: 10.1080/01494929.2016.1247761. Self-esteem: Pinquart, M. and Gerke, D. C. (2019). Associations of parenting styles with self-esteem in children and adolescents: A meta-analysis. *Journal of Child and Family Studies* 28, 2017–35. doi: 10.1007/s10826-019-01417-5. Perfectionism: Yıldız, M., Duru, H., and Eldeleklioğlu, J. (2020). Relationship between parenting styles and multidimensional perfectionism: a meta-analysis study. *Educational Sciences: Theory & Practice* 20(4), 16–35. doi: 10.12738/jestp.2020.4.002. Behaviour: Pinquart, M. (2017b). Associations of parenting dimensions and styles with externalizing problems of children and adolescents: an updated meta-analysis. *Developmental Psychology* 53(5), 873–932. doi: 10.1037/dev0000295. Aggression: Masud, H. et al. (2019). Parenting styles and aggression among young adolescents: a systematic review of literature. *Community Mental Health Journal* 55(6), 1015–30. doi: 10.1007/s10597-019-00400-0. Social mindedness: Wong, T. K., Konishi, C., and Kong, X. (2021). Parenting and prosocial behaviors: a meta-analysis. *Social Development* 30(2), 343–73. doi: 10.1111/sode.12481. School: Pinquart, M. (2016). Associations of parenting styles and dimensions with academic achievement in children and adolescents: a meta-analysis. *Educational Psychology Review* 28(3), 475–93. doi: 10.1007/s10648-015-9338-y. Parent relationships: Neal, J. and Frick-Horbury, D. (2001). The effects of parenting styles and childhood attachment patterns on intimate relationships. *Journal of Instructional Psychology* 28(3), 178. Sibling relationships: Van Volkom, M., Dirmeitis, D. and Cappitelli, S. (2019). An investigation of the connection between parenting styles, birth order, personality, and sibling relationships. *Journal of Psychology and Behavioral Science* 7(1), 55–63. doi: 10.15640/jpbs.v7n1a7. Friendships: Llorca, A., Richaud, M. C. and Malonda, E. (2017). Parenting, peer relationships, academic self-efficacy, and academic achievement: direct and mediating effects. *Frontiers in Psychology* 8, 2120. doi: 10.3389/fpsyg.2017.02120. Bullying: Lereya, S. T., Samara, M. and Wolke, D. (2013). Parenting behavior and the risk of becoming a victim and a bully/victim: a meta-analysis study. *Child Abuse & Neglect* 37(12), 1091–108. doi: 10.1016/j.chiabu.2013.03.001. Exercise and weight: Sleddens, S. F. et al. (2011). General parenting, childhood overweight and obesity-inducing behaviors: a review. *International Journal of Pediatric Obesity* 6(sup3), e12–27. doi: 10.3109/17477166.2011.566339. Smoking: Stephenson, M. T. and Helme, D. W. (2006). Authoritative parenting and sensation seeking as predictors of adolescent cigarette and marijuana use. *Journal of Drug Education* 36(3), 247–70. doi: 10.2190/Y223-2623-7716-22.

3   Winnicott, D. W. (1971). *Playing and Reality*. Tavistock Publications.

You

1   Roeters, A. and Gracia, P. (2016). Child care time, parents' well-being, and gender: evidence from the American time use survey. *Journal of Child and Family Studies* 25, 2469–79. doi: 10.1007/s10826-016-0416-7.

2   Autism spectrum disorder/developmental delay: Barroso, N. E. et al. (2018). Parenting stress through the lens of different clinical groups: a systematic review & meta-analysis. *Journal of Abnormal Child Psychology* 46(3), 449–61. doi: 10.1007/s10802-017-0313-6. Postnatal depression: Leigh, B. and Milgrom, J. (2008). Risk factors for antenatal depression, postnatal depression and parenting stress. *BMC Psychiatry* 8(1), 1–11. doi: 10.1186/1471-244X-8-24. Ill child: Golfenshtein, N., Srulovici, E. and Medoff-Cooper, B. (2016). Investigating parenting stress across pediatric health conditions – a systematic review. *Comprehensive Child and Adolescent Nursing* 39(1), 41–79. doi: 10.3109/01460862.2015.1078423. Financial problems and relationship difficulties: Nelson, S. K., Kushlev, K. and Lyubomirsky, S. (2014). The pains and pleasures of parenting: when, why, and how is parenthood associated with more or less well-being? *Psychological Bulletin* 140(3), 846. doi: 10.1037/a0035444. Family policies: Nomaguchi, K. and Milkie, M. A. (2020). Parenthood and well-being: A decade in review. *Journal of Marriage and Family* 82(1), 198–223. doi: 10.1111/jomf.12646.

3 Murphy, M. H. et al. (2019). The effects of continuous compared to accumulated exercise on health: a meta-analytic review. *Sports Medicine* 49, 1585–607. doi: 10.1007/s40279-019-01145-2.

4 Hu, T. et al. (2014). Relation between emotion regulation and mental health: a meta-analysis review. *Psychological Reports* 114(2), 341–62. doi: 10.2466/03.20. PR0.114k22w4.

5 Lack of confidence due to tiredness: Chau, V. and Giallo, R. (2015). The relationship between parental fatigue, parenting self-efficacy and behaviour: implications for supporting parents in the early parenting period. *Child: Care, Health and Development* 41(4), 626–33. doi: 10.1111/cch.12205. Getting up after twenty minutes: e.g. Stahl, S. M. and Sigua, N. L. (2016). Healthy sleep in adults. *American Journal of Respiratory and Critical Care Medicine* 193(5), 7–8. doi: 10.1164/rccm.1935P7.

6 Burgdorf, V., Szabó, M. and Abbott, M. J. (2019). The effect of mindfulness interventions for parents on parenting stress and youth psychological outcomes: a systematic review and meta-analysis. *Frontiers in Psychology* 10, 1336. doi: 10.3389/fpsyg.2019.01336. Note that the evidence base, though, was weak.

7 Gunderson, J. and Barrett, A. (2017). Emotional cost of emotional support? The association between intensive mothering and psychological well-being in midlife. *Journal of Family Issues* 38(7), 992–1009. doi: 10.1177/0192513X15579502.

8 Jang, S., Zippay, A. and Park, R. (2012). Family roles as moderators of the relationship between schedule flexibility and stress. *Journal of Marriage and Family* 74(4), 897–912. doi: 10.1111/j.1741-3737.2012.00984.x.

9 Wang, D., Hagger, M. S. and Chatzisarantis, N. L. (2020). Ironic effects of thought suppression: a meta-analysis. *Perspectives on Psychological Science* 15(3), 778–93. doi: 10.1177/1745691619898795.

10 Mindfulness practice in research on emotions: Brockman, R. et al. (2017). Emotion regulation strategies in daily life: mindfulness, cognitive reappraisal and emotion suppression. *Cognitive Behaviour Therapy* 46(2), 91–113. doi: 10.1080/16506073.2016.1218926. Showing feelings to your child: Karnilowicz, H. R., Waters, S. F. and Mendes, W. B. (2019). Not in front of the kids: effects of parental suppression on socialization behaviors during cooperative parent–child interactions. *Emotion* 19(7), 1183–91. doi: 10.1037/emo0000527. Impact of hiding feelings: Brockman et al. (2017).

11 Biringen, Z. (2000). Emotional availability: conceptualization and research findings. *American Journal of Orthopsychiatry* 70(1), 104–14. doi: 10.1037/h0087711.

12 Brown, B, 'The Power of Vulnerability | Brené Brown | TEDxHouston' [video], YouTube (recorded 6 Oct. 2010), https://youtu.be/X4Qm9cGRub0.

13 Fraiberg, S., Adelson, E. and Shapiro, V. (1975). Ghosts in the nursery. A psychoanalytic approach to the problems of impaired infant–mother relationships. *Journal of the American Academy of Child Psychiatry* 14(3), 387–421, p. 429. doi: 10.1016/s0002-7138(09)61442-4.

14 Rijlaarsdam, J. et al. (2014). Maternal childhood maltreatment and offspring emotional and behavioral problems: maternal and paternal mechanisms of risk transmission. *Child Maltreatment* 19(2), 67–78. doi: 10.1177/1077559514527639.

15 Garon-Bissonnette, J. et al. (2022). Maternal childhood abuse and neglect predicts offspring development in early childhood: the roles of reflective functioning and child sex. *Child Abuse & Neglect* 128, 105030. doi: 10.1016/j. chiabu.2021.105030.

16 Cunningham-Burley, S., Backett-Milburn, K. and Kemmer, D. (2005). Balancing work and family life: mothers' views. In L. McKie and S. Cunningham-Burley (eds). *Families in Society: Boundaries and Relationships*. Policy Press.

17 Conflict of commitments: Hess, S., and Pollmann-Schult, M. (2020). Associations between mothers' work–family conflict and children's psychological well-being: the mediating role of mothers' parenting behavior. *Journal of Child and Family Studies* 29, 1561–71. doi: 10.1007/s10826-019-01669-1. Tiredness from work: Danner-Vlaardingerbroek, G., Kluwer, E., Van Steenbergen, E., and Van der Lippe, T. (2013). The psychological availability of dual-earner parents for their children after work. *Family Relations* 62(5), 741–54. doi: 10.1111/fare.12039.

18 Lapierre, L. M. et al. (2016). Juggling work and family responsibilities when involuntarily working more from home: a multiwave study of financial sales professionals. *Journal of Organizational Behavior* 37(6), 804–22. doi: 10.1002/job.2075.

19 Basile, K. A. and Beauregard, T. A. (2016). Strategies for successful telework: how effective employees manage work/home boundaries. *Strategic HR Review* 15(3), 106–11. doi: 10.1108/SHR-03-2016-0024.

20 'Self-efficacy' as a term: Vance, A. J. and Brandon, D. H. (2017). Delineating among parenting confidence, parenting self-efficacy and competence. *ANS: Advances in Nursing Science* 40(4), E18–E37. doi: 10.1097/ANS.0000000000000179. Reduced likelihood of harsh, permissive or inconsistent discipline: Sanders, M. R. and Woolley, M. L. (2005). The relationship between maternal self-efficacy and parenting practices: implications for parent training. *Child: Care, Health and Development* 31(1), 65–73. doi: 10.1111/j.1365-2214.2005.00487.x. Parenting stress: Bloomfield, L. and Kendall, S. (2012). Parenting self-efficacy, parenting stress and child behaviour before and after a parenting programme. *Primary Health Care Research & Development* 13(4), 364–72. doi: 10.1017/S1463423612000060; Chau and

Giallo (2015). Better outcomes: Mouton, B. et al. (2018). Confident parents for easier children: a parental self-efficacy program to improve young children's behavior. *Education Sciences* 8(3), 134. doi: 10.3390/educsci8030134.

21 Xue, A. et al. (2021). New parents experienced lower parenting self-efficacy during the COVID-19 pandemic lockdown. *Children* 8(2), 79. doi: 10.3390/children8020079.

22 Manguel, A. (2014). *A Reading Diary: A Year of Favourite Books* [Kindle edn].Canongate.

23 Mouton et al. (2018).

24 Waters, L. and Sun, J. (2016). Can a brief strength-based parenting intervention boost self-efficacy and positive emotions in parents? *International Journal of Applied Positive Psychology* 1(1), 41–56. doi: 10.1007/s41042-017-0007-x.

25 Merrifield, K. A. and Gamble, W. C. (2013). Associations among marital qualities, supportive and undermining coparenting, and parenting self-efficacy: testing spillover and stress-buffering processes. *Journal of Family Issues* 34(4), 510–33. doi: 10.1177/0192513X12445561.

Home life

1 Laible, D. J. and Thompson, R. A. (2002). Mother–child conflict in the toddler years: lessons in emotion, morality, and relationships. *Child Development* 73(4), 1187–203. doi: 10.1111/1467-8624.00466.

2 Canary, D. J. (2021). Relationship conflict and communication. In *Oxford Research Encyclopedia of Communication* [online publication]. doi: 10.1093/acrefore/9780190228613.013.759.

3 Emotionally focused couples' therapy: Beasley, C. C. and Ager, R. (2019). Emotionally focused couples therapy: a systematic review of its effectiveness over the past 19 years. *Journal of Evidence-Based Social Work* 16(2), 144–59. doi: 10.1080/23761407.2018.1563013. Constructive conflict: Cummings, E. M. et al. (2008). Evaluating a brief prevention program for improving marital conflict in community families. *Journal of Family Psychology* 22(2), 193–202. doi: 10.1037/0893-3200.22.2.193.

4 Olson, D. H. and Olson, A. K. (2013) PREPARE/ENRICH program: version 2000. In R. Berger and M. Hannah (eds). *Preventive Approaches in Couples Therapy*. Routledge, p. 204.

5 MacDonald, G., Zanna, M. P. and Holmes, J. G. (2000). An experimental test of the role of alcohol in relationship conflict. *Journal of Experimental Social Psychology* 36(2), 182–93. doi: 10.1006/jesp.1999.1412.

6 Golombok, S. et al. (2016). Single mothers by choice: mother–child relationships and children's psychological adjustment. *Journal of Family Psychology* 30(4), 409–18. doi: 10.1037/fam0000188.

7 Germo, G. R. et al. (2007). Child sleep arrangements and family life: perspectives from mothers and fathers. *Infant and Child Development: An International Journal of Research and Practice* 16(4), 433–56. doi: 10.1002/icd.521.

8 Education programmes: Blanchard, V. L. et al. (2009). Investigating the effects of marriage and relationship education on couples' communication skills: a meta-analytic study. *Journal of Family Psychology* 23(2), 203. doi: 10.1037/a0015211. Couples' groups: Cowan, C. P., Cowan, P. A. and Barry, J. (2011). Couples' groups for parents of preschoolers: ten-year outcomes of a randomized trial. *Journal of Family Psychology* 25(2), 240. doi: 10.1037/a0023003. DVDs: Bodenmann, G. et al. (2014). Enhancement of couples' communication and dyadic coping by a self-directed approach: a randomized controlled trial. *Journal of Consulting and Clinical Psychology* 82(4), 580. doi: 10.1037/a0036356.

9 Olson and Olson (2013), p. 203.

10 Olson and Olson (2013), p. 206.

11 Finkel, E. J. et al. (2013). A brief intervention to promote conflict reappraisal preserves marital quality over time. *Psychological Science* 24(8), 1595–601. doi: 10.1177/0956797612474938.

12 Finkel, E. J. et al. (2014). The suffocation of marriage: climbing Mount Maslow without enough oxygen. *Psychological Inquiry* 25(1), 1–41. doi: 10.1080/1047840X.2014.863723.

13 Gottman, J. and Silver, N. (2007). *The Seven Principles for Making Marriage Work*. Hachette.

14 Olson and Olson (2013), p. 203.

15 Germo et al. (2007).

16 Vanderbleek, L. et al. (2011). The relationship between play and couple satisfaction and stability. *Family Journal* 19(2), 132–9. doi: 10.1177/1066480711399729.

17 Marsh, S., Dobson, R. and Maddison, R. (2020). The relationship between household chaos and child, parent, and family outcomes: a systematic scoping review. *BMC Public Health* 20(1), 1–27. doi: 10.1186/s12889-020-08587-8.

18 Relationship: Kirkorian, H. L. et al. (2009). The impact of background television on parent–child interaction. *Child Development* 80(5), 1350–9. doi: 10.1111/j.1467-8624.2009.01337.x. Aggression: Martin, A., Razza, R. A. and Brooks-Gunn, J. (2012). Specifying the links between household chaos and preschool children's development. *Early Child Development and Care* 182(10), 1247–63. doi: 10.1080/03004430.2011.605522.

Being a parent: what to avoid

1 Poor outcomes for children who are hit: Alampay, L. P. et al. (2017). Severity and justness do not moderate the relation between corporal punishment and negative child outcomes: a multicultural and longitudinal study. *International Journal of Behavioral Development* 41(4), 491–502. doi: 10.1177/0165025417697852. Increase in risk after being spanked: MacKenzie, M. J. et al. (2015). Spanking and children's externalizing behavior across the first decade of life: evidence for transactional processes. *Journal of Youth and Adolescence* 44(3), 658–69. doi: 10.1007/s10964-014-0114-y.

2 Fairchild and Erwin (1977), cited in Durrant, J. and Ensom, R. (2012). Physical punishment of children: lessons from 20 years of research. *Canadian Medial Association Journal* 184(12), 1373–7. doi: 10.1503/cmaj.101314.

3 Smith, A. B. (2006). The state of research on the effects of physical punishment. *Social Policy Journal of New Zealand* 27, 114.

4 Long-term negative effects: Gershoff, E. T. (2016). Should parents' physical punishment of children be considered a source of toxic stress that affects brain development? *Family Relations* 65(1), 151–62. doi: 10.1111/fare.12177. Stress and higher cortisol levels: Gershoff, E. T. and Bitensky, S. H. (2007). The case against corporal punishment of children: converging evidence from social science research and international human rights law and implications for U.S. public policy. *Psychology, Public Policy, and Law* 13(4), 231. doi: 10.1037/1076-8971.13.4.231. Links to mental health issues: Smoller, J. W. (2016). The genetics of stress-related disorders: PTSD, depression, and anxiety disorders. *Neuropsychopharmacology* 41(1), 297–319. doi: 10.1038/npp.2015.266.

5 Vulnerability to depression: Hooley, J. M., Siegle, G. and Gruber, S. A. (2012). Affective and neural reactivity to criticism in individuals high and low on perceived criticism. *PLoS ONE* 7(9), e44412. doi: 10.1371/journal.pone.0044412. Responses to winning and losing: James, K. M. et al. (2021). Maternal criticism and children's neural responses to reward and loss. *Journal of Experimental Child Psychology* 211, 105226. doi: 10.1016/j.jecp.2021.105226.

6 Swenson, S. et al. (2016). Parents' use of praise and criticism in a sample of young children seeking mental health services. *Journal of Pediatric Health Care* 30(1), 49–56. doi: 10.1016/j.pedhc.2015.09.010.

7 Ideal ratio: Gottman, J. M. (1994). *What Predicts Divorce? The Relationship between Marital Processes and Marital Outcomes*. Psychology Press. Parental increase in positive comments: Armstrong, A. B. and Field, C. E. (2012). Altering positive/negative interaction ratios of mothers and young children. *Child & Family Behavior Therapy* 34(3), 231–42. doi: 10.1080/07317107.2012.707094.

8 Difficult childhood: Lotto, C. R., Altafim, E. R. P. and Linhares, M. B. M. (2021). Maternal history of childhood adversities and later negative parenting: a systematic review. *Trauma, Violence, & Abuse* 24(2), 662–83. doi: 10.1177/15248380211036076. Being easily overwhelmed and difficulty calming down: Mence, M. et al. (2014). Emotional flooding and hostile discipline in the families of toddlers with disruptive behavior problems. *Journal of Family Psychology* 28(1), 12–21. doi: 10.1037/a0035352. Shouting when stressed or angry: Poole, E. et al. (2014). Father involvement with children and couple relationships [briefing paper for the organisation Modern Fatherhood: Fathers, Work and Families in the 21st Century].

9 Jimenez, M. E. et al. (2019). Early shared reading is associated with less harsh parenting. *Journal of Developmental and Behavioral Pediatrics* 40(7), 530. doi: 10.1097/DBP.0000000000000687.

10 Markham, L. (2012). *Peaceful Parent, Happy Kids: How to Stop Yelling and Start Connecting.* TarcherPerigee.

11 Developed from Barber, B. K. (2002). *Intrusive Parenting: How Psychological Control Affects Children and Adolescents.* American Psychological Association.

12 Child feeling lack of influence: Nanda, M. M., Kotchick, B. A. and Grover, R. L. (2012). Parental psychological control and childhood anxiety: the mediating role of perceived lack of control. *Journal of Child and Family Studies* 21, 637–45. doi: 10.1007/s10826-011-9516-6. Seeing situations as threatening: Rapee, R. M. (2001). The development of generalized anxiety. In M. W. Vasey and M. R. Dadds (eds). *The Developmental Psychopathology of Anxiety.* Oxford University Press, pp. 481–503. Less able to develop secure sense of self: Soenens, B. and Vansteenkiste, M. (2010). A theoretical upgrade of the concept of parental psychological control: proposing new insights on the basis of self-determination theory. *Developmental Review* 30(1), 74–99. doi: 10.1016/j.dr.2009.11.001.

13 Perfectionism: Soenens, B., Vansteenkiste, M. and Luyten, P. (2010). Toward a domain-specific approach to the study of parental psychological control: distinguishing between dependency-oriented and achievement-oriented psychological control. *Journal of Personality* 78(1), 217–56. doi: 10.1111/j.1467-6494.2009.00614.x. Sensitivity to hurt: Walling, B. R., Mills, R. S. and Freeman, W. S. (2007). Parenting cognitions associated with the use of psychological control. *Journal of Child and Family Studies* 16(5), 642–59. doi: 10.1007/s10826-006-9113-2. Risk factor: Soenens, B. et al. (2006). In search of the sources of psychologically controlling parenting: the role of parental separation anxiety and parental maladaptive perfectionism. *Journal of Research on Adolescence* 16(4), 539–59. doi: 10.1111/j.1532-7795.2006.00507.x. Bonding: Soenens and Vansteenkiste (2010).

14 Walling, Mills and Freeman (2007).

15 Murray, K. W. et al. (2014). Parent–child relationships, parental psychological control, and aggression: maternal and paternal relationships. *Journal of Youth and Adolescence* 43(8), 1361–73. doi: 10.1007/s10964-013-0019-1.

16 Wischerth, G. A. et al. (2016). The adverse influence of permissive parenting on personal growth and the mediating role of emotional intelligence. *Journal of Genetic Psychology* 177(5), 185–9. doi: 10.1080/00221325.2016.1224223.

17 Patterson, G. R. and Fisher, P. A. (2002). Recent developments in our understanding of parenting: bidirectional effects, causal models, and the search for parsimony. In M. H. Borstein (ed.). *Handbook of Parenting, Volume 5: Practical Issues in Parenting*. Lawrence Erlbaum Associates.

18 Setting out appropriate boundaries: see the Introduction for sources outlining the difference between permissive and authoritative parenting. Effect of taking a mindful parenting approach: Gouveia, M. J. et al. (2016). Self-compassion and dispositional mindfulness are associated with parenting styles and parenting stress: the mediating role of mindful parenting. *Mindfulness* 7(3), 700–12. doi: 10.1007/s12671-016-0507-y.

19 Garcia, F. and Gracia, E. (2009). Is always authoritative the optimum parenting style? Evidence from Spanish families. *Adolescence* 44(173), 101–31.

20 Turner, K. A. et al. (2023). Too much of a good thing? Associations among parenting profiles and helicopter parenting. *Family Journal* 31(2), 296–307. doi: 10.1177/10664807221123554.

21 Ungar, M. (2009). Overprotective parenting: helping parents provide children the right amount of risk and responsibility. *American Journal of Family Therapy* 37(3), 258–71. doi: 10.1080/01926180802534247.

22 Taylor, C. T. and Alden, L. E. (2006). Parental overprotection and interpersonal behavior in generalized social phobia. *Behavior Therapy* 37(1), 14–24. doi: 10.1016/j.beth.2005.03.001.

23 Mental health: e.g. Yap, M. B. H. and Jorm, A. F. (2015). Parental factors associated with childhood anxiety, depression, and internalizing problems: a systematic review and meta-analysis. *Journal of Affective Disorders* 175, 424–40. doi: 10.1016/j.jad.2015.01.050. Physical health: e.g. Yerkes, M. A. et al. (2019). In the best interests of children? The paradox of intensive parenting and children's health. *Critical Public Health* 31(3), 349–60. doi: 10.1080/09581596.2019.1690632.

24 Doepke, M. and Zilibotti, F. (2019). The economic roots of helicopter parenting. *Phi Delta Kappan* 100(7), 22–7. doi: 10.1177/0031721719841334.

25 Doepke and Zilibotti (2019).

26 Main link: Jones, L. B. et al. (2021). Systematic review of the link between maternal anxiety and overprotection. *Journal of Affective Disorders* 295, 541–51. doi: 10.1016/j.jad.2021.08.065. Separation anxiety: Cooklin, A. R. et al. (2013). Postpartum maternal separation anxiety, overprotective parenting, and children's social-emotional well-being: longitudinal evidence from an Australian cohort. *Journal of Family Psychology* 27(4), 618–28. doi: 10.1037/a0033332.

27 Child prematurity and overprotectiveness: Faleschini, S. et al. (2020). Trajectories of overprotective parenting and hyperactivity-impulsivity and inattention among moderate–late preterm children: a population-based study. *Journal of Abnormal Child Psychology* 48(12), 1555–68. doi: 10.1007/s10802-020-00704-w. Time/energy cost of intensive parenting: Faircloth, C. (2014). Intensive parenting and the expansion of parenting. In E. Lee, J. Bristow and J. Macvarish (eds). *Parenting Culture Studies*. Palgrave Macmillan, pp. 25–50.

28 Ungar (2009).

Being a parent: things that work

1 Health: e.g. Alen, N. V. et al. (2020). Childhood parental warmth and heart rate variability in midlife: implications for health. *Personal Relationships* 27(3), 506–25. doi: 10.1111/pere.12329. Behaviour: e.g. Pinquart, M. (2017b). Associations of parenting dimensions and styles with externalizing problems of children and adolescents: an updated meta-analysis. *Developmental Psychology* 53(5), 873–932. doi: 10.1037/dev0000295. Well-being: e.g. Khaleque, A. (2013). Perceived parental warmth, and children's psychological adjustment, and personality dispositions: a meta-analysis. *Journal of Child and Family Studies* 22(2), 297–306. doi: 10.1007/s10826-012-9579-z. Poverty-related stress: Thompson, R.A. (2014). Stress and child development. *Future of Children* 24(1), 41–59. doi: 10.1353/foc.2014.0004.

2 Luangrath, A. and Hiscock, H. (2011). Problem behaviour in children – an approach for general practice. *Australian Family Physician* 40(9), 678–81.

3 One study has found, counter-intuitively, that better understanding of emotions in children is linked to slightly worse psychological well-being. The authors speculate that children with worse mental health spend more time trying to work out what others are thinking and feeling – they train themselves to understand emotions better. See: Göbel, A. et al. (2016). The relationship between emotion comprehension and internalizing and externalizing behavior in 7- to 10-year-old children. *Frontiers in Psychology* 7, 1917. doi: 10.3389/fpsyg.2016.01917.

4 Tantrum frequency: Potegal, M. and Davidson, R. J. (2003). Temper tantrums in young children: 1. behavioural composition. *Developmental and Behavioral Pediatrics* 24(3), 140–7. doi: 10.1097/00004703-200306000-00002.

5 Eisenberg, N. and Fabes, R. (1994). Mothers' reactions to children's negative emotions: relations to children's temperament and anger behavior. *Merrill-Palmer Quarterly* 40(1), 138–56. http://www.jstor.org/stable/23087912.

6 Faber, A. and Mazlish, E. (2012). *How to Talk So Kids Will Listen and Listen So Kids Will Talk.* Piccadilly Press, p. 30.

7 Moed, A. et al. (2017). Expressing negative emotions to children: mothers' aversion sensitivity and children's adjustment. *Journal of Family Psychology* 31(2), 224–33. doi: 10.1037/fam0000239.

8 Playful parents: Shorer, M. et al. (2019). Parental playfulness and children's emotional regulation: the mediating role of parents' emotional regulation and the parent–child relationship. *Early Child Development and Care* 191(2), 210–20. doi: 10.1080/03004430.2019.1612385. Improved self-soothing abilities: Garner, P. W. (1995). Toddlers' emotion regulation behaviours: the roles of social conduct and family expressiveness. *Journal of Genetic Psychology* 156(4), 417–30. doi: doi: 10.1080/00221325.1995.9914834.

9 Karreman, A. et al. (2006). Parenting and self-regulation in preschoolers: a meta-analysis. *Infant and Child Development* 15(6), 561–79. doi: 10.1002/icd.478.

10 Cited in Lansbury, J. (2013). *No Bad Kids: Toddler Discipline without Shame* [Kindle edn]. JLML Press.

11 Ackerlund Brandt, J. A. et al. (2015). The value of choice as a reinforcer for typically developing children. *Journal of Applied Behavior Analysis* 48(2), 344–62. doi: 10.1002/jaba.199.

12 Froiland, J. M. (2015). Parents' weekly descriptions of autonomy supportive communication: promoting children's motivation to learn and positive emotions. *Journal of Child and Family Studies* 24(1), 117–26. doi: 10.1007/s10826-013-9819-x.

Relationships

1 Rodwell, H. and Norris, V. (2017). *Parenting with Theraplay®: Understanding Attachment and How to Nurture a Closer Relationship with Your Child.* Jessica Kingsley Publishers.

2 Pressures of schoolwork: Noack, P. and Buhl, H. M. (2004). Child–parent relationships. In F. R. Lang and K. L. Fingerman (eds). *Growing Together: Personal Relationships Across the Life Span.* Cambridge University Press, pp.

45–75. Complexity of parents' work: Danner-Vlaardingerbroek, G. et al. (2013). The psychological availability of dual-earner parents for their children after work. *Family Relations* 62(5), 741–54. doi: 10.1111/fare.12039. Fatigue: White, C. P. et al. (2015). Does maternal fatigue influence maternal verbal control in a stressful parenting task with toddlers? *Journal of Child and Family Studies* 24, 351–62. doi: 10.1007/s10826-013-9843-x. Finances: Ramdahl, M. E. et al. (2018). Family wealth and parent–child relationships. *Journal of Child and Family Studies* 27, 1534–43. doi: 10.1007/s10826-017-1003-2.

3   Coached parents: Thomas, R. et al. (2017). Parent–child interaction therapy: a meta-analysis. *Pediatrics* 140(3), e20170352. doi: 10.1542/peds.2017-0352. (Note that other elements formed part of this coaching too.) Considering child's thoughts and feelings: Rostad, W. L. and Whitaker, D. J. (2016). The association between reflective functioning and parent–child relationship quality. *Journal of Child and Family Studies* 25, 2164–77. doi: 10.1007/s10826-016-0388-7.

4   Lindo, N. A. et al. (2012). Child parent relationship therapy: exploring parents' perceptions of intervention, process, and effectiveness. *International Journal of Humanities and Social Science* 2(1), 51–61.

5   Booth, P. B. and Jernberg, A. M. (2010). *Theraplay: Helping Parents and Children Build Better Relationships through Attachment-Based Play*. Jossey-Bass.

6   Damour, L. (2017). *Untangled: Guiding Teenage Girls through the Seven Transitions into Adulthood*. Ballantine Books.

7   Duncan, L. G., Coatsworth, J. D. and Greenberg, M. T. (2009). A model of mindful parenting: implications for parent–child relationships and prevention research. *Clinical Child and Family Psychology Review* 12, 255–70. doi: 10.1007/s10567-009-0046-3.

8   Support in developing healthy independence level: Hodges, E. V. E., Finnegan, R. A. and Perry, D. G. (1999). Skewed autonomy–relatedness in preadolescents' conceptions of their relationships with mother, father, and best friend. *Developmental Psychology* 35(3), 737–48. doi: 10.1037//0012-1649.35.3.737. Secretiveness: Hawk, S. T. et al. (2013). 'I still haven't found what I'm looking for': parental privacy invasion predicts reduced parental knowledge. *Developmental Psychology* 49(7), 1286–98. doi: 10.1037/a0029484.

9   Stein and Albro (1997), cited in Stein, N. L. and Albro, E. R. (2001). The origins and nature of arguments: studies in conflict understanding, emotion, and negotiation. *Discourse Processes* 32(2–3), 113–13. doi: 10.1080/0163853X.2001.9651594.

10   Hastings, P. D. and Grusec, J. E. (1998). Parenting goals as organizers of responses to parent–child disagreement. *Developmental Psychology* 34(3), 465–79. doi: 10.1037/0012-1649.34.3.465.

11 Fauchier, A. and Margolin, G. (2004). Affection and conflict in marital and parent–child relationships. *Journal of Marital and Family Therapy* 30(2), 197–211. doi: 10.1111/j.1752-0606.2004.tb01234.x.

12 Laible, D. J. and Thompson, R. A. (2002). Mother–child conflict in the toddler years: lessons in emotion, morality, and relationships. *Child Development* 73(4), 1187–203. doi: 10.1111/1467-8624.00466.

13 Shy and withdrawn children, and best friends: Rubin, K. H. et al. (2006). The best friendships of shy/withdrawn children: prevalence, stability, and relationship quality. *Journal of Abnormal Child Psychology* 34(2), 143–57. doi: 10.1007/s10802-005-9017-4. Making and maintaining friendships: Ladd, G. et al. (2011). Characterizing and comparing the friendships of anxious-solitary and unsociable preadolescents. *Child Development* 82(5), 1434–53. doi: 10.1111/j.1467-8624.2011.01632.x.

14 MacEvoy, J. et al. (2016). Friendship expectations and children's friendship-related behavior and adjustment. *Merrill-Palmer Quarterly* 62(1), 74–104. doi: 10.13110/merrpalmquar1982.62.1.0074.

15 Black, B. and Logan, A. (1995). Links between communication patterns in mother–child, father–child, and child–peer interactions and children's social status. *Child Development* 66, 255–71. doi: 10.2307/1131204.

16 Dunn and Slomkowski (1992), cited in Canary, D. J., Cupach, W. R. and Messman, S. J. (1995). *Relationship Conflict: Conflict in Parent–Child, Friendship, and Romantic Relationships.* Sage Publications, p. 55.

17 Whiteman, S. D., Becerra Bernard, J. M. and Jensen, A. C. (2011). Sibling influence in human development. In J. Caspi (ed.). *Sibling Development: Implications for Mental Health Practitioners.* Springer Publishing Co., pp. 1–16.

18 Bascoe, S., Davies, P. and Cummings, E. (2012). Beyond warmth and conflict: the developmental utility of a boundary conceptualization of sibling relationship processes. *Child Development* 83(6), 2121–38. doi: 10.1111/j.1467-8624.2012.01817.x. See also https://dictionary.apa.org/enmeshment.

19 Pike, A. and Oliver, B. R. (2017). Child behavior and sibling relationship quality: a cross-lagged analysis. *Journal of Family Psychology* 31(2), 250–5. doi: 10.1037/fam0000248.

20 Effects of non-intervention: Tucker, C. J. and Kazura, K. (2013). Parental responses to school-aged children's sibling conflict. *Journal of Child and Family Studies* 22(5), 737–45. doi: 10.1007/s10826-013-9741-2. Intervention and closeness with teenagers: Kramer, L., Perozynski, L. A. and Chung, T. Y. (1999). Parental responses to sibling conflict: the effects of development and parent gender. *Child Development* 70(6), 1401–14. doi: 10.1111/1467-8624.00102.

21 Smith, J. and Ross, H. (2007). Training parents to mediate sibling disputes affects children's negotiation and conflict understanding. *Child Development* 78(3), 790–805. doi: 10.1111/j.1467-8624.2007.01033.x.

22 Smith and Ross (2007).

23 Ross, H. (2014). Parent mediation of sibling conflict: addressing issues of fairness and morality. In C. Wainryb and H. Recchia (eds). *Talking about Right and Wrong: Parent–Child Conversations as Contexts for Moral Development.* Cambridge University Press, pp. 143–67.

24 Tucker, C. J. and Finkelhor, D. (2017). The state of interventions for sibling conflict and aggression: a systematic review. *Trauma, Violence, and Abuse* 18(4), 396–406. doi: 10.1177/1524838015622438.

25 Adams, C. D. and Kelley, M. L. (1992). Managing sibling aggression: overcorrection as an alternative to time-out. *Behavior Therapy* 23(4), 707–17. doi: 10.1016/S0005-7894(05)80230-8.

26 Gass, K., Jenkins, J. and Dunn, J. (2007). Are sibling relationships protective? A longitudinal study. *Journal of Child Psychology and Psychiatry* 48(2), 167–75. doi: 10.1111/j.1469-7610.2006.01699.x.

27 Health problems: e.g. Copeland, W. E. et al. (2014). Childhood bullying involvement predicts low-grade systemic inflammation into adulthood. *Proceedings of the National Academy of Sciences* 111(21), 7570–5. doi: 10.1073/pnas.1323641111. Mental health problems: e.g. Christina, S. et al. (2021). The bidirectional relationships between peer victimization and internalizing problems in school-aged children: an updated systematic review and meta-analysis. *Clinical Psychology Review* 85, 101979. doi: 10.1016/j.cpr.2021.101979. Long-lasting impacts: e.g. Schäfer, M. et al. (2004). Lonely in the crowd: recollections of bullying. *British Journal of Developmental Psychology* 22(3), 379–94. doi: 10.1348/0261510041552756.

28 Children in the US: Lebrun-Harris, L. A. et al. (2019). Bullying victimization and perpetration among U.S. children and adolescents: 2016 National Survey of Children's Health. *Journal of Child and Family Studies* 28, 2543–57. doi: 10.1007/s10826-018-1170-9. Children in the UK: Muijs, D. (2017). Can schools reduce bullying? The relationship between school characteristics and the prevalence of bullying behaviours. *British Journal of Educational Psychology* 87(2), 255–72. doi: 10.1111/bjep.12148. Prevalence of online bullying: DePaolis, K. J. and Williford, A. (2019). Pathways from cyberbullying victimization to negative health outcomes among elementary school students: a longitudinal investigation. *Journal of Child and Family Studies* 28, 2390–403. doi: 10.1007/s10826-018-1104-6.

29 Davis, S. and Nixon, C. L. (2014). *Youth Voice Project: Student Insights into Bullying and Peer Mistreatment.* Research Press.

30 Davis and Nixon (2014).

31 Bullied children and exercise: Sibold, J. et al. (2020). Bullying environment moderates the relationship between exercise and mental health in bullied US children. *Journal of School Health* 90(3), 194–9. doi: 10.1111/josh.12864. Forgiveness: Watson, H., Rapee, R. and Todorov, N. (2017). Forgiveness reduces anger in a school bullying context. *Journal of Interpersonal Violence* 32(11), 1642–57. doi: 10.1177/0886260515589931.

32 Waasdorp, T. E. and Bradshaw, C. P. (2009). Child and parent perceptions of relational aggression within urban predominantly African American children's friendships: examining patterns of concordance. *Journal of Child and Family Studies* 18, 731. doi: 10.1007/s10826-009-9279-5.

Behaviour

1 Swiss study: Moses Passini, C., Pihet, S. and Favez, N. (2014). Assessing specific discipline techniques: a mixed-methods approach. *Journal of Child and Family Studies* 23, 1389–402. doi: 10.1007/s10826-013-9796-0. Criticism-to-praise ratio: Swenson, S. et al. (2016). Parents' use of praise and criticism in a sample of young children seeking mental health services. *Journal of Pediatric Health Care* 30(1), 49–56. doi: 10.1016/j.pedhc.2015.09.010.

2 Delgado, B. et al. (2018). Temperament and behavioral problems in young children: the protective role of extraversion and effortful control. *Journal of Child and Family Studies* 27, 3232–40. doi: 10.1007/s10826-018-1163-8.

3 Parenting intervention: Westwood, S., Faelling, J. and Sutton, C. (2021). 'Catch them being good': preliminary findings from a brief parenting intervention. *Early Child Development and Care* 191(10), 1613–23, p. 1613. doi: 10.1080/03004430.2019.1663184. Specific instructions: Everett, G. et al. (2005). The contributions of eye contact and contingent praise to effective instruction delivery in compliance training. *Education and Treatment of Children* 28(1), 48–62.

4 Increase in self-blame: Kamins, M. L. and Dweck, C. S. (1999). Person versus process praise and criticism: implications for contingent self-worth and coping. *Developmental Psychology* 35(3), 835–47. doi: 10.1037/0012-1649.35.3.835. Persistence levels: Zentall, S. R. and Morris, B. J. (2010). 'Good job, you're so smart': the effects of inconsistency of praise type on young children's motivation. *Journal of Experimental Child Psychology* 107(2), 155–63. doi: 10.1016/j.jecp.2010.04.015.

5 Scott, S. and Humayun, S. (2011). Parenting programmes for conduct problems. In Skuse, D. et al. (eds). *Child Psychology and Psychiatry: Frameworks for Practice*. John Wiley & Sons, pp. 387–93.

6 Hood, M. (2016). *Real Parenting for Real Kids: Enabling Parents to Bring out the Best in Their Children*. Practical Inspiration Publishing.

7 Kazdin, A. E. (2005). *Parent Management Training: Treatment for Oppositional, Aggressive, and Antisocial Behaviour in Children and Adolescents*. Oxford University Press.

8 Mageau, G. A. et al. (2018). Effectiveness and acceptability beliefs regarding logical consequences and mild punishments. *Journal of Applied Developmental Psychology* 54, 12–22. doi: 10.1016/j.appdev.2017.11.001.

9 Leijten, P. et al. (2019). Meta-analyses: key parenting program components for disruptive child behavior. *Journal of the American Academy of Child and Adolescent Psychiatry* 58(2), 180–90. doi: 10.1016/j.jaac.2018.07.900.

10 Effective tool: Leijten, P. et al. (2018). Parenting behaviors that shape child compliance: a multilevel meta-analysis. *PLoS ONE* 13(10), e0204929. doi: 10.1371/journal.pone.0204929. No harm: Knight, R. M. et al. (2020). Longitudinal relationship between time-out and child emotional and behavioral functioning. *Journal of Developmental and Behavioral Pediatrics* 41(1), 31–7. doi: 10.1097/DBP.0000000000000725.

11 Single warning: Roberts (1972a), cited in Larzelere, R. E. et al. (2020). Causal evidence for *Exclusively Positive Parenting* and for timeout: rejoinder to Holden, Grogan-Kaylor, Durrant, and Gershoff (2017). *Marriage & Family Review* 56(4), 287–319. doi: 10.1080/01494929.2020.1712304. Length of time out: Drayton, A. K. et al. (2014). Internet guidance on time out: inaccuracies, omissions, and what to tell parents instead. *Journal of Developmental and Behavioral Pediatrics* 35(4), 239–46. doi: 10.1097/DBP.0000000000000059.

12 Hembree-Kigin, T. L. and McNeil, C. B. (2013). *Parent–Child Interaction Therapy*. Springer Science & Business Media.

13 Phelan, T. W. (2010). *1-2-3 Magic: Effective Discipline for Children 2–12*. ParentMagic, Inc.

14 Ducharme, J. M. (2007). Success-based, non-coercive treatment of oppositional behavior. In C. Schaefer and J. Briesmeister (eds). *Handbook of Parent Training*. John Wiley & Sons, pp. 268–304.

15 Knight et al. (2020).

16 Deci, E. L., Koestner, R. and Ryan, R. M. (1999). A meta-analytic review of experiments examining the effects of extrinsic rewards on intrinsic motivation. *Psychological Bulletin* 125(6), 627–68. doi: 10.1037/0033-2909.125.6.627.

17 Deci, Koestner and Ryan (1999).

18 Adapted from Perry, P. (2019). *The Book You Wish Your Parents Had Read (and Your Children Will Be Glad That You Did)*. Penguin UK, pp. 191–2.

19 Searcy, Y. D. (2007). Placing the horse in front of the wagon: toward a conceptual understanding of the development of self-esteem in children and adolescents. *Child and Adolescent Social Work Journal* 24, 121–31. doi: 10.1007/s10560-006-0070-9.

20 Nieman, P. and Shea, S. (2004). Effective discipline for children. *Paediatrics & Child Health* 9(1), 37–41. doi: 10.1093/pch/9.1.37.

21 Zeytinoglu, S. et al. (2017). Pathways from maternal effortful control to child self-regulation: the role of maternal emotional support. *Journal of Family Psychology* 31(2), 170–80. doi: 10.1037/fam0000271.

22 Bowker, J. C. et al.(2010). Distinguishing children who form new best-friendships from those who do not. *Journal of Social and Personal Relationships* 27(6), 707–25. doi: 10.1177/0265407510373259.

23 Vaish, A., Carpenter, M. and Tomasello, M. (2009). Sympathy through affective perspective taking and its relation to prosocial behavior in toddlers. *Developmental Psychology* 45(2), 534–43. doi: 10.1037/a0014322.

24 Svetlova, M., Nichols, S. R. and Brownell, C. A. (2010). Toddlers' prosocial behavior: from instrumental to empathic to altruistic helping. *Child Development* 81(6), 1814–27. doi: 10.1111/j.1467-8624.2010.01512.x.

25 Friends: Eivers, A. R. et al. (2012). Concurrent and longitudinal links between children's and their friends' antisocial and prosocial behavior in preschool. *Early Childhood Research Quarterly* 27(1), 137–46. doi: 10.1016/j.ecresq.2011.05.001. Siblings: Smorti, M. and Ponti, L. (2018). How does sibling relationship affect children's prosocial behaviors and best friend relationship quality? *Journal of Family Issues* 39(8), 2413–36. doi: 10.1177/0192513X18755195. Parents: Ferreira, T. et al. (2016). Preschool children's prosocial behavior: the role of mother–child, father–child and teacher–child relationships. *Journal of Child and Family Studies* 25(6), 1829–39. doi: 10.1007/s10826-016-0369-x.

26 Lora, K. R. et al. (2014). Frequency of family meals and 6–11-year-old children's social behaviors. *Journal of Family Psychology* 28(4), 577–82. doi: 10.1037/fam0000014.

27 Hastings, P. D., Utendale, W. T. and Sullivan, C. (2007). The socialization of prosocial development. In J. E. Grusec and P. D. Hastings (eds). *Handbook of Socialization: Theory and Research*. Guilford Press, pp. 638–64.

28 Kirschner, S. and Tomasello, M. (2010). Joint music making promotes prosocial behavior in 4-year-old children. *Evolution and Human Behavior* 31(5), 354–64. doi: 10.1016/j.evolhumbehav.2010.04.004.

29 Hastings, Utendale and Sullivan (2007).

30 Avoiding information overload: Walker, L., Hennig, K. and Krettenauer, T. (2000). Parent and peer contexts for children's moral reasoning development.

Child Development 71(4), 1033–48. doi: 10.1111/1467-8624.00207. Giving clear explanations: Laible, D. J. and Thompson, R. A. (2002). Mother–child conflict in the toddler years: lessons in emotion, morality, and relationships. *Child Development* 73(4), 1187–203. doi: 10.1111/1467-8624.00466.

31 Aggressive behaviour when quick to anger: Joussemet, M. et al. (2008). Controlling parenting and physical aggression during elementary school. *Child Development* 79(2), 411–25. doi: 10.1111/j.1467-8624.2007.01133.x. Camel-shaped curve: Wahl, K. and Metzner, C. (2012) Parental influences on the prevalence and development of child aggressiveness: *Journal of Child and Family Studies* 21, 344–55. doi: 10.1007/s10826-011-9484-x.

32 Boys more aggressive than girls: Joussemet et al. (2008). Girls harming relationships: Crick et al. (1999), cited in Kroneman, L. M. et al. (2008). Girls' disruptive behavior and its relationship to family functioning: a review. *Journal of Child and Family Studies* 18(3), 259–73. doi: 10.1007/s10826-008-9226-x. Differences in dealing with aggression: Golden, B. (2006). *Healthy Anger: How to Help Children and Teens Manage their Anger*. Oxford University Press.

33 Dadds, M. R. and Salmon, K. (2003). Punishment insensitivity and parenting: temperament and learning as interacting risks for antisocial behavior. *Clinical Child and Family Psychology Review* 6(2), 69–86. doi: 10.1023/A:1023762009877.

34 Rhee, S. H. and Waldman, I. D. (2002). Genetic and environmental influences on antisocial behavior: a meta-analysis of twin and adoption studies. *Psychological Bulletin* 128(3), 490–529. doi: 10.1037/0033-2909.128.3.490.

35 Prescott, A. T., Sargent, J. D. and Hull, J. G. (2018). Metaanalysis of the relationship between violent video game play and physical aggression over time. *Proceedings of the National Academy of Sciences* 115(40), 9882–8. doi: 10.1073/pnas.1611617114.

36 Collier, K. M. et al. (2016). Does parental mediation of media influence child outcomes? A meta-analysis on media time, aggression, substance use, and sexual behavior. *Developmental Psychology* 52(5), 798–812. doi: 10.1037/dev0000108.

37 DeGangi, G. A. (2017). *Pediatric Disorders of Regulation in Affect and Behavior: A Therapist's Guide to Assessment and Treatment*. Academic Press.

38 Sulking links with unfairness and hurt feelings: Hardecker, D. J. K. and Haun, D. B. M. (2020). Approaching the development of hurt feelings in childhood. *New Ideas in Psychology* 59, 100796. doi: 10.1016/j.newideapsych.2020.100796. Hurt feelings as lack of perceived value: Leary, M. R. et al. (1998). The causes, phenomenology, and consequences of hurt feelings. *Journal of Personality and Social Psychology* 74(5), 1225–37. doi: 10.1037/0022-3514.74.5.1225. Sense of abandonment and sibling favouritism: Hardecker and Haun (2020).

39 Rogers, B. and McPherson, E. (2014). *Behaviour Management with Young Children: Crucial First Steps with Children 3–7 Years*. Sage. (Note that this book is aimed at teachers rather than parents.)

40 Owen, D. J., Slep, A. M. S. and Heyman, R. E. (2012). The effect of praise, positive nonverbal response, reprimand, and negative nonverbal response on child compliance: a systematic review. *Clinical Child and Family Psychology Review* 15(4), 364–85. doi: 10.1007/s10567-012-0120-0.

41 Owen, Slep and Heyman (2012).

42 General effectiveness recommendation: Radley, K. C. and Dart, E. H. (2015). Antecedent strategies to promote children's and adolescents' compliance with adult requests: a review of the literature. *Clinical Child and Family Psychology Review* 19(1), 39–54. doi: 10.1007/s10567-015-0197-3. Eye contact, physical proximity, speaking quietly and giving time to respond: Ford, A. D. et al. (2001). The sequential introduction of compliance training components with elementary-aged children in general education classroom settings. *School Psychology Quarterly* 16(2), 142–57. doi: 10.1521/scpq.16.2.142.18702. (Note the educational focus of this study.) Speaking calmly, giving one instruction at a time and framing requests positively: Scott, S. and Humayun, S. (2011). Parenting programmes for conduct problems. In Skuse, D. et al. (eds). *Child Psychology and Psychiatry: Frameworks for Practice*. John Wiley & Sons, pp. 387–93.

43 Radley and Dart (2015).

44 Radley and Dart (2015).

45 Owen, Slep and Heyman (2012).

46 Characteristics of children who bully others: Cook, C. R. et al. (2010). Predictors of bullying and victimization in childhood and adolescence: a meta-analytic investigation. *School Psychology Quarterly* 25(2), 65–83. doi: 10.1037/a0020149. Secure relationship: Walden, L. M. and Beran, T. N. (2010). Attachment quality and bullying behavior in school-aged youth. *Canadian Journal of School Psychology* 25(1), 5–18. doi: 10.1177/0829573509357046. Domestic violence: Chesworth, B., Lanier, P. and Rizo, C. F. (2019). The association between exposure to intimate partner violence and child bullying behaviors. *Journal of Child and Family Studies* 28(12). doi: 10.1007/s10826-019-01439-z. Authoritarian parents: Baldry, A. C. and Farrington, D. P. (2000). Bullies and delinquents: personal characteristics and parental styles. *Journal of Community & Applied Social Psychology* 10(1), 17–31. doi: 10.1002/(SICI)1099-1298(200001/02)10:1<17::AID-CASP526>3.0.CO;2-M. Boys more often bully than girls: Cook et al. (2010).

47 'Bully/victims' bullied more and do more bullying: Demaray, M. K. and Malecki, C. K. (2003). Perceptions of the frequency and importance of social support by students classified as victims, bullies, and bully/victims in an urban middle school. *School Psychology Review* 32(3), 471–89. doi: 10.1080/02796015.2003.12086213. Bad behaviour, performance and depression in bully/victims: Haynie, D. L. et al. (2001). Bullies, victims, and bully/victims: distinct groups of at risk youth. *Journal of Early Adolescence* 21(1), 29–49. doi: 10.1177/0272431601021001002.

48 Fewer parental activities with bully/victims: Bowes, L. et al. (2009). School, neighborhood, and family factors are associated with children's bullying involvement: a nationally representative longitudinal study. *Journal of the American Academy of Child & Adolescent Psychiatry* 48(5), 545–53. doi: 10.1097/chi.0b013e31819cb017. Bullies' perception of less parental support: Demaray and Malecki (2003).

49 Cook et al. (2010).

50 The details of effective instruction delivery are drawn from lower-quality research.

Physical health

1 This was actually my partner, four weeks too late for me to decide not to procreate with him.

2 World Health Organization (2021). WHO remains firmly committed to the principles set out in the preamble to the Constitution, https://www.who.int/about/governance/constitution.

3 Weight beliefs: Tompkins, C. L., Seablom, M. and Brock, D. W. (2015). Parental perception of child's body weight: a systematic review. *Journal of Child and Family Studies* 24(5), 1384–91. doi: 10.1007/s10826-014-9945-0. Underfeeding: Pugliese, M. T. et al. (1987). Parental health beliefs as a cause of nonorganic failure to thrive. *Pediatrics* 80(2), 175–82. The second study focused on very young children.

4 Dumuid, D. et al. (2017). Health-related quality of life and lifestyle behavior clusters in school-aged children from 12 countries. *Journal of Pediatrics* 183, 178–83. doi: 10.1016/j.jpeds.2016.12.048.

5 Sitting down not a concern: Cliff, D. P. et al. (2016). Objectively measured sedentary behaviour and health and development in children and adolescents: systematic review and meta-analysis. *Obesity Reviews* 17(4), 330–44. doi: 10.1111/obr.12371. Sitting as bad for children's health: Tremblay, M. S. et al. (2011). Systematic review of sedentary behaviour and health indicators in school-aged children and youth. *International Journal of Behavioral Nutrition and Physical Activity* 8(1), 1–22. doi: 10.1186/1479-5868-8-98.

6 Smith, J. J. et al. (2014). The health benefits of muscular fitness for children and adolescents: a systematic review and meta-analysis. *Sports Medicine* 44(9), 1209–23. doi: 10.1007/s40279-014-0196-4.

7 Gunnar, M. et al. (2010). The rise in cortisol in family day care: associations with aspects of care quality, child behavior, and child sex. *Child Development* 81(3), 851–69. doi: 10.1111/j.1467-8624.2010.01438.x.

8 Healthier arteries: Lydakis, C. et al. (2012). Correlation of blood pressure, obesity, and adherence to the Mediterranean diet with indices of arterial stiffness in children. *European Journal of Pediatrics* 171(9), 1373–82. doi: 10.1007/s00431-012-1735-3. Wheezing: Castro-Rodriguez, J. A. et al. (2008). Mediterranean diet as a protective factor for wheezing in preschool children. *Journal of Pediatrics* 152(6), 823–8. doi: 10.1016/j.jpeds.2008.01.003. Gut microbiome: Ou, Y. et al. (2022). Development of the gut microbiota in healthy children in the first ten years of life: associations with internalizing and externalizing behavior. *Gut Microbes* 14(1), 2038853. doi: 10.1080/19490976.2022.2038853.

9 Spector, T. (2020). *Spoon-Fed: Why Almost Everything We've Been Told about Food Is Wrong.* Random House.

10 Dairy: O'Sullivan, T. A., Schmidt, K. A. and Kratz, M. (2020). Whole-fat or reduced-fat dairy product intake, adiposity, and cardiometabolic health in children: a systematic review. *Advances in Nutrition* 11(4), 928–50. doi: 10.1093/advances/nmaa011. Sugar: Wolraich, M. L., Wilson, D. B. and White, J. W. (1995). The effect of sugar on behavior or cognition in children: a meta-analysis. *Jama* 274(20), 1617–21. doi: 10.1001/jama.1995.03530200053037.

11 Dallacker, M., Hertwig, R. and Mata, J. (2018). The frequency of family meals and nutritional health in children: a meta-analysis. *Obesity Reviews* 19(5), 638–53.

12 Fuentes-Leonarte, V., Tenías, J. M. and Ballester, F. (2009). Levels of pollutants in indoor air and respiratory health in preschool children: a systematic review. *Pediatric Pulmonology* 44(3), 231–43. doi: 10.1002/ppul.20965.

13 Aggio, D. et al. (2012). Temporal relationships between screen-time and physical activity with cardiorespiratory fitness in English schoolchildren: a 2-year longitudinal study. *Preventive Medicine* 55(1), 37–9. doi: 10.1016/j.ypmed.2012.04.012.

14 Hatam-Nahavandi, K. et al. (2020). Pediculosis capitis among school-age students worldwide as an emerging public health concern: a systematic review and meta-analysis of past five decades. *Parasitology Research* 119(10), 3125–43. doi: 10.1007/s00436-020-06847-5.

15 Coating with jelly or oils: Flores-Genuino, R. N. S., Gnilo, C. M. S. and Dofitas, B. L. (2020). Occlusive versus neurotoxic agents for topical treatment of head lice infestation: a systematic review and meta-analysis. *Pediatric Dermatology* 37(1), 86–92. doi: 10.1111/pde.14016. Herbal treatments and combing: Grieve, K. A. et al. (2007). A randomised, double-blind, comparative efficacy trial of three head lice treatment options: malathion, pyrethrins with piperonyl butoxide and MOOV Head Lice Solution. *Australian Pharmacist* 26(9), 738–43. Kunzea oil: Williams, C. R. et al. (2016). Can kunzea oil (Kunzea ambigua) control head lice (Pediculus humanus capitis)? *Parasitology Open* 2. doi: 10.1017/pao.2015.2. Tea tree oil and nerolidol: Di Campli, E. et al. (2012). Activity of tea tree oil and nerolidol alone or in combination against Pediculus capitis (head lice) and its eggs. *Parasitology Research* 111(5), 1985–92. doi: 10.1007/s00436-012-3045-0.

16 Åslund, L. et al. (2018). Cognitive and behavioral interventions to improve sleep in school-age children and adolescents: a systematic review and meta-analysis. *Journal of Clinical Sleep Medicine* 14(11), 1937–47. doi: 10.5664/jcsm.7498.

17 One in five children: Montgomery, P. and Dunne, D. (2007). Sleep disorders in children. *BMJ Clinical Evidence*, 2007, 2304. Health: Williamson, A. A. et al. (2021). Sleep problems, internalizing and externalizing symptoms, and domains of health-related quality of life: bidirectional associations from early childhood to early adolescence. *Sleep* 44(1), zsaa139. doi: 10.1093/sleep/zsaa139. Weight: Chaput, J. et al. (2016). Systematic review of the relationships between sleep duration and health indicators in school-aged children and youth. *Applied Physiology, Nutrition, and Metabolism* 41(6), S266–S282. doi: 10.1139/apnm-2015-0627. Children who sleep badly as babies: Byars, K. C. et al. (2012). Prevalence, patterns, and persistence of sleep problems in the first 3 years of life. *Pediatrics* 129(2), e276–e284. doi: 10.1542/peds.2011-0372. Child's sleep affecting parents' sleep: Meltzer, L. J. and Mindell, J. A. (2007). Relationship between child sleep disturbances and maternal sleep, mood, and parenting stress: a pilot study. *Journal of Family Psychology* 21(1), 67–73. doi: 10.1037/0893-3200.21.1.67.

18 Hale, L. et al. (2011). A longitudinal study of preschoolers' language-based bedtime routines, sleep duration, and well-being. *Journal of Family Psychology* 25(3), 423–33. doi: 10.1037/a0023564.

19 Common elements: Staples, A. D., Bates, J. E. and Petersen, I. T. (2015). Bedtime routines in early childhood: prevalence, consistency, and associations with nighttime sleep. *Monographs of the Society for Research in Child Development* 80(1), 141–59. doi: 10.1111/mono.12149. An hour more of sleep: Mindell, J. A. et al. (2009). Developmental aspects of sleep hygiene: findings from the

2004 National Sleep Foundation Sleep in America Poll. *Sleep Medicine* 10(7), 771–9. doi: 10.1016/j.sleep.2008.07.016. Self-care routines: Spilsbury, J. C. et al. (2005). Effects of the home environment on school-aged children's sleep. *Sleep* 28(11), 1419–27. doi: 10.1093/sleep/28.11.1419. Link between strictness and bedtime stress: Golem, D. et al. (2019). 'My stuffed animals help me': the importance, barriers, and strategies for adequate sleep behaviors of school-age children and parents. *Sleep Health* 5(2), 152–60. doi: 10.1016/j.sleh.2018.11.003. Link between bedtime stress and sleep: Mindell, J. A. et al. (2015). Bedtime routines for young children: a dose-dependent association with sleep outcomes. *Sleep* 38(5), 717–22. doi: 10.5665/sleep.4662.

20 Mindell et al. (2009).

21 Mindell et al. (2009).

22 Screens in bedrooms: Carter, B. et al. (2016). Association between portable screen-based media device access or use and sleep outcomes: a systematic review and meta-analysis. *JAMA Pediatrics* 170(12), 1202–8. doi: 10.1001/jamapediatrics.2016.2341. Twenty minutes' sleep: Mindell et al. (2009).

23 Golem et al. (2019).

24 Link to sleep: Mindell et al. (2009). Sensitivity: Torres-Ugalde, Y. C. et al. (2020). Caffeine consumption in children: innocuous or deleterious? A systematic review. *International Journal of Environmental Research and Public Health* 17(7), 2489. doi: 10.3390/ijerph17072489.

25 Nutritious food and better sleep: Golley, R. K. et al. (2013). Sleep duration or bedtime? Exploring the association between sleep timing behaviour, diet and BMI in children and adolescents. *International Journal of Obesity* 37(4), 546–51. doi: 10.1038/ijo.2012.212. Carbohydrate and calcium: Galland, B. C. and Mitchell, E. A. (2010). Helping children sleep. *Archives of Disease in Childhood* 95(10), 850–3. doi: 10.1136/adc.2009.162974.

26 CBT sessions: Åslund et al. (2018). Teaching yourself about sleep: San Ng, A. et al. (2013). The relationship between parent and child dysfunctional beliefs about sleep and child sleep. *Journal of Child and Family Studies* 22(6), 827–35. doi: 10.1007/s10826-012-9637-6.

27 Forty-seven minutes: Magee, L. et al. (2022). Nonpharmacological interventions to lengthen sleep duration in healthy children: a systematic review and meta-analysis. *JAMA Pediatrics* 176(11), 1084–97. doi: 10.1001/jamapediatrics.2022.3172. Getting out of bed: Stores, G. (1999). Sleep disorders in children and adolescents. *Advances in Psychiatric Treatment* 5, 19–29. doi: 10.1192/apt.5.1.19.

28 No long-term harm/benefit: Price, A. M. et al. (2012). Five-year follow-up of harms and benefits of behavioral infant sleep intervention: randomized trial.

Pediatrics 130(4), 643–51. doi: 10.1542/peds.2011-3467. Not intervening: Williams, K. E. et al. (2017). A developmental cascade model of behavioral sleep problems and emotional and attentional self-regulation across early childhood. *Behavioral Sleep Medicine* 15(1), 1–21. doi: 10.1080/15402002.2015.1065410.

29 Fangupo, L. J. et al. (2021). Do sleep interventions change sleep duration in children aged 0–5 years? A systematic review and meta-analysis of randomised controlled trials. *Sleep Medicine Reviews* 59, 101498. doi: 10.1016/j. smrv.2021.101498.

30 e.g. Montgomery and Dunne (2007).

31 Moore, B. A. et al. (2007). Brief report: evaluating the Bedtime Pass Program for child resistance to bedtime – a randomized, controlled trial. *Journal of Pediatric Psychology* 32(3), 283–7. doi: 10.1093/jpepsy/jsl025.

32 Studies of babies: e.g. Kuhn, B. R. and Elliott, A. J. (2003). Treatment efficacy in behavioral pediatric sleep medicine. *Journal of Psychosomatic Research* 54(6), 587–97. doi: 10.1016/s0022-3999(03)00061-8. Waking at night: e.g. Newton, A. T., Honaker, S. M. and Reid, G. J. (2020). Risk and protective factors and processes for behavioral sleep problems among preschool and early school-aged children: a systematic review. *Sleep Medicine Reviews* 52, 101303. doi: 10.1016/j.smrv.2020.101303.

33 Boreham, C. and Riddoch, C. (2001). The physical activity, fitness and health of children. *Journal of Sports Sciences* 19(12), 915–29. doi: 10.1080/026404101317108426.

34 Aerobic, muscle and bone-strengthening exercise: Janssen, I. and LeBlanc, A. G. (2010). Systematic review of the health benefits of physical activity and fitness in school-aged children and youth. *International Journal of Behavioral Nutrition and Physical Activity* 7(1), 1–16. doi: 10.1186/1479-5868-7-40. Bone mineral: Hind, K. and Burrows, M. (2007). Weight-bearing exercise and bone mineral accrual in children and adolescents: a review of controlled trials. *Bone* 40(1), 14–27. doi: 10.1016/j.bone.2006.07.006. Jumping: Gómez- Bruton, A. et al. (2017). Plyometric exercise and bone health in children and adolescents: a systematic review. *World Journal of Pediatrics* 13(2), 112–21. doi: 10.1007/s12519-016-0076-0. Bunny hops and frog jumps: Faigenbaum, A. D. et al. (2020). Making a strong case for prioritizing muscular fitness in youth physical activity guidelines. *Current Sports Medicine Reports* 19(12), 530–6. doi: 10.1249/JSR.0000000000000784.

35 Showing importance of exercise: Welk, G. (1999). *Promoting Physical Activity in Children: Parental Influences*. ERIC Clearinghouse on Teaching and Teacher Education. Providing exercise opportunities: Dale, D., Corbin, C. B. and Dale, K. S. (2000). Restricting opportunities to be active during school time: do children compensate by increasing physical activity levels after school? *Research Quarterly for Exercise and Sport* 71(3), 240–8. doi: 10.1080/02701367.2000.10608904. (Note that the research underpinning this recommendation took place in an educational setting, not at home.) Fitness and time spent outdoors: Gray, C. et al. (2015). What is the relationship between outdoor time and physical activity, sedentary behaviour, and physical fitness in children? A systematic review. *International Journal of Environmental Research and Public Health* 12(6), 6455–74. doi: 10.3390/ijerph120606455.

36 Ramer, J. D. et al. (2021). Enjoyment of physical activity – not MVPA during physical education – predicts future MVPA participation and sport self-concept. *Sports* 9(9), 128. doi: 10.3390/sports9090128.

37 Petersen, T. L. et al. (2020). Association between parent and child physical activity: a systematic review. *International Journal of Behavioral Nutrition and Physical Activity* 17(1), 67. doi: 10.1186/s12966-020-00966-z.

38 Good relationships and responsiveness: Pinquart, M. (2014). Associations of general parenting and parent–child relationship with pediatric obesity: a meta-analysis. *Journal of Pediatric Psychology* 39(40), 381–93. doi: 10.1093/jpepsy/jst144. Healthy diet: Sallis, J. F., Prochaska, J. J. and Taylor, W. C. (2000). A review of correlates of physical activity of children and adolescents. *Medicine and Science in Sports and Exercise* 32(5), 963–75. doi: 10.1097/00005768-200005000-00014. Screens: Aggio et al. (2012).

39 Zabinski, M. F. et al. (2003). Overweight children's barriers to and support for physical activity. *Obesity Research* 11(2), 238–46. doi: 10.1038/oby.2003.37.

40 Lonely children struggling with social activities: e.g. Barkley, J. E., Salvy, S. J. and Roemmich, J. N. (2012). The effect of simulated ostracism on physical activity behavior in children. *Pediatrics* 129(3), e659–e666. doi: 10.1542/peds.2011-0496. Increased exercise and decreased loneliness: Page, R. M. et al. (1992). Children's feelings of loneliness and social dissatisfaction: relationship to measures of physical fitness and activity. *Journal of Teaching in Physical Education* 11(3), 211–19. doi: 10.1123/jtpe.11.3.211.

41 Kercood, S. et al. (2015). Parent rules, barriers, and places for youth physical activity vary by neighborhood walkability and income. *Children, Youth and Environments* 25(1), 100–18. doi: 10.7721/chilyoutenvi.25.1.0100.

42 Mascola, A. J., Bryson, S. W. and Agras, W. S. (2010). Picky eating during childhood: a longitudinal study to age 11 years. *Eating Behaviors* 11(4), 253–7. doi: 10.1016/j.eatbeh.2010.05.006.

43 Tatangelo, G. et al. (2016). A systematic review of body dissatisfaction and sociocultural messages related to the body among preschool children. *Body Image* 18, 86–95. doi: 10.1016/j.bodyim.2016.06.003.

44 Girls: Phares, V., Steinberg, A. R. and Thompson, J. K. (2004). Gender differences in peer and parental influences: body image disturbance, self-worth, and psychological functioning in preadolescent children. *Journal of Youth and Adolescence* 33(5), 421–9. doi: 10.1023/B:JOYO.0000037634.18749.20. Boys: Cohane, G. H. and Pope Jr, H. G. (2001). Body image in boys: a review of the literature. *International Journal of Eating Disorders* 29(4), 373–9. doi: 10.1002/eat.1033. CBeebies output: All 118 programmes listed on 7 April 2022 at https://www.bbc.co.uk/tv/cbeebies/a-z were analysed.

45 Harriger, J. A. et al. (2019). You can buy a child a curvy Barbie doll, but you can't make her like it: young girls' beliefs about Barbie dolls with diverse shapes and sizes. *Body Image* 30, 107–13. doi: 10.1016/j.bodyim.2019.06.005.

46 Yee, A. Z., Lwin, M. O. and Ho, S. S. (2017). The influence of parental practices on child promotive and preventive food consumption behaviors: a systematic review and meta-analysis. *International Journal of Behavioral Nutrition and Physical Activity* 14(1), 1–14. doi: 10.1186/s12966-017-0501-3.

47 Pearson, N. et al. (2012). Maternal and best friends' influences on meal-skipping behaviours. *British Journal of Nutrition* 108(5), 932–8. doi: 10.1017/S000711451100612X.

48 Cooke, L. (2007). The importance of exposure for healthy eating in childhood: a review. *Journal of Human Nutrition and Dietetics* 20(4), 294–301. doi: 10.1111/j.1365-277X.2007.00804.x.

49 Joseph, Reed and Mennella (2016), cited in Herz, R. (2017). *Why You Eat What You Eat: The Science behind Our Relationship with Food.* W. W. Norton & Company.

50 Dallacker, Hertwig and Mata (2018).

51 Orrell-Valente, J. K. et al. (2007). 'Just three more bites': an observational analysis of parents' socialization of children's eating at mealtime. *Appetite* 48(1), 37–45. doi: 10.1016/j.appet.2006.06.006.

52 Sadness, guilt and shame: Fisher, J. O. and Birch, L. L. (2000). Parents' restrictive feeding practices are associated with young girls' negative self-evaluation of eating. *Journal of the American Dietetic Association* 100(11), 1341–6. doi: 10.1016/S0002-8223(00)00378-3. Restrictiveness at age five: Birch, L. L., Fisher, J. O. and Davison, K. K. (2003). Learning to overeat: maternal use of restrictive feeding practices promotes girls' eating in the absence of hunger. *American Journal of Clinical Nutrition* 78(2), 215–20. doi: 10.1093/ajcn/78.2.215.

53 Cormack, J. (2017). *Helping Children Develop a Positive Relationship with Food: A Practical Guide for Early Years Professionals.* Jessica Kingsley Publishers, p. 25.

54 Gardening and vegetable-eating: Dudley, D. A., Cotton, W. G. and Peralta, L. R. (2015). Teaching approaches and strategies that promote healthy eating in primary school children: a systematic review and meta-analysis. *International Journal of Behavioral Nutrition and Physical Activity* 12(1), 1–26. doi: 10.1186/s12966-015-0182-8. Twitter graph: Andy Ryan (@itsandyryan), 'I formulated this while trying to get help in the garden' [Twitter post], 13 May 2016, https://twitter.com/ItsAndyRyan/status/995747509866725379.

55 Gillison, F. B. et al. (2016). Can it be harmful for parents to talk to their child about their weight? A meta-analysis. *Preventive Medicine* 93, 135–46. doi: 10.1016/j.ypmed.2016.10.010.

56 Hart, L. M., Damiano, S. R. and Paxton, S. J. (2016). Confident body, confident child: a randomized controlled trial evaluation of a parenting resource for promoting healthy body image and eating patterns in 2- to 6-year old children. *International Journal of Eating Disorders* 49(5), 458–72. doi: 10.1002/eat.22494.

57 Handford, C. M., Rapee, R. M. and Fardouly, J. (2018). The influence of maternal modeling on body image concerns and eating disturbances in preadolescent girls. *Behaviour Research and Therapy* 100, 17–23. doi: 10.1016/j.brat.2017.11.001.

58 Women's magazines and body dissatisfaction: Dohnt and Tiggemann (2006). Body image concerns in young girls: the role of peers and media prior to adolescence. *Journal of Youth and Adolescence* 35(2), 135–45. doi: 10.1007/s10964-005-9020-7. *iCarly*: Kirsch and Murnen (2015), cited in Slater, A. and Tiggemann, M. (2016). Little girls in a grown-up world: Exposure to sexualized media, internalization of sexualization messages, and body image in 6–9 year-old girls. *Body Image* 18, 19–22. doi: 10.1016/j.bodyim.2016.04.004. Social networking sites and body dissatisfaction: Holland, G. and Tiggemann, M. (2016). A systematic review of the impact of the use of social networking sites on body image and disordered eating outcomes. *Body Image* 17, 100–10. doi: 10.1016/j.bodyim.2016.02.008.

59 Bray, I. et al. (2018). Promoting positive body image and tackling overweight/obesity in children and adolescents: a combined health psychology and public health approach. *Preventive Medicine* 116, 219–21. doi: 10.1016/j.ypmed.2018.08.011.

Learning and play

1 Seeking out nature as adults: Snell, T. L. et al. (2016). Contact with nature in childhood and adult depression. *Children, Youth and Environments* 26(1), 111–24. doi: 10.7721/chilyoutenvi.26.1.0111. Environmental commitment as adults: Gill, T. (2014). The benefits of children's engagement with nature: a systematic literature review. *Children, Youth and Environments* 24(2), 10–34. doi: 10.7721/chilyoutenvi.24.2.0010.

2   Physical and cognitive development: Tovey, H. (2010). Playing on the edge: perceptions of risk and danger in outdoor play. In P. Broadhead, J. Howard and E. Wood (eds). *Play and Learning in the Early Years: From Research to Practice*. Sage, pp. 79–94. Learning from the environment: Dowdell, K. et al. (2011). Nature and its influence on children's outdoor play. *Journal of Outdoor and Environmental Education* 15(2), 24–35. doi: 10.1007/BF03400925. Behaviour and feeling regulation: Colliver, Y. et al. (2022). Free play predicts self-regulation years later: longitudinal evidence from a large Australian sample of toddlers and preschoolers. *Early Childhood Research Quarterly* 59, 148–61. doi: 10.1016/j. ecresq.2021.11.011.

3   Gill (2014).

4   Reading adventure stories: Clements, R. (2004). An investigation of the status of outdoor play. *Contemporary Issues in Early Childhood* 5(1), 68–80. doi: 10.2304/ciec.2004.5.1.10. Parental encouragement: Cleland, V. et al. (2010). Predictors of time spent outdoors among children: 5-year longitudinal findings. *Journal of Epidemiology and Community Health* 64(5), 400–6. doi: 10.1136/jech.2009.087460.

5   Risk as crucial for healthy development: Tremblay, M. S. et al. (2015). Position statement on active outdoor play. *International Journal of Environmental Research and Public Health* 12(6), 6475–505. doi: 10.3390/ijerph120606475. Canadian Mounted Police survey: Dalley and Ruscoe (2003), cited in Lee, H. et al. (2015). A meta-study of qualitative research examining determinants of children's independent active free play. *International Journal of Behavioral Nutrition and Physical Activity* 12(5), 1–12. doi: 10.1186/s12966-015-0165-9. Benefits outweighing health risks: Brussoni, M. et al. (2015). What is the relationship between risky outdoor play and health in children? A systematic review. *International Journal of Environmental Research and Public Health* 12(6), 6423–54. doi: 10.3390/ijerph120606423.

6   Parent, N. et al. (2021). Social determinants of playing outdoors in the neighbourhood: family characteristics, trust in neighbours and daily outdoor play in early childhood. *Canadian Journal of Public Health* 112, 120–27. doi: 10.17269/s41997-020-00355-w.

7   Lee et al. (2015).

8   Perry, P. (2019). *The Book You Wish Your Parents Had Read (and Your Children Will Be Glad That You Did)*. Penguin UK.

9   e.g. Aggio, D. et al. (2012). Temporal relationships between screen-time and physical activity with cardiorespiratory fitness in English schoolchildren:

a 2-year longitudinal study. *Preventive Medicine* 55(1), 37–9. doi: 10.1016/j.ypmed.2012.04.012.

10 Motor skills: Martzog, P. and Suggate, S. P. (2022). Screen media are associated with fine motor skill development in preschool children. *Early Childhood Research Quarterly* 60, 363–73. doi: 10.1016/j.ecresq.2022.03.010. Mental imagery: Suggate, S. P. and Martzog, P. (2022). Preschool screen-media usage predicts mental imagery two years later. *Early Child Development and Care* 192(10), 1659–72. doi: 10.1080/03004430.2021.1924164.

11 Mallawaarachchi, S. R. et al. (2022). Associations of smartphone and tablet use in early childhood with psychosocial, cognitive and sleep factors: a systematic review and meta-analysis. *Early Childhood Research Quarterly* 60, 13–33. doi: 10.1016/j.ecresq.2021.12.008.

12 Academic achievement: Hofferth, S. (2010). Home media and children's achievement and behavior. *Child Development* 81(5), 1598–619. doi: 10.1111/j.1467-8624.2010.01494.x. Language skills: Madigan, S. et al. (2020). Associations between screen use and child language skills: a systematic review and meta-analysis. *JAMA Pediatrics* 174(7), 665–75. doi: 10.1001/jamapediatrics.2020.0327. Visual–spatial and problem-solving skills: Schmidt, M. E. and Vandewater, E. A. (2008). Media and attention, cognition, and school achievement. *Future of Children* 18(1), 63–85. doi: 10.1353/foc.0.0004.

13 Less screen time, less aggression and less likely to view harmful content: Gentile, D. A. et al. (2014). Protective effects of parental monitoring of children's media use: a prospective study. *JAMA Pediatrics* 168(5), 479–84. doi: 10.1001/jamapediatrics.2014.146. Smartphone limits and reduced online harassment: Schmuck, D. et al. (2021). Out of control? How parents' perceived lack of control over children's smartphone use affects children's self-esteem over time. *New Media & Society* 25(1), 1–21. doi: 10.1177/14614448211011452.

14 Altruism, tolerance and cooperation: Wilson, B. J. (2008). Media and children's aggression, fear, and altruism. *The Future of Children* 18(1), 87–118. doi: 10.1353/foc.0.0005. On-screen relationships engaging children: Richert, R., Robb, M. and Smith, E. (2011). Media as social partners: the social nature of young children's learning from screen media. *Child Development* 82(1), 82–95. doi: 10.1111/j.1467-8624.2010.01542.x.

15 Language development: Madigan et al. (2020). Family connection: Padilla-Walker, L., Coyne, S. and Fraser, A. (2012). Getting a high-speed family connection: associations between family media use and family connection. *Family Relations* 61(3), 426–40. doi: 10.2307/41495220. Parents spending time watching TV with children: Gentile et al. (2014).

16 Raudaskoski, S., Mantere, E. and Valkonen, S. (2017). The influence of parental smartphone use, eye contact and 'bystander ignorance' on child development. In A. R. Lahikainen et al. (eds). *Media, Family Interaction and the Digitalization of Childhood*. Edward Elgar Publishing.

17 Lauricella, A. R. and Cingel, D. P. (2020). Parental influence on youth media use. *Journal of Child and Family Studies* 29(2), 1927–37. doi: 10.1007/s10826-020-01724-2.

18 Less time reading and doing number-based activities: Baker, M. and Milligan, K. (2016). Boy–girl differences in parental time investments: evidence from three countries. *Journal of Human Capital* 10(4), 399–441. doi: 10.1086/688899. Difference in reading and maths ability: Baker and Milligan (2016). Children between three and five: Abelson, P. (1996). Preparing children for the future. *Science* 274, 1819.

19 Merga, M. K. (2014). Exploring the role of parents in supporting recreational book reading beyond primary school. *English in Education* 48(2), 149–63. doi: 10.1111/17548845.2014.11912512.

20 Merga, M. K. and Mat Roni, S. (2018). Empowering parents to encourage children to read beyond the early years. *Reading Teacher* 72(2), 213–21. doi: 10.1002/trtr.1703.

21 Link to learning: Burnette, J. L. et al. (2013). Mind-sets matter: a meta-analytic review of implicit theories and self-regulation. *Psychological Bulletin* 139(3), 655–701. doi: 10.1037/a0029531; Yeager, D. S. and Dweck, C. S. (2020). What can be learned from growth mindset controversies? *American Psychologist* 75(9), 1269–84. doi: 10.1037/amp0000794. Findings on study quality: Macnamara, B. N. and Burgoyne, A. P. (2023). Do growth mindset interventions impact students' academic achievement? A systematic review and meta-analysis with recommendations for best practices. *Psychological Bulletin* 149(3–4), 133–73. doi: 10.1037/bul0000352.

22 'Scaffolding': Neitzel, C. and Stright, A. D. (2003). Mothers' scaffolding of children's problem solving: establishing a foundation of academic self-regulatory competence. *Journal of Family Psychology* 17(1), 147–59. doi: 10.1037/0893-3200.17.1.147. Reduced persistence: Leonard, J. A. et al. (2021). Children persist less when adults take over. *Child Development* 92(4), 1325–36. doi: 10.1111/cdev.13492. Symbolic play: Creaghe, N. and Kidd, E. (2022). Symbolic play as a zone of proximal development: an analysis of informational exchange. *Social Development* 31(4), 1138–56. doi: 10.1111/sode.12592.

23 Stright, A. D. et al. (2001). Instruction begins in the home: relations between parental instruction and children's self-regulation in the classroom. *Journal of Educational Psychology* 93(3), 456–66. doi: 10.1037/0022-0663.93.3.456.

24 Rich language: Landry, S. H., Smith, K. E. and Swank, P. R. (2006). Responsive parenting: establishing early foundations for social, communication, and independent problem-solving skills. *Developmental Psychology* 42(4), 627–42. doi: 10.1037/0012-1649.42.4.627. High expectations and improved attainment: Fan, X. and Chen, M. (2001). Parental involvement and students' academic achievement: a meta-analysis. *Educational Psychology Review* 13(1), 1–22. doi: 10.1023/A:1009048817385.

25 Mills, C. M. et al. (2022). 'Why do dogs pant?': characteristics of parental explanations about science predict children's knowledge. *Child Development* 93(2), 326–40. doi: 10.1111/cdev.13681.

26 Touchscreen devices: Xie, H. et al. (2018). Can touchscreen devices be used to facilitate young children's learning? A meta-analysis of touchscreen learning effect. *Frontiers in Psychology* 9, 2580. doi: 10.3389/fpsyg.2018.02580. Number games and easy sums: Susperreguy, M. I. et al. (2020). Children's home numeracy environment predicts growth of their early mathematical skills in kindergarten. *Child Development* 91(5), 1663–80. doi: 10.1111/cdev.13353.

27 IQ: Protzko, J. (2017). Raising IQ among school-aged children: five meta-analyses and a review of randomized controlled trials. *Developmental Review* 46, 81–101. doi: 10.1016/j.dr.2017.05.001. (Note that IQ is heavily contested as a measure of intelligence.) Conscientiousness, ambition and openness: Hille, A. and Schupp, J. (2015). How learning a musical instrument affects the development of skills. *Economics of Education Review* 44, 56–82. doi: 10.1016/j.econedurev.2014.10.007. Music training: Bolduc, J. et al. (2021). The impact of music training on inhibition control, phonological processing, and motor skills in kindergarteners: a randomized control trial. *Early Child Development and Care* 191(12), 1886–95. doi: 10.1080/03004430.2020.1781841.

28 Jorgensen, B. and Savla, J. (2010). Financial literacy of young adults: the importance of parental socialization. *Family Relations* 59(4), 465–78. doi: 10.1111/j.1741-3729.2010.00616.x.

29 Lewis, A. and Scott, A. J. (2000). The economic awareness, knowledge and pocket money practices of a sample of UK adolescents: a study of economic socialisation and economic psychology. *Citizenship, Social and Economics Education* 4(1), 34–46. doi: 10.2304/csee.2000.4.1.34.

30 Nguyen, H. T. et al. (2022). Gender differences in time allocation contribute to differences in developmental outcomes in children and adolescents. *Economics of Education Review* 89, 102270. doi: 10.1016/j.econedurev.2022.102270.

31 Frey, B. S. and Jegen, R. (2001). Motivation crowding theory. *Journal of Economic Surveys*, 15(5), 589–611. doi: 10.1111/1467-6419.00150.

Happiness and well-being

1 School's effect on well-being: Fazel, M. et al. (2014). Mental health interventions in schools in high-income countries. *Lancet Psychiatry* 1(5), 377–87. doi: 10.1016/S2215-0366(14)70312-8. Bullying and friendships: Gutman, L. and Feinstein, L. (2008). Children's well-being in primary school: pupil and school effects [Wider Benefits of Learning Research Report No. 25]. Centre for Research on the Wider Benefits of Learning, Institute of Education, University of London. Girls' mental health: Kaye-Tzadok, A., Kim, S. S. and Main, G. (2017). Children's subjective well-being in relation to gender – what can we learn from dissatisfied children? *Children and Youth Services Review* 80, 96–104. doi: 10.1016/j.childyouth.2017.06.058.

2 Mental health in cities vs rural areas: Evans, B. E. et al. (2018.) Urbanicity is associated with behavioral and emotional problems in elementary school-aged children. *Journal of Child and Family Studies* 27, 2193–205 (2018). doi: 10.1007/s10826-018-1062-z. Green space: Vanaken, G. J. and Danckaerts, M. (2018). Impact of green space exposure on children's and adolescents' mental health: a systematic review. *International Journal of Environmental Research and Public Health* 15(12), 2668. doi: 10.3390/ijerph15122668. Traffic noise: Schubert, M. et al. (2019). Behavioral and emotional disorders and transportation noise among children and adolescents: a systematic review and meta-analysis. *International Journal of Environmental Research and Public Health* 16(18), 3336. doi: 10.3390/ijerph16183336. Air pollution: Braithwaite, I. et al. (2019). Air pollution (particulate matter) exposure and associations with depression, anxiety, bipolar, psychosis and suicide risk: a systematic review and meta-analysis. *Environmental Health Perspectives* 127(12), 126002. doi: 10.1289/EHP4595.

3 Proximity to water: Barton, J. and Pretty, J. (2010). What is the best dose of nature and green exercise for improving mental health? A multi-study analysis. *Environmental Science and Technology* 44(10), 3947–55. doi: 10.1021/es903183r. Less freedom: Jack, G. (2010). Place matters: the significance of place attachments for children's well-being. *British Journal of Social Work* 40(3), 755–71. doi: 10.1093/BJSW/BCN142.

4 Suppression of angry feelings: Zeman, J., Shipman, K. and Suveg, C. (2002). Anger and sadness regulation: predictions to internalizing and externalizing symptoms in children. *Journal of Clinical Child and Adolescent Psychology* 31(3), 393–8. doi: 10.1207/153744202760082658. Being a more competent parent: Gurdo, L. et al. (2020). Do parental reflective functioning and parental competence affect the socioemotional adjustment of children? *Journal of Child and Family Studies* 19(12), 3621–31. doi: 10.1007/s10826-020-01840-z.

5 Greater self-compassion: Cheang, R., Gillions, A. and Sparkes, E. (2019). Do mindfulness-based interventions increase empathy and compassion in children and adolescents: a systematic review. *Journal of Child and Family Studies* 28(7), 1765–79. doi: 10.1007/s10826-019-01413-9. Active coping mechanisms: Steele, R. G. et al. (2008). Profiles and correlates of children's self-reported coping strategies using a cluster analytic approach. *Journal of Child and Family Studies* 17(1), 140–53. doi: 10.1007/s10826-007-9153-2.

6 Kouros, C. D. et al. (2020). Children's self-blame appraisals about their mothers' depressive symptoms and risk for internalizing symptoms. *Journal of Family Psychology* 34(5), 534–43. doi: 10.1037/fam0000639.

7 Intelligence as changed through effort: Schleider, J. L. et al. (2016). Parents' intelligence mindsets relate to child internalizing problems: moderation through child gender. *Journal of Child and Family Studies* 25(12), 3627–36. doi: 10.1007/s10826-016-0513-7. Witnessing racism: Heard-Garris, N. J. et al. (2018). Transmitting trauma: a systematic review of vicarious racism and child health. *Social Science & Medicine* 199, 230–40. doi: 10.1016/j. socscimed.2017.04.018.

8 Adamsons, K. and Johnson, S. K. (2013). An updated and expanded meta-analysis of nonresident fathering and child well-being. *Journal of Family Psychology* 27(4), 589–99. doi: 10.1037/a0033786

9 Sensitive, attuned childcare staff: de Vet, S. M. et al. (2023). Young children's cortisol levels at out-of-home child care: a meta-analysis. *Early Childhood Research Quarterly* 63, 204–18. doi: 10.34894/LVAYR7. Learning: e.g. Weiland, C. and Yoshikawa, H. (2013). Impacts of a prekindergarten program on children's mathematics, language, literacy, executive function, and emotional skills. *Child Development* 84(6), 2112–30. doi: 10.1111/cdev.12099. Social competence: D'Onise, K. et al. (2010). Can preschool improve child health outcomes? A systematic review. *Social Science & Medicine* 70(9), 1423–40. doi: 10.1016/j.socscimed.2009.12.037.

10 CAMHS service: YoungMinds (n.d.). Guide to CAMHS, https:// youngminds.org.uk/find-help/your-guide-to-support/guide-to-camhs/. CAMHS resources: CAMHS (n.d.). CAMHS Resources. https://www.camhs-resources.co.uk.

11 Ryan-Wenger, A. et al. (2011). Stress, coping, and health in children. In Rice, V. H. (ed.). *Handbook of Stress, Coping, and Health: Implications for Nursing Research, Theory, and Practice.* Sage Publications.

12 Active coping mechanisms and social competence: Clarke, A. T. (2006). Coping with interpersonal stress and psychosocial health among children and adolescents: a meta-analysis. *Journal of Youth and Adolescence* 35(1), 10–23. doi:

10.1007/s10964-005-9001-x. Inappropriate use of active coping mechanisms: Wadsworth, M. E. (2015). Development of maladaptive coping: a functional adaptation to chronic, uncontrollable stress. *Child Development Perspectives* 9(2), 96–100. doi: 10.1111/cdep.12112.

13 Corraliza, J. A., Collado, S. and Bethelmy, L. (2012). Nature as a moderator of stress in urban children. *Procedia – Social and Behavioral Sciences* 38, 253–63. doi: 10.1016/j.sbspro.2012.03.347.

14 Hanewald, R. (2011). Reviewing the literature on 'at-risk' and resilient children and young people. *Australian Journal of Teacher Education* 36(2), 16–29. doi: 10.14221/ajte.2011v36n2.2.

15 Empathy, strengths and expectations: Brooks, R. (2012). The power of parenting. In S. Goldstein and R. B. Brooks (eds.) *Handbook of Resilience in Children*. Kluwer Academic/Plenum Publishers. Quote: Elizabeth Day. *How to Fail with Elizabeth Day* [podcast; all episodes], https://howtofail.podbean.com.

16 Pallas, A. et al. (1990). Social structure and the development of self-esteem in young children. *Social Psychology Quarterly* 53(4), 302–15. doi: 10.2307/2786736.

17 DeHart, T., Pelham, B. W. and Tennen, H. (2006). What lies beneath: parenting style and implicit self-esteem. *Journal of Experimental Social Psychology* 42(1), 1–17. doi: 10.1016/j.jesp.2004.12.005.

18 Clarke, J. I. (2011). *Self-Esteem: A Family Affair*. Hazelden, p. 19.

19 Brummelman, E. et al. (2017). When parents' praise inflates, children's self-esteem deflates. *Child Development* 88(6), 1799–809. doi: 10.1111/cdev.12936.

20 Brummelman et al. (2017) and Brummelman, E. et al. (2014). On feeding those hungry for praise: person praise backfires in children with low self-esteem. *Journal of Experimental Psychology: General* 143(1), 9–14. doi: 10.1037/a0031917.

21 Adapted from Foxman, P. (2004). *The Worried Child: Recognizing Anxiety in Children and Helping them Heal*. Hunter House, pp. 22–3. Note that 'dark' for age 5 and 'thunder and lightning' for age 7–8 were both inferred from the original source due to their listing in the age bands above and below. 'Fears based on television viewing' (age 7–8) was omitted as it seems unlikely that this would be relevant to a single age band.

22 Several factors in anxiety: Appleton, P. (2008). A developmental framework for understanding children's anxiety. In Appleton, P. (ed.). *Children's Anxiety: A Contextual Approach*. Routledge, pp. 3–39. Small impact of parenting on children's anxiety: McLeod, B. D., Wood, J. J. and Weisz, J. R. (2007). Examining the association between parenting and childhood anxiety: a meta-analysis. *Clinical Psychology Review* 27(2), 155–72. doi: 10.1016/j.cpr.2006.09.002.

23 Shimshoni, Y. et al. (2020). Anxious-irritable children: a distinct subtype of childhood anxiety? *Behavior Therapy* 51(2), 211–22. doi: 10.1016/j.beth.2019.06.005.

24 Top physical symptoms: Sharrer, V. W. and Ryan-Wenger, N. A. (2002). School-age children's self-reported stress symptoms. *Pediatric Nursing* 28(1), 21–7. Shy children: Laurin, J. C. et al. (2015). Early forms of controlling parenting and the development of childhood anxiety. *Journal of Child and Family Studies* 24, 3279–92. doi: 10.1007/s10826-015-0131-9. Children with learning disabilities: Emerson (2003), cited in Appleton (2008). Confirmation of fears: Dibbets, P., Fliek, L. and Meesters, C. (2015). Fear-related confirmation bias in children: a comparison between neutral- and dangerous-looking animals. *Child Psychiatry & Human Development* 46(3), 418–25. doi: 10.1007/s10578-014-0481-3.

25 Parfitt, G. and Eston, R. G. (2005). The relationship between children's habitual activity level and psychological well-being. *Acta Paediatrica* 94(12), 1791–7. doi: 10.1111/j.1651-2227.2005.tb01855.x.

26 Herren, C., In-Albon, T. and Schneider, S. (2013). Beliefs regarding child anxiety and parenting competence in parents of children with separation anxiety disorder. *Journal of Behavior Therapy and Experimental Psychiatry* 44(1), 53–60. doi: 10.1016/j.jbtep.2012.07.005.

27 Wei, C. and Kendall, P. C. (2014). Parental involvement: contribution to childhood anxiety and its treatment. *Clinical Child and Family Psychology Review* 17, 319–39. doi: 10.1007/s10567-014-0170-6.

28 Fisak, B. and Grills-Taquechel, A. E. (2007). Parental modeling, reinforcement, and information transfer: risk factors in the development of child anxiety? *Clinical Child and Family Psychology Review* 10(3), 213–31. doi: 10.1007/s10567-007-0020-x.

29 Sori, C. F. and Biank, N. (2014). Soaring above stress: using relaxation, visualization, and music with children who display signs of anxiety or hyperactivity. In Sori, C. F., Hecker, L. L. and Bachenberg, M. E. (eds). *The Therapist's Notebook for Children and Adolescents: Homework, Handouts, and Activities for Use in Psychotherapy*. Routledge.

30 Rapee, R. M., Abbott, M. J. and Lyneham, H. J. (2006). Bibliotherapy for children with anxiety disorders using written materials for parents: a randomized controlled trial. *Journal of Consulting and Clinical Psychology* 74(3), 436. doi: 10.1037/0022-006X.74.3.436. The book was Rapee, R. et al. (2008). *Helping Your Anxious Child: A Step-by-Step Guide for Parents*. New Harbinger Publications.

31 Smith, M. M. et al. (2022). Parenting behaviors and trait perfectionism: a meta-analytic test of the social expectations and social learning models. *Journal of Research in Personality* 96, 104180. doi: 10.1016/j.jrp.2021.104180.

32 Mothers' self-criticism: Clark, S. and Coker, S. (2009). Perfectionism, self-criticism and maternal criticism: a study of mothers and their children. *Personality and Individual Differences* 47(4), 321–5. doi: 10.1016/j.paid.2009.03.020. Parental pressure: Smith et al. (2022).

33 Flett, G. L. and Hewitt, P. L. (2020). The perfectionism pandemic meets COVID-19: understanding the stress, distress, and problems in living for perfectionists during the global health crisis. *Journal of Concurrent Disorders* 2, 80–105. doi: 10.54127/AXGJ8297.

34 Will, G. J. et al. (2016). Chronic childhood peer rejection is associated with heightened neural responses to social exclusion during adolescence. *Journal of Abnormal Child Psychology* 44(1), 43–55. doi: 10.1007/s10802-015-9983-0.

35 Dyregrov, A. (2010). *Grief in Children: A Handbook for Adults*. Jessica Kingsley Publishers. Cronin Favazza, P. and Munson, L. J. (2010); Loss and grief in young children. *Young Exceptional Children* 13(2), 86–99. doi: 10.1177/1096250609356883.

36 Age-appropriate book: Rosen, M. and Blake, Q. (2005). *Michael Rosen's Sad Book*. Candlewick Press. Complex grief: e.g. Griese, B. et al. (2017). Comprehensive grief care for children and families: policy and practice implications. *American Journal of Orthopsychiatry* 87(5), 540–8.

Appendix 2

1 There are links between work–family conflict and children's sleep, but these were excluded as the focus of the relevant section is on parents setting boundaries between their home and their work, not the presence of conflict between work and home life (which is common, and over which parents have little control).